Careers in Law Enforcement

SAGE was founded in 1965 by Sara Miller McCune to support the dissemination of usable knowledge by publishing innovative and high-quality research and teaching content. Today, we publish over 900 journals, including those of more than 400 learned societies, more than 800 new books per year, and a growing range of library products including archives, data, case studies, reports, and video. SAGE remains majority-owned by our founder, and after Sara's lifetime will become owned by a charitable trust that secures our continued independence.

Los Angeles | London | New Delhi | Singapore | Washington DC | Melbourne

Careers in Law Enforcement

Coy H. Johnston
Arizona State University

Los Angeles | London | New Delhi
Singapore | Washington DC | Melbourne

FOR INFORMATION:

SAGE Publications, Inc.

2455 Teller Road

Thousand Oaks, California 91320

E-mail: order@sagepub.com

SAGE Publications Ltd.

1 Oliver's Yard

55 City Road

London, EC1Y 1SP

United Kingdom

SAGE Publications India Pvt. Ltd.

B 1/I 1 Mohan Cooperative Industrial Area

Mathura Road, New Delhi 110 044

India

SAGE Publications Asia-Pacific Pte. Ltd.

3 Church Street

#10-04 Samsung Hub

Singapore 049483

Acquisitions Editor: Jerry Westby

Editorial Assistant: Laura Kirkhuff

Production Editor: Olivia Weber-Stenis

Copy Editor: Cathy Kottwitz

Typesetter: Hurix Systems Pvt. Ltd.

Proofreader: Tricia Currie-Knight

Indexer: J. Naomi Linzer Indexing Services

Cover Designer: Anupama Krishnan

Marketing Manager: Terra Schultz

Printed in the United States of America

ISBN 978-1-4833-7906-7

This book is printed on acid-free paper.

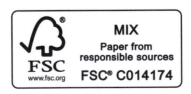

16 17 18 19 20 10 9 8 7 6 5 4 3 2 1

Brief Contents_____

Detailed Contents_____

Preface _____

Career development is a lifelong process students go through that includes their personality, interests, values, abilities, circumstances, and background. It is something that is constantly taking place regardless of the student's awareness to it. *Career counseling* is something a student can receive, usually from an individual who is trained and has tools to use. The counseling process helps students become more aware of themselves and how they fit into the work ambit, ultimately helping them make educational, career, and life choices. Combining development with counseling and applying it specifically to criminal justice is the crux of this book. *The themes of planning, pursuing, and preparing* imply three important components to this lifelong process. Without devoting attention to all three, students may find themselves behind their peers in the job hunt.

Many students find it difficult to decide early on what they want to do for a career. They sometimes take irrelevant elective classes as fodder for needed credit hours. They may miss or dismiss unique opportunities. Like a game of chess, if students have no purposeful strategy, the moves they make may be of little benefit, or counterproductive. By using some of the same tools as career counselors, professors can combine development with counseling and play a huge role in helping students be realistic in their aspirations.

Although everything a student ever wants to know is right in front of them in a device called a laptop, they don't always take advantage of it. Every career imaginable is right at their fingertips, but they don't know what they don't know. They rarely have the time or initiative to do more than the required homework. Being aware of this reality, professors try to include some career and hiring information in their lectures. By having a book containing career and hiring information, professors can utilize it for homework assignments, thus nudging students in their pursuit for happiness.

After students learn about the criminal justice system and decide where they hope to fit in, they enter the world of applying, interviewing, facing disappointment, learning from their experience, trying again and again, and for some, settling for less than what they hoped for. Students compete against other students for jobs, and universities compete against other universities for rankings. Providing students with tools for preparation gives them an edge and enhances their confidence. It offers a great feeling of vicariousness and satisfaction when a professor gets a thank you letter from prior students who landed their dream jobs.

In response to the needs of professors and students, I have provided this textbook as a supplement to law enforcement–related courses, preferably in the introduction stages of the degree program. This issue offers the key tools of career counseling to help students plan their path, core information about law enforcement careers, and advanced training for the hiring process. Students who are introduced to this "hiring-focused" book will be better prepared for the hiring process of their dream job.

Acknowledgments _____

I would like to thank Jerry Westby (acquisitions editor) and editorial assistant Laura Kirkhuff, as well as the various other staff members at SAGE who dedicated their time to preparing this book. Collectively, the team at SAGE transformed a collection of unrefined material into a polished supplemental textbook.

I would like to acknowledge the experts I interviewed about their respective careers. Their written dialogue is just a small part of their overall contribution to the quality of the book.

Additionally, I would like to acknowledge my wife and my children and their spouses: Coy and Tanya Johnston, Tyler and Hawli Landvatter, Cody and Kacie Backus, and Colton and Samantha Johnston. As former college students, they provided me with valuable insight to the realities students face in the job search. Thanks to their applicable advice, I have been able to hone my orientation toward the hiring processes.

About the Author _____

Coy Johnston is a professor in the School of Criminology and Criminal Justice at Arizona State University (ASU). He earned his bachelor's degree in business management at University of Phoenix and his master's degree in community counseling from Northern Arizona University. He has been a nationally certified counselor since 2004. For more than 27 years, Johnston worked in law enforcement, specializing in sexual crimes and domestic violence. During his career, he co-organized several nonprofit organizations and specialized law enforcement programs and networks. Noteworthy awards during his law enforcement career included the Distinguished Service Award of Victims of Crime and a Certificate of Recognition from Arizona Governor Janet Napolitano for the Law Enforcement DV Roundup. Johnston has served on the governor's grant approval committee for STOP and RECOVERY grants since 2007. Since retiring from law enforcement in 2007, Johnston has taught psychology and criminal justice classes at University of Phoenix, ITT Technical Institute, Chandler-Gilbert Community College, Everest College, the CARLOTA Police Academy, and Arizona State University. This book is his third official publication.

SECTION 1

Planning

1

Know Yourself

Two questions that regularly stump candidates in hiring interviews are "What are your strengths?" and "What are your weaknesses?" An interviewee who has been well coached may offer some scripted examples of strengths, such as being a great communicator or having a fun personality or being a quick thinker. A well-coached interviewee will also know better than to give a long list of weaknesses. As discussed in more detail in the final chapter, there is nothing wrong with being coached for an interview, and it is actually highly recommended.

One important purpose of the hiring interview is to give an employer an opportunity to assess certain personality and character traits of an individual that can't be sufficiently discovered through a written test or from the application paperwork. The ability to communicate well and to think quickly and to be a fun person may be exactly what an agency is looking for. It is refreshing for interviewers when candidates meet their criteria and are self-aware and genuinely know who they are. Other traits commonly sought by most agencies include assertiveness, ability to work well with others, willingness to work hard, capacity for independent thought, ability to follow a chain of command, and a high level of integrity, which is often determined through background checks and polygraph tests.

When answering interview questions, it is always a good idea to be truthful. However, truth is somewhat subjective in the area of self-awareness. Too often students aren't fully aware of their own strengths and weaknesses. An uncoached student with desirable qualities might not adequately describe his or her strengths in an interview and might subsequently be passed over in favor of others who are better prepared. Sadly, some well-qualified students don't feel ready and therefore don't even apply. The opposite is also true. There are those who aren't ready (or are not a good fit for the jobs they seek) and are not aware of it.

The overall usefulness of this book depends largely on how well you know yourself. This first chapter is dedicated to helping students become more in touch with their individual personalities, their temperaments, their strengths and weaknesses, their biases and beliefs, and what types of careers might be a good fit. Just as a house needs a good foundation to be built upon, learning about oneself is the right place to start if the best results are to be achieved. It is fundamentally important, and when self-assessment exercises are used in college courses, students report them as among their favorite activities.

What You Don't Know Can Hurt You

Self-awareness is the gateway to self-improvement. Learning should be a life-long interest, but the biggest stumbling block for some students is the belief that they already have a handle on the way things are. This way of thinking is normal, especially in early adulthood. It develops naturally from everything a person has experienced throughout his or her life using the five senses coupled with reassurance and confirmations from peers. This type of person is stagnant. Stagnant people have slowed their growth and sometimes never crawl out of the hole they dig for themselves. Stagnant people feel comfortable around others who think as they do. It is a natural tendency for people to consider someone who thinks as they do as normal or even intelligent. Instead of desiring and trying to understand everyone and appreciate the differences, stagnant individuals tend to divide people into "us versus them." This poem by John Godfrey Saxe (1873) helps demonstrate how people get stuck in such a rut:

I.

It was six men of Indostan

To learning much inclined,

Who went to see the Elephant

(Though all of them were blind),

That each by observation

Might satisfy his mind.

II.

The *First* approach'd the Elephant,

And happening to fall

Against his broad and sturdy side,

At once began to bawl:

"God bless me!—but the Elephant

Is very like a wall!"

III.

The *Second*, feeling of the tusk,

Cried, "Ho!—what have we here

So very round and smooth and sharp?

To me 't is mighty clear

This wonder of an Elephant

Is very like a spear!"

IV.

The *Third* approached the animal,

And happening to take

The squirming trunk within his hands,

Thus boldly up and spake:

"I see," quoth he, "the Elephant

Is very like a snake!"

V.

The *Fourth* reached out his eager hand,

And felt about the knee.

"What most this wondrous beast is like

Is mighty plain," quoth he;

"Tis clear enough the Elephant

Is very like a tree!"

VI.

The *Fifth*, who chanced to touch the ear,

Said: "E'en the blindest man

Can tell what this resembles most;

Deny the fact who can,

This marvel of an Elephant

Is very like a fan!"

VII.

The *Sixth* no sooner had begun

About the beast to grope,

Than, seizing on the swinging tail

That fell within his scope,

"I see," quoth he, "the Elephant

Is very like a rope!"

VIII.

And so these men of Indostan

Disputed loud and long,

Each in his own opinion

Exceeding stiff and strong,

Though each was partly in the right,

And all were in the wrong!

MORAL.

So, oft in theologic wars,

The disputants, I ween,

Rail on in utter ignorance

Of what each other mean,

And prate about an Elephant

Not one of them has seen!

This poem has an important message for all of us. There is so much we do not know and will never have the opportunity to know. It is the realization of our vulnerabilities and inefficiencies that prepares us for learning, changing, and improving. Narcissistic people we may come across in our lives would benefit greatly from self-awareness, but they will never realize that they don't already have it.

What You Don't Know

To learn more about ourselves, we should first put our own existence into the proper perspective. Current estimates suggest that there are over 165 billion galaxies in the universe, each with hundreds of billions of stars (National

Aeronautics and Space Administration, n.d.). The universe is estimated to be over 12 billion years old (National Aeronautics and Space Administration, 2012). Compare that with the average life span of humans, which is estimated at 78 years (U.S. Census Bureau, 2012).

Let's just consider what we can learn about our own planet. There are seven continents, containing 193 countries, on which approximately 7 billion people reside, speaking over 6,000 different languages (O'Neil, 2013). Our planet has an estimated 146 million books (Taychir, 2010). If someone were to read one book per day between the ages of 6 and 86 years, he or she could read only 29,200 of those books in a lifetime. In reality, the average American reads only about 15 books a year.

There are hundreds of degrees available, but according to the U.S. Census Bureau (Stoops, 2004), only 29% of young adults in America receive a bachelor's degree or higher. Seldom does anyone devote the time and money to obtain more than one bachelor's or master's degree. Like the blind men who each felt only one part of the elephant, there is so much we don't know. Realizing and accepting this truth is the key to having the learning attitude we need. "Do you wish to rise? Begin by descending. You plan a tower that will pierce the clouds? Lay first the foundation of humility" (Saint Augustine, 354–430 CE).

Self-Assessments

Working in the criminal justice field can be a very rewarding and exciting career. Many students entering criminal justice degree programs already have a particular career in mind. They hope to land the job they have always desired or something equally attractive. A common question for a professor to ask a group of students is "What do you want to do with your degree?" Then there are the follow-up questions that solicit the raising of hands: "Who is interested in being a police officer?" "Who is interested in being an attorney?" "How many want to work in the forensic field?" "How many want to work in corrections?" Other typical interests usually include the Federal Bureau of Investigation, the Drug Enforcement Administration, the U.S. Marshals Service, victim services, child interviews, and criminal profiling. There are also those students who are not sure where they want to work or are not sure what they are a good fit for.

As students progress through their bachelor's degrees in criminal justice, they learn more about the types of jobs available as well as the positive and negative aspects of each field. It is common for a professor to hear comments such as "I don't think I could ever defend a murderer in court" or "I could never interview child molesters because I would want to strangle them." Students start to become aware of personal issues that might affect their job performance or their happiness in certain careers. Similarly, professors have the opportunity to recognize students' strengths and weaknesses and could either confirm that students are a good fit for the careers they wish to pursue or direct students to better choices. This is easier to do if the students are somewhat aware of their own strengths, preferences, and natural tendencies. The ideal situation is for students to learn about themselves at the earliest point possible.

There are several tools available to help us realize our own temperaments, personalities, likes and dislikes, strengths and weaknesses, and even what types of people we would be happiest with and what careers we would be best fit for. These tools (and some useful books) will be discussed throughout the rest of this chapter. It is highly recommended that you learn all you can about yourself (and what makes you happy) before progressing far into your degree program. Having true insight early on will help you search out the best volunteer positions or internships that will get your foot not just in the door but in the right door.

What Color Is Your Parachute?

Richard Bolles published a book in 1970 titled *What Color Is Your Parachute?* It has been a very successful job hunter's book, with a new edition appearing each year, and it continues to be revised and reissued. The 2015 edition can be found on Amazon for as little as $10. More than 10 million copies have been sold, including one copy of the 30th edition that I purchased and read. The ideas and concepts in the book are very helpful and easy to retain.

Chapter 4 is titled "What Do You Have to Offer the World?" Bolles (2000) states, "You must figure out which of your skills you most delight to use." Bolles gives these three steps to job-hunting success:

1. What: You must decide exactly what you have to offer to the world.

2. Where: You must decide where you want to use your skills.

3. How: You must go after the organizations that interest you the most, whether or not they are known to have vacancies.

These three steps are in line with the focus of the present book, *Careers in Law Enforcement*, in which we plan, pursue, and prepare. The first step, planning, is essential, but that is not to say that everyone goes through an identical, meticulous process. It is highly recommended, however, that students figure out their own preferences and skills, and ultimately their ideal career paths, at the earliest point possible. According to Bolles, everyone has skills, but "there is such a thing as being deeply unaware of our skills." I have witnessed students' unawareness when they have been asked to write self-reflection essays to articulate the skills they use to accomplish group work. The assignment is didactic, intended to trigger students' awareness of the skills they possess and how they use them to influence, encourage, and motivate others. The essays usually end up being more of a description of the work they've done or what they normally do. The essays rarely include actual skills. They are usually very short accounts of what results have been accomplished instead of how they were accomplished. What Bolles wrote about, people being deeply unaware of their skills, is surprisingly ubiquitous. Candidates who are not ready for questions about their own strengths and weaknesses in hiring interviews often find themselves surprised at how hard it is to articulate one's own skills. We will visit this issue again in Section 3.

Keirsey Temperament Sorter

In 1984, David Keirsey and Marilyn Bates published *Please Understand Me*. The book focuses on the concept that everyone is fundamentally different and that differences are neither good nor bad. They asserted that self-assessment is foreign to most people, so using some kind of examination tool is very helpful. Keirsey and Bates created the Keirsey Temperament Sorter, consisting of 70 questions, which can be found on page 5 of their book. The questions each offer two choices, for example,

20. On the job do you want your activities

___(a) scheduled   ___(b) unscheduled

The value of this tool hinges on the test taker being as honest as possible. The answers are recorded on a scoring form that ultimately identifies where the test taker fits among 16 different personality types. The book follows up with detailed information about each type, which assists a person in understanding more about what the results of the assessment mean.

Keirsey wrote a follow-up book in 1998 titled *Please Understand Me II*. The newer book is 140 pages longer than the first version. The 70 Keirsey Temperament Sorter II questions and score sheet are available in the book on page 4. The questions are similar to those in the original book, but the follow-up information is more comprehensive.

A website was created allowing people to answer the Keirsey Temperament Sorter II questions online, free of charge, and to receive a scored report (Keirsey.com, n.d.). The report has minimal information to help students better understand their own temperaments and styles. For a more detailed report on the results, one would have to pay a small fee. The free report includes your basic personality type (Artisan, Guardian, Idealist, or Rationalist) and four subtypes. As an example of the details, if your results show that you are a Guardian, you will find out that the four types of Guardians are supervisors, protectors, inspectors, and providers. A few things the free report briefly explains about Guardians are that they pride themselves on being dependable, helpful, and hardworking. They make loyal mates and reasonable parents, and they are stabilizing leaders. A Guardian is also a concerned citizen who trusts authority, joins groups, seeks security, and dreams of meting out justice.

Jamie Gissel: SWAT – Mesa Police Department

CJ: What is your current position?

JG: I am a member of the SWAT team. On our team, every member is trained in all basic aspects of being a SWAT officer such as entry, perimeter, and immediate action team. SWAT officers are able to also specialize in other areas such as sniper, rappel team, explosive breaching, etc. My current specialty on the team is explosive breacher.

CJ: What are your typical job duties?

JG: As a member of the SWAT team, we have five main duties: provide security for dignitaries, perform rescue missions for both officers and citizens, provide assistance during high-risk warrant service, provide assistance to other law enforcement agencies and other units within the department, and provide assistance during barricaded situations. As a full-time SWAT team, we try to meet the National Tactical Officers Association's standard of 40 hours of training a month. We typically train a few hours at the beginning of each shift. We also assist in training officers not only in our department, but we provide training to other agencies as well. When we are not busy with any of those responsibilities, we will typically hit the street and help out patrol or look for any crimes in progress.

CJ: How long have you been at your current assignment?

JG: I was selected to the team in 2008. I became a member of the explosive breaching team in 2011.

CJ: What other positions have you held prior to this one?

JG: Prior to joining the SWAT team I worked as a nighttime patrol officer for 3 years.

CJ: What are the requirements/qualifications for your job as a police officer and as a SWAT member?

JG: The selection process for our SWAT team is quite a process. The test starts out with a physical test and obstacle course, three different shooting evaluations, a written test, and an interview with several senior members of the team. After all of the initial testing is done, a peer and supervisor review is performed. From the results of all the testing to that point, officers are selected to go to an eight day SWAT school. If the officer passes SWAT school, they are able to come to the team as a probationary member for a year. During that year the officer must pass several other schools including entry weapons school and hostage rescue school. Once the year of probation is completed, the team votes whether or not to take the officer as a member of the team. Even after an officer is selected to the team, we are required to pass the physical test and several shooting qualifications throughout the year. Our policy states that a SWAT officer can be removed from the team at any time so we must do our best at all times.

CJ: What steps did you go through during hiring?

JG: Prior to being hired, I talked to a lot of people in law enforcement. I wanted to get as much information prior to testing so I knew what to expect during the testing process and also what the job entailed. I was able to do a ride-along and see what it was like to be a police officer. I wanted to make sure I knew what I was in for. I also got myself in the best shape I could so I could excel during the physical test. I also made sure I stayed out of trouble and kept my recorded clean so I could pass the background phase of the testing. I can still remember the day I was notified I was being hired. I have loved every day since.

CJ: What advice can you offer students who might be interested in pursuing a similar career and becoming a member of the SWAT team?

JG: Develop work ethic. Being a police officer and a member of the SWAT team is a lot of work. It is both physically and mentally demanding. Your reputation will make or break your career in any aspect of law enforcement, especially SWAT. If you have a reputation of being lazy or you are not a team player, the team will find out. Be a leader. As a SWAT officer, when you arrive on a scene officers and supervisors will look to you to take charge of the scene. Keep in shape. Being a SWAT officer team is physical job. You must be in great shape in order to perform your duties. Have a good attitude and treat others with respect. You will go a lot further with both peers and people if you treat them with respect.

To get detailed information on the four subtypes, you would need to pay a fee for the type of report you want. You can order the 18-page "Classic Temperament" report ($14.95), the 18-page "Career Temperament" report ($19.95), the 15-page "Learning Style Temperament" report ($14.95), or the 3-page "Temperament Discovery" report ($4.95) at www.keirsey.com. The Keirsey Temperament Sorter II can also be accessed at that website. It takes only about 20 to 25 minutes to answer the questions, and the results come back immediately and can be printed out.

It is important to remember that you can buy the book, which contains the Keirsey Temperament Sorter II questions and score sheet, several pages of detailed information about each type of personality, careers you would be best fit for, and what type of person you are a good match for. The book can be found on Amazon for as little as $5.

True Colors

Roger Birkman published his book *True Colors* in 1995. The book can be purchased new at https://store.birkman.com/?items=books for $15 or used on Amazon for as little as $4. Birkman was fascinated with the topic of perception and posited that our perceptions, whether right or wrong, influence everything we do. He felt that by gaining the proper perspective on one's own perceptions, other things would start to fall into place. According to Birkman, there are no criteria anywhere that define what is normal, and so "nobody is normal, and everyone is." Birkman also suggested that "there is great freedom in knowing one's own strengths and weaknesses, for as soon as these are identified, it becomes a much simpler matter to focus on the things you do well and look for help in your weaker areas" (p. 31).

In *True Colors*, Birkman explains that there is no limit on the number of "normal" or "right" behaviors but that the unlimited number of normal and right behaviors can be categorized to some extent. Birkman categorizes people in four quadrants using the colors red, yellow, green, and blue. He explains in the book what these colors represent. He also notes that the best way to learn which of the four quadrants is the most indicative of one's own personality is to take a personalized, individual assessment. Birkman also gives two other ways to help someone determine his or her self-perception. He includes in the book (pp. 42–43) 16 true-or-false questions as well as instructions on how to score the answers. The other way to determine your perceptions is to read the explanations and examples throughout the book. On page 44, there is a chart that gives just a few examples of what falls under the different quadrants. If you fall under the red quadrant, you are friendly, decisive, energetic, frank, and logical. If you favor the yellow quadrant, you are orderly, concentrative, cautious, and insistent. Green people are competitive, assertive, flexible, and enthusiastic about new things. Blues are insightful, selective sociable, thoughtful, reflective, and optimistic.

Chances are that you could look at these examples and guess what color you would fall in before you even take the 16-question test. You might also find that you have some characteristics from more than one quadrant. Birkman dedicated many pages to explaining how to interpret the results. In the book, there are details about different operating styles, what motivates you, understanding your needs, how to relate to people of other colors, and several other categories of helpful information.

In *True Colors*, Birkman lists 10 classifications of interest with possible occupations that are a good fit for each category. Here are some examples:

Artistic: photographer, architect, artist, florist, designer, painter, or decorator

Clerical: secretary, typist, office worker, or financial manager

Literary: writer, editor, literary scholar, reporter, or librarian

Mechanical: engineer, machine designer, auto mechanic, carpenter, pilot, or plumber

Musical: professional singer, musician, or songwriter

Numerical: cashier, accountant, mathematician, or administrative office worker

Outdoor: carpenter, farmer, animal trainer, sportsman, forest ranger, or field engineer

Persuasive: salesperson, teacher, counselor, public relations director, politician, or auctioneer

Scientific: scientist, lab worker, detective, meteorologist, doctor, or dentist

Social services: teacher, social worker, counselor, or personnel or employment manager

Birkman states in his book (pp. 58–59) that strong interests have the same status as a need and that our interests influence us more than we realize.

What Type Am I?

In 1998, Renee Baron published a book titled *What Type Am I?* This book can be purchased on Amazon new for under $7. Baron also wrote a followup book titled *The Four Temperaments*, which we will explore later. In *What Type Am I?* Baron tells us that she began to learn about personality temperaments when she came upon the book *Please Understand Me* by Keirsey and Bates. She explains that learning her own temperament gave her a strong sense of relief to finally identify her real self. It was this great feeling of selfworth that inspired her to teach it to others for the next 18 years. In this book, Baron shares the Myers-Briggs system the way it was first taught to her. She starts her book with an overview of the Myers-Briggs system, which is one of the most popular and comprehensive personality assessments to date.

The Myers-Briggs scheme measures both preferences and temperaments. The first part of the book deals with preferences. The four pairs of preferences are listed as opposites:

Extraversion (E) and Introversion (I)

Sensing (S) and Intuiting (N)

Thinking (T) and Feeling (F)

Judging (J) and Perceiving (P)

Baron wrote full chapters on each of these opposite pairs. She starts each of the chapters with a 20-question inventory to help the reader distinguish which preference is dominant. The second part of the book delves into temperament, which is "a pattern of characteristic behaviors that reflect a person's natural disposition" (Baron, 1998, p. 51). Myers-Briggs lists the four temperaments themes as follows:

SJ–Sensing Judging: duty seekers

SP–Sensing Perceiving: action seekers

NT–Intuiting Thinking: knowledge seekers

NF–Intuiting Feeling: ideal seekers

Ultimately, the Myers-Briggs system classifies a person into 1 of the following 16 categories:

ESTP	ESFP	ISTJ	ISFJ
ENTP	ENFP	INTJ	INFJ
ESTJ	ENTJ	ISTP	INTP
ESFJ	ENFJ	ISFP	INFP

Baron explains the meaning of these types in great detail. She says in the last paragraph of the book that this valuable information changed her life. She says that it started her on the path to acceptance and "that it was alright to be me, an ENFP" (Baron, 1998).

The Four Temperaments

Baron's 2004 follow-up was titled *The Four Temperaments*. The book can be purchased on Amazon (used) for under $5. This book contains a personality inventory that starts on page 9 and consists of 80 questions. These 80 questions are divided into four different groups of 20 questions each.

The four groups are Security Seeker, Experience Seeker, Knowledge Seeker, and Ideal Seeker. You answer each question with one of these three choices:

0—Not like me

1—Somewhat like me

2—Exactly like me

An example item is "I dislike wasting time talking about policies and procedures. I want to take immediate action." At the end of the inventory, you total your points and mark on a chart where you fall in each of the four categories. The remainder of the book gives an in-depth description of the four temperaments.

Security Seekers make up approximately 40% of the U.S. population (Baron, 2004). Baron tells us that Security Seekers are responsible, dependable, and solid citizens. They feel obligated to do their part and work hard. They respect customs, traditions, and social standards. Security Seekers place a high value on family and are the most marriage minded of all the temperaments. This type of person is also organized and thrives on routine and structure. Security Seekers like to communicate in a clear way, with things stated specifically, without having to draw assumptions. As teens, they are generally cooperative and respect authority. As parents, they provide a secure and consistent home environment. Security Seekers are well suited for careers in health care, finance, clerical work, sales, education, social service, counseling, legal or civil service, and a variety of creative fields, such as painting and photography.

Experience Seekers make up approximately 40% of the U.S. population (Baron, 2004). According to Baron, Experience Seekers have the need to act spontaneously for fun and also for problem solving. They value independence and freedom. They don't like to be burdened by obligations. Experience Seekers thrive in crisis situations. They feel comfortable acting spontaneously in the moment. As teens, Experience Seekers learn best in a hands-on setting, such as building, playing instruments, and playing sports. As parents, Experience Seekers like to expose their children to adventures and encourage them to be physically active. Experience Seekers are well suited for careers in sports, entertainment, creative fields, sales, service, travel, health care, education, social service, and miscellaneous related fields, including the law and private investigation.

Knowledge Seekers make up approximately 10% of the U.S. population (Baron, 2004). Baron tells us that Knowledge Seekers need competency and seek understanding of things such as the world and universal truths. Knowledge Seekers see patterns and connections and the relationship between things. They thrive on developing theories and focus on long-range goals. As teens, Knowledge Seekers are challenged by learning and are bright and clever. They can become bored if not challenged mentally. They are curious and inquisitive and constantly investigating and experimenting. As parents, Knowledge Seekers expect their children to challenge themselves intellectually. They challenge their children to accept responsibility, but they can be so busy that they neglect the normal tasks of family life. Knowledge Seekers are well suited for careers in education, medicine, science, engineering, business, finance, creative fields, and miscellaneous professions including the law, organizational consulting, and computer programming.

Ideal Seekers make up approximately 10% of the U.S. population (Baron, 2004). Baron writes that Ideal Seekers need to express themselves authentically and genuinely. They are passionate about things they believe in and spend a lot of time fostering relationships. They are insightful, perceptive, and sensitive. As teens, Ideal Seekers can have rich imaginations and are usually cooperative. They do their best when competing against themselves because competing against others causes disharmony. They try to be like those they admire. As parents, Ideal Seekers are concerned about their children's emotional development. They encourage their children's individuality and allow the children their free expression. Ideal Seekers are well suited for careers in helping professions, education, creative fields, health care, business, sales, and professional positions such as fund-raiser, conference planner, program coordinator, and public relations specialist.

Baron includes some closing thoughts at the end of her book in which she says, "Although temperaments do not explain everything about people, they certainly give us a great deal of practical insight into human behavior, which can have a life-transforming effect on our relationships with ourselves and others" (Baron, 2004, p. 109). I agree wholeheartedly with this message. We can better understand and relate to others after we sufficiently understand ourselves.

What Color Is Your Personality?

Carol Ritberger published *What Color Is Your Personality?* in 1999. This petite and colorful book can be purchased on Amazon new for under $9. Ritberger's book includes a personality assessment that helps you determine if you are a red, orange, yellow, or green personality type. She explains that it is more crucial to understand ourselves than it is to understand others. By paying attention to our own habits, why we do what we do, and how we respond to challenges, we can see what characteristics are stumbling blocks and need to be changed.

Ritberger categorizes the colors briefly for the reader prior to the actual personality assessment. She tells us that red is a personality style in which a person needs to be in control. This need causes stress, which could be released through physical activity. Individuals with the orange personality always need to be doing things for others, so there is hardly any time for themselves. People with this personality type could pamper themselves more, perhaps learn yoga. Yellow types find themselves frustrated by indecision because they can see both sides very well. Such individuals could help themselves by creating stimulating mind diversions such as reading a book or even playing video games. Greens can get angry when they feel disorganized or out of control; they could read books on how to better manage time and how to get better organized.

The personality assessment Ritberger uses is found on pages 60 to 65 and consists of 60 statements. Each statement has a letter next to it: A, B, C, or D. When taking this assessment, you are asked to circle any of the 60 statements that represent your most frequent and habitual patterns. An example of one of the statements is "I have a lot of thoughts in my head simultaneously, and I am often accused of not listening or of being preoccupied." At the end of the assessment, the total circled answers are added up separately for the As, Bs, Cs, and Ds. The last step is to combine As and Cs to get a red score, Bs and Cs to get a yellow score, As and Ds to get an orange score, and Bs and Ds to get a green score. One of the strong points of Ritberger's assessment tool is her coverage of the weak side of each personality type and potential health issues. She states at the end of her book that the "state of our mind directly affects the chemistry of the body in such a way that we are either becoming ill or overcoming illness every moment of our lives" (Ritberger, 1999, p. 163). She further explains that our health is directly related to our success and happiness, which is in direct relation to understanding ourselves and changing unhealthy habits and thoughts.

Jung Typology Test

Another free online personality test is the HumanMetrics (2013) Jung Typology Test. The test is based on Carl Jung's and Isabel Briggs Myers's typological approach to personality. To take this assessment, you answer 72 yes-or-no questions and then submit the test for grading. An example question is

2. You like to be engaged in an active and fast-paced job.

The results of your answers come back immediately. I answered the questions honestly, and according to the results, I am an INTJ, preferring Introversion (33%), Intuition (12%), Thinking (1%), and Judging (44%). The following analysis was provided:

- You have *moderate* preference of Introversion over Extraversion (33%)
- You have *slight* preference of Intuition over Sensing (12%)
- You have *marginal or no* preference of Thinking over Feeling (1%)
- You have *moderate* preference of Judging over Perceiving (44%)

On the same screen with your results, you can choose other free results. By clicking on the career choices for your type, you will be directed to another screen with helpful career information. The information for INTJs is as follows:

> Generally, INTJs have successful careers in areas requiring intensive intellectual efforts, presenting intellectual challenge, and creative approach. Due to the characteristics mentioned above, successful INTJs are found in technological companies, particularly in research and development, and also found among corporate lawyers, high- and mid-rank managers in technology companies and financial institutions.

The various careers suggested for INTJs fall into areas of computer programming, natural science, teaching, engineering, management, entrepreneurship, the law, and libraries. The results even list the names of famous personalities who share the same personality type. Some other INTJs include these individuals:

- Stephen Hawking, a theoretical physicist, cosmologist, and author
- Andrew Grove, a businessman, engineer, and author
- Marie Curie, a physicist and chemist famous for her pioneering research on radioactivity
- Guy Kawasaki, a venture capitalist, best-selling author, and Apple fellow
- Igor Sikorsky, a pioneer of aviation
- Hillary Clinton, the 67th U.S. secretary of state
- Arnold Schwarzenegger, ex-governor of California

Another option from the results screen is to access a profile of your personality type. The profile of the INTJ is a comprehensive report of 1,400 words. This is one of the paragraphs from the INTJ profile:

> INTJs are perfectionists, with a seemingly endless capacity for improving upon anything that takes their interest. What prevents them from becoming chronically bogged down in this pursuit of perfection is the pragmatism so characteristic of the type: INTJs apply (often ruthlessly) the criterion "Does it work?" to everything from their own research efforts to the prevailing social norms. This in turn produces an unusual independence of mind, freeing the INTJ from the constraints of authority, convention, or sentiment for its own sake.

GAcollege411

Another website with a career assessment tool and free results is GAcollege411 (Xap Corporation, 2009). At this site, you can choose several different assessments. A good option is the Career Cluster Survey, which takes 15 to 25 minutes. You are first asked to choose (from a list of several options) the activities you would like to do in the future, and the ones you're interested in or able to do right now. An example of an activity from this list is "Come up with a new way to do something." If this were something you are interested in, you would click on the box next to that activity. After this section, you are asked to choose words from a list that describe you best. A few of the words on the list are *dependable, determined,* and *cooperative.* The last section of the inventory asks you to choose a few of the school subjects that you enjoy most. You are provided a list of the typical college subjects, such as English, mathematics, music, and drama. After submitting the last screen, you are provided a cluster (or a rank order) of the top 10 to 12 careers that fit your profile. Along with the cluster chart, you are provided with all the answers you gave during the assessment exercise.

Another option on this website besides the Career Cluster Survey is the Career Key, which takes 10 to 15 minutes. The Career Key introduction tells you that you will answer a few questions about yourself in five categories and then see your personality types (or interest areas) and discover related careers. The first section of the Career Key asks you to select careers of interest from a list. The instructions tell you to check every career that interests you or attracts you in some way. It tells you not to click a career that you are undecided about, that does not sound interesting to you, or that you would dislike. The next section is "Interests." The directions ask you to read each statement and decide how much it describes you. If the statement is a very accurate description of you, you are asked to click the "True" button. If it is mostly true of you, there is also a button for that. If it does not describe you, then you are asked to click "Not True." An example of one of these questions is "I like to lead and persuade people, and to sell things and ideas." The next section is "Abilities." The directions tell you to compare yourself with other persons your age. Decide the extent to which each statement is true of you. An example statement is "I am good at leading people and selling things or ideas." You would again click on "True," "Mostly True," or "Not True." The last two sections are answered the same way. Those sections are titled "How You See Yourself" and "Your Values." The results of the Career Key give you the areas in which you scored the highest, and a new button allows you to view your best career options. I scored highest in the following two areas:

Social

- You are a "Helper."
- You enjoy assisting people in various ways.
- You like working in groups.
- You find that verbal and communication skills come naturally to you.

Enterprising

- You are a "Persuader."
- You enjoy leading or managing other people.
- You often respond well to competition and enjoy leading teams.

- You are willing to take risks.
- You value status, power, money and material possessions.
- You describe yourself as ambitious or energetic.

Here are some comments from students at Arizona State University who took the GAcollege411 assessment in April 2013:

I have always known that I have been fond of "toys" at work, school and home. The results of my test indicated this. However, it also said that ENTPs replace these "toys" once they become too familiar or "solved." I never noticed this about myself but I often do replace things that do not need to be replaced just because I get bored of them. Almost all of the results seemed to be accurate to my personality. (Lucas Burruel)

Overall this survey was right on with who I am and the career that I chose. It is interesting how answering fewer than 100 questions can explain so much about whom you are and the career you should pursue. (Jake Petronzio)

I must say that I actually learned quite a bit about myself after taking this test. I think that, first of all, it's quite fascinating that a set amount of questions can actually determine, with some accuracy, what type of personality type you fall under. I definitely learned a bit about why I seem to do things and the motivation behind them. For example, the results and overview pointed out that I often "neglect [myself] and [my] own needs for others." While I never really realized this, it definitely makes sense and really is a big part of who I am. I never really realized that this detail defined who I am and made such a big impact on my overall personality and profile. (Alex Segal)

It says that ESPJ's have the tendency to be very emotional and fragile. I'm definitely like that—secretly of course! I tend to have sympathy with people that have done much wrong to me or even to many people. Over all, I feel like this is right on point. (Judith Ornelas)

I found this to be spot on with my career choice. I was very surprised that answering those simple questions could get results that were so fitting with me. I am actually going to school to be a social worker. I then want to go back to get my masters in order to be a counselor. I would not have thought I would be good in the teaching environment. I do enjoy being involved in a lot of direct interaction with others. I currently am a server and love it because I am able to meet and converse with new people everyday. This exercise helped me realize that I do enjoy being in that type of setting and also like to be involved in responsibility for critical task. I really enjoyed reading my personality type and was pleasantly surprised that the results were so accurate. (Taylor Buckner)

It surprised me that the analysis said that INFJs have the ability to "deduce the inner workings of the mind, will, and emotions of others" because as a psychology major that is exactly what I want to do with my career. I have always known I am introverted, but the analysis gave me greater clarity as to what this means besides being shy and quiet. I also learned that people like me are more careful in choosing the people they spend time with, which would explain why I have just a handful of close friends and family members rather than a ton of acquaintances. The results are very accurate. The careers chosen for my personality type include social services and counseling, which makes sense because I want to become a substance abuse counselor. (Marlee Seymore)

This test proved that I am an extrovert, but I already knew that much. What shocked me was that it proved that I choose Perceiving over Judging. It also said that I prefer work with creativity, which I don't find myself as the creative type. It did say though that my top career choice was journalism, which is what I'm majoring in! So at least I know I'm on the right track! (Jordan Young)

Summary

Two questions that stump applicants in an interview are "What are your strengths?" and "What are your weaknesses?" Sometimes a person has great strengths and skills but has trouble articulating them in an interview. Many students aren't adequately aware of their own strengths and weaknesses. Just as a house needs a good foundation to be built upon, learning about oneself is the right place to start if the best results are to be achieved. Some people lack self-awareness and are stuck in a rut. They are not likely to change and improve their lives, simply because they feel as if they already know enough. In reality, there is so much we do not know and will never have the opportunity to know. It is the realization of our vulnerabilities and inefficiencies that prepares us for learning, changing, and improving.

Professors come to recognize students' strengths and weaknesses and could either confirm to students that they are a good fit for the careers they are pursuing or help direct them to better choices. It is best if students are aware of their own strengths, preferences, and natural tendencies. The ideal situation is for students to learn more about themselves at the earliest point possible.

There are several books and self-assessment tools available to assist students in reaching a deeper understanding of their strengths and weaknesses, including other people who might be a good fit for them and what types of jobs they might be best suited for. Some online assessment tools are free and offer concise reports of the results. There are books available to clarify the results with much more comprehensive information. Once you gain a deeper understanding of your own strengths and weaknesses, you can have the insight early on that will help you search out the best volunteer positions or internships that will get your foot not just in the door but in the right door.

DISCUSSION QUESTIONS

1. What is the difference between group skills we possess and use and the actual work we do in group projects?

2. Do you agree with the statement "Self-awareness is the gateway to self improvement"? Why or why not?

3. What is the moral of the poem about the six blind men from Indostan?

4. Do you agree with Bolles's statement that "everyone has skills, but there is such a thing as being deeply unaware of our skills"? Why or why not?

5. What does Birkman mean when he says, "Nobody is normal, and everyone is"?

6. Do you agree with Ritberger when she explains, "It is more crucial to understand ourselves than it is to understand others"? Why or why not?

7. Do you agree with the results you got from the free online Jung Typology Test (http://www.humanmetrics.com/cgi-win/JTypes2.asp)? Were there any surprises?

REFERENCES

Baron, R. (1998). *What type am I? Discover who you really are.* London, UK: Penguin Group.

Baron, R. (2004). *The four temperaments: A fun and practical guide to understanding yourself and the people in your life.* New York, NY: St. Martin's.

Birkman, R. W. (1995). *True colors: Get to know yourself and others better with the highly acclaimed Birkman method.* Nashville, TN: Thomas Nelson, Inc.

Bolles, R. (2000). *What color is your parachute? A practical manual for job-hunters and career changers* (30th ed.). Berkeley, CA: Ten Speed.

HumanMetrics. (2013). *Jung typology test.* Retrieved from http://www.humanmetrics.com/cgi-win/JTypes2.asp

Keirsey, D. (2000). *Please understand me II: Temperament character intelligence* (Kindle ed.). Del Mar, CA: Prometheus Nemesis.

Keirsey, D., & Bates, M. M. (1984). *Please understand me: Character & temperament types* (5th ed.). Del Mar, CA: Prometheus Nemesis.

Keirsey.com. (n.d.). *Welcome to the Keirsey Temperament Sorter II (KTS-II).* Retrieved from http://keirsey.com/sorter/register.aspx

National Aeronautics and Space Administration. (n.d.). *Counting galaxies with the Hubble Space Telescope.* Retrieved from http://spacemath.gsfc.nasa.gov/weekly/6Page14.pdf

National Aeronautics and Space Administration. (2012). *How old is the Universe?* Retrieved from http://map.gsfc.nasa.gov/universe/uni_age.html

O'Neil, D. (2013). Introduction. In *Language and culture: An introduction to human communication*. Retrieved from http://anthro.palomar.edu/language/language_1.htm

Ritberger, C. (1999). *What color is your personality? Red, orange, yellow, green*. Carlsbad, CA: Hay House.

Saxe, J. (1873). *The poems of John Godfrey Saxe*. Washington, DC: Library of Congress.

Stoops, N. (2004). Educational attainment in the United States: 2003. *Current Population Reports*, pp. 1–10.

Taychir, L. (2010). Books of the world, stand up and be counted! All 129,864,880 of You [Web log post]. Retrieved from http://booksearch.blogspot.com/2010/08/books-of-world-stand-up-and-be-counted.html

U.S. Census Bureau. (2012). *Births, deaths, marriages, & divorces: Life expectancy*. Retrieved from http://www.census.gov/compendia/statab/cats/births_deaths_marriages_divorces/life_expectancy.html

Xap Corporation. (2009). *GAcollege411*. Retrieved from https://secure.gacollege411.org/Career_Planning/Learn_About_Yourself/Learn_About_Yourself.aspx

2 Setting Realistic Goals

Career development is a process that takes time, patience, hard work, and—for those without a full-ride scholarship—money. Like climbing a ladder, the process involves a beginning step. Trying to skip the first step and going straight to the second is very arduous and, for most, not possible. Trying to start on the third step is almost impossible, leaving those attempting it with feelings of disappointment and failure. In this analogy, we can factor in those who get a boost and can actually reach the second or third rung immediately. Boosters include family members or friends who are already in position and willing to give a boost. Our analogy also includes supporters who help people with steadiness and therefore enable them to climb each step more quickly and with less difficulty. This chapter is important for those who can't depend on boosters and supporters to land that dream job.

The two factors that affect your happiness the most are your relationships and your job. These areas each have a profound effect on the other. It is common for a person who is not happy at work to bring the discord home and make others miserable as well. The same happens when a person is experiencing difficulty at home and then tries to muster up some positive energy at work. Without our jobs and our relationships being in harmony, we can't be our happiest, and our trials are more difficult to overcome.

The self-assessment tests in Chapter 1 can show you a multitude of information if you actively seek it. If you are searching for understanding in relationships, those types of tests can bring more clarity as to what kind of person might be a good fit for you and why. If you are looking for happiness in a career, self-assessments can accomplish the same thing. If you seek a career that is not a good fit, you may find yourself unhappy at work and at home. If you are afraid of needles, you might need to reevaluate your dream of being a doctor. If you get sick to your stomach before giving a presentation in front of your college class, being a prosecutor might not be something you would be happy doing.

Desire to do a particular job doesn't necessarily translate into being good at it, and disinterest doesn't mean that you're deficient in the skills needed to do the job. However, people tend to like doing what they are good at, and people excel at things they like to do. Therefore, being or becoming good at what you choose to do for your job correlates with being happy in your career. Some people become knowledgeable and somewhat skillful in certain areas through exposure, and they subsequently transition into careers without much trouble. This type of experience is common when someone follows in the footsteps of a parent or older sibling. Someone raised by a parent who is an attorney would develop insight into that type of thinking, just as the daughter of a police officer is likely to be somewhat familiar with the police personality. How does a person who has not had these learning opportunities choose a career? How do you know what you can be good at if you haven't tried it?

Set Realistic Goals

A popular quotation from Laurence J. Peter (1919–1988) goes like this: "If you don't know where you are going, you'll probably end up somewhere else." In 2007, David P. Campbell published a book titled *If You Don't Know Where You're Going, You'll Probably End Up Somewhere Else: Finding a Career and Getting a Life*. According to Campbell, we all want choices, but to create choices, we must have goals. To reach your goals and expand your choices, you need assets, and the more the better. These assets can include a good education, good health, broadening experiences, talents, and—as mentioned in our ladder analogy—help from family and friends. In fact, Campbell puts assets in this order of importance for having the greatest impact on your future choices:

1. Talents and skills

2. Intellectual intelligence

3. Emotional intelligence

4. Education

5. Friends

6. Family

7. Experiences

8. Appearance

9. Health

The more assets you have going for you, the more choices you will have. What talents and skills do you already have? As we discussed at the beginning of this book, one of the questions many applicants are the least prepared for is "What are your strengths?" Often applicants have the relevant skills needed for a job but can't articulate them. Likewise, some applicants are dreadfully lacking the necessary skills for a job but unfortunately do not realize it. For example, consider some of the popular talent shows, such as *American Idol*, *America's Got Talent*, and *So You Think You Can Dance*. Before the judges select the final competitors, they view hundreds to thousands of tryouts, including many that are embarrassingly humorous. Professionals in the criminal justice system witness similar humorous tryouts. If some of the interviews were televised, they would make for an entertaining television show.

To set realistic goals, you should evaluate the talents and skills you already have as well as those you need for the career you are interested in. You then need to be realistic with your goals. One advantage of getting a degree is improving your knowledge and skills for a career. Improving in your abilities often means stepping outside your comfort zone. Consider public speaking, which is a valuable skill for many professions. How does a person who is frightful of public speaking become skilled at it? Those who are afraid to speak in public generally avoid it. Some people have handicaps that hinder their ability to become great public speakers no matter how much they practice.

Sometimes improving ourselves involves altering our way of thinking first. There is a prayer by American theologian Reinhold Niebuhr (1892–1971) that has been adopted by Alcoholics Anonymous and other 12-step programs. It has become known as the Serenity Prayer. The part of the prayer most widely used goes like this: "God, grant me the serenity to accept the things I cannot change, the courage to change the things I can, and the wisdom to know the difference."

Once you know the difference between what you can and can't change, you can concentrate more time and effort in the areas that will be of the most benefit. Most of our skills are improvable with practice. Some traits are not easily changeable, such as our demeanor and personality, but depending on your career choice, these may be the most important areas to concentrate on.

There are special talents and skills specific to particular jobs in the criminal justice field. Some say you practically need to walk on water to become a police officer. Some lawyers would tell you that it is equally challenging to be accepted to a top 40 law school. Employees in correctional facilities would likewise agree that special skills are needed to succeed, including the gift of gab, in which the wrong candidate would get swallowed up amid the argot working as a corrections officer. Throughout the remainder of this chapter, we will explore certain skills needed to work in the law enforcement arena. In subsequent chapters we will explore specific careers in more detail at agencies of all levels.

Issues With Police Work

Law enforcement is a highly sought after career, which makes it extremely difficult to get hired. It encompasses the federal, state, county, and city levels, as well as other miscellaneous agencies such as campus police and gaming officers. As we explore the skills necessary for state, county, and city law enforcement, we will refer to it broadly as *police work*. By understanding some of the more advanced matters in police work, you can better appreciate what skills are needed and determine if it is a career you could actually excel in and enjoy. The more one knows about what a police officer is and does, the better one can understand what type of person an agency is looking for. This knowledge can help you decide if you are a good fit for police work and can help you prepare for the hiring interview. It is important to note that it is not possible to fully comprehend the jobs and thought processes of police officers by reading a textbook. A graduate of an 18-week police academy, with another 18 weeks of field training and over 5 years on the street, would tell you that every call is different, and doing the job requires a variety of new approaches and techniques every shift. Additionally, most officers with 5 years or more of experience would say that they are confident they can handle anything that comes along. Police agencies are looking for that type of person.

Agencies invest a lot of time in the hiring process and a substantial amount of money in the training of their recruits. They want a person who, after sufficient training, can handle the variety of incidents that occur. What types of things do police officers have to handle? Do you have an adequate understanding of what is expected of you as a police officer?

Some of the best introductory textbooks on policing are comprehensive and cover the topic in a way that is easy to understand (e.g., Scaramella, Cox, & McCamey, 2010). I recommend studying an all-inclusive textbook for a basic understanding of policing. However, getting hired as a law enforcement officer and performing the job with competence requires a deeper insight. Knowledge of topics such as evidence-based policing and intelligence-led policing is good, but not exactly what recruiters are looking for at the hiring stage. Although a degree and a strong knowledge base are great assets, recruiters will be looking for someone who can do the job at the entry level with the potential to be great. Factors such as an appropriate thought process, uplifting personality, astute communication skills, and stable temperament are of higher importance to recruiters.

If you have not yet had a chance to study from an introductory policing textbook, you should ask yourself what you already know about police work. Ask yourself where you got that knowledge. The average citizen has not taken the opportunity to experience a police ride-along, nor have most people taken any criminal justice classes in college. The average citizen knows about police work only through the media, stories from family and friends, and brief observations or encounters during traffic incidents or reporting a crime.

To get the most out of this chapter, it is recommended that you consider the poem in Chapter 1 about the blind men and the elephant. Be open-minded to the reality that there is more to learn and, thanks to selective and fragmented media coverage, plenty to unlearn.

An example of how police work is distorted by the media is the illusion that police often use force against citizens. In reality, there is relatively little use of force by police officers in the United States. In fact, according to a database of the International Association of Chiefs of Police (2001), law enforcement officers in 1995 used some level of force only 4.19 times every 10,000 calls for service. The data in 1999 showed that force was used only 3.61 times for every 10,000 calls for service.

The following information is intended to help you better understand the police reality, which can help you start developing the necessary way of thinking to stand out in the hiring interview or, as a possible consequence, sway you to consider a different career. Some of the skills and expectations relative to police work might shock you as we visit some important and controversial issues in the field of policing.

The Use of Deception

An important paradox in policing that might be too conflicting for some to appreciate and accept is that an exceptional law enforcement officer is one who can use deception in the appropriate settings and yet be conclusively honest enough to pass a polygraph test. As mentioned earlier, it is difficult for interviewees to articulate their strengths in hiring interviews if they are not prepared. You can imagine the irony in an interview were you to answer the strength question by saying that you are a really good liar. It is not recommended that you answer the question that way, but recruiters are essentially looking for honest people who can be actors, including the ability to deceive. A person who has never done anything wrong might be a great bank teller or a priest but might lack the unusual characteristics that are needed to be a proficient law enforcement officer. However, anybody in law enforcement will tell you that dishonesty will get you fired as fast as committing crimes or other serious misconduct.

This contradiction can put police work in a bad light if not clearly understood. Mothers usually teach their children that they can trust certain professionals, such as teachers, doctors, and police officers, but you will rarely see a mother after her child tells a lie say to her child, "You would make a great police officer!" When trickery is used by law enforcement to develop criminal cases, defense attorneys often enjoy letting the jury know about it in a way that shocks them. Some citizens believe that police officers should never lie. Some citizens also feel that the police should disarm knife-wielding suspects using martial arts techniques and should shoot the gun out of the hands of a would-be cop killer. If you are one of these citizens, police work might not be the right job for you. However, if you can develop a "reality" mind-set like that of a police officer, you will not be far out of your wheelhouse during the hiring interview.

When is it okay for a police officer to lie? One of the few allowable circumstances is when it is done for the purpose of obtaining the truth. Police officers are fact finders. Regardless of the purpose at hand, such as to prevent crime or to protect and serve citizens, police officers must report the facts of an incident as accurately as possible. This includes honestly reporting any trickery or lies that were used to accomplish the task. If an officer obtains a confession from a suspect by falsely telling him that there were witnesses who saw him commit the crime, the officer must be honest and accurate in the report and in court testimony about the lie told to the suspect. When police are faced with a child molestation case in which there is little or no physical evidence, a confession from the suspect is likely the only way justice will be served. It is common for the police to ask a young victim to make a phone call (monitored and recorded) and deceive the perpetrator in an effort to solicit incriminating comments. This type of trickery by the police can shock people who are naive to police strategies. In such a situation, an officer may need to educate the jury on police tactics to help them understand that deception is allowable and necessary. Some jury members may still be appalled. Police officers also work a variety of undercover-type operations in which deception is the norm. You need to decide how you feel about the methods police use to achieve their goals. Can you, in good conscience, lie to a suspect in an investigation to gain a confession?

Regardless of the need to use deception in police work, there are ethical issues and gray areas that officers learn to work with (and work around) through experience. However, when it comes to a suspect's rights, reporting incidents, testifying in court, or answering questions during internal investigations, an officer must always be as honest as possible. Like so many other aspects of a police officer's job, the allowable situations for lying and deceiving are not specifically spelled out in policy. If you get hired as a recruit officer, you will need to learn how to survive in a fine-line career with vague and volatile guidelines. Most officers don't stress over the ambiguity and just survive on faith that they will be treated fairly if their behavior is ever questioned. They continue to learn from veteran officers, court decisions, and trial and error.

The Role of Acting in Police Work

Being a good deceiver correlates with being a good actor. The necessity to act isn't limited to police work only, but it is a big part of a police officer's job. Some refer to it as the ability to wear different hats. It is important that an interviewer knows that you have the ability to be an actor. If you can't show some level of fluctuation in your persona during your hiring interview, the recruiter might not feel that you can show it on the street. The interview is your one shot to demonstrate that you can. An officer needs to be able to leave a death scene where she just spoke softly and soothingly to the victim's family and arrive at a scene of melee and discord, shouting commands to unruly citizens in an authoritative fashion. This same officer may then need to interview a woman who was kidnapped by a stranger and brutally raped and then, 2 hours later, interview the perpetrator of the attack. Each of these scenarios requires a different demeanor on the officer's part. To do the job of a police officer well, one needs to be able to change hats from one call to the next. An officer might go home and have a good cry after handling a drowned baby incident earlier in the day, but during the shift, officers are expected to remain professional and wear whatever hat is necessary.

The Use of Discretion

Some of the toughest scenario-based questions that are asked in a hiring interview involve some kind of discretionary decision. These questions generally include issues such as use of force, integrity, critical thinking, and teamwork. To be prepared for these types of questions, one needs to be aware of the scope of an officer's discretionary powers. Police officers must constantly make decisions in situations in which there are several options. Even though there are many ways to accomplish things, the personnel who developed the interview questions have already decided what they feel would be the best answers. If a police officer makes a traffic stop, she can decide when and where to actually turn on the overhead lights to signal the driver to pull over. The officer can then decide whether to approach the car from the driver's side or the passenger's side. The officer may choose to have the driver step out of the car. There may be passengers to deal with. The officer might see or smell something in the car that brings in new options to choose from.

Depending on the circumstances, the driver may get a warning, be ticketed, or be arrested. If the driver is arrested and transported to jail, the officer would have to decide what to do about the suspect's vehicle. She may choose to have the car towed, call someone to come get it, or lock it and leave it at the scene. The officer may choose to read the Miranda warnings to the suspect and can decide when and where to do so. If the officer decides to conduct an interview, another group of choices is introduced. In many cases, officers can choose between booking suspects in jail or citing and releasing them with future court dates. The decision tree is significantly larger for incidents that aren't as routine as this example.

A difficult area for anyone to fully comprehend, including currently active police officers, is exactly what types of crimes are okay to give a citizen a free pass on. There is rarely a clear rule or policy that explains it. Protocols for these types of decisions are normally unwritten and passed down from veteran officers and supervisors through the years. A problem with this type of structure is that not all officers and supervisors agree on what should be tolerated and what should be strictly enforced. Police personnel bring their own opinions and values to the job. What is okay to overlook and what is not can become somewhat clouded throughout a career of working with different officers and supervisors. This tremendous discretionary power can result in situations of unfairness to citizens, such as racial bias, gender bias, age bias, and other similar instances of inequity. It also opens up possibilities for corruption, whereby officers may succumb when solicited with favors in exchange for a release without an arrest.

It is important to understand that a department's policy doesn't explicitly give permission for an officer to give a break to a citizen on anything. When an officer pours alcohol on the ground and tells underage drinkers to go home with no record made of the incident, the officer puts his job on the line by not following the policy of the department. Most agencies in this scenario would require a police report, for charges to be filed if appropriate, and for the alcohol to be placed into evidence until trial or proper destruction. A police officer today might choose to be lenient simply because another police officer in the past did the same thing for him or her. If an officer opts not to arrest a driver who is under the influence of alcohol and lets the driver call for a ride home, the officer is actually taking the risk of being disciplined. Again, there is no specific permission given in department policies to allow officers to make that type of decision, but this kind of discretion takes place all the time. Officers face the dilemma every shift of trying to balance what they feel they should do and what policy tells them to do.

Just as with the example of underage drinking, when an officer chooses a certain course of action, it could be for numerous reasons. If the jail is over-crowded and the dispatcher is holding several high-priority calls, an officer may choose to cut some slack to a driver who is inebriated. That same officer, during a slow shift on the following day, might arrest four to five people for driving under the influence of alcohol and give absolutely no breaks. In the busy night scenario with the overcrowded jail, there may be other officers who do not cut any slack for any reason. They might not want to risk answering to a supervisor who doesn't agree with their decisions. The lenient officers might end up taking a beating from the workload and may even find themselves without sufficient backup because other officers are busy with the lengthy procedures involved with booking suspects. There may even be serious calls, such as robberies or aggravated assault cases, waiting on hold for long periods of time because officers are unavailable. Police officers often must choose between the letter of the law and the spirit of the law, but there is no express written permission allowing officers to make many of the discretionary decisions they make.

One of the main reasons a police department has standards and policies is to protect it from lawsuits. If an officer follows his training and adheres to these policies, the department will likely back him up on lawsuits or citizen complaints. If the officer violates a policy, the department might not stand behind him in a civil lawsuit and could choose to discipline him, which can include termination. Even with this lose-lose quandary officers are faced with, they continue to make discretionary decisions on whom to arrest and whom to let go without documented permission to do so.

All officers bring in their own principles based on their life experiences. They have different agendas and preferable violations they specifically look for and enforce. They have different strengths and weaknesses. They have different personalities and approaches. They have different biases, too. If you enter the police world, you too will add to the diversity and bring your own heart and soul to the work. Can you survive in this type of work environment, with vast degrees of freedom and empowerment, yet with such ambiguity and, consequently, insecurity?

One more peculiar fact about discretion in the police world is that the higher ranking a person is in a department, the less discretion that person can exercise. As a police officer climbs the supervisory ladder in a department (from operations to middle management to upper management), her hands are tied more and more the higher she gets. The chief of police must follow the standards, policies, and procedures to a tee, with little or no deviation. This bit of information is very important, because you will want to answer questions in the hiring interview as though you are talking directly to the chief. In other words, for questions in which discretion is asked for, it is best to lean in the direction of what the chief would want to hear, not toward what you think most officers actually do in reality. We will be discussing this further in Chapter 11.

The Use of Force

Police officers periodically get shot and sometimes must shoot people. Do you have the fortitude to use lethal force against another human being? Do you comprehend when it is appropriate to do so? Use of force is closely linked to the topic of discretion. There are often scenario questions in the hiring interview that involve a use-of-force decision. Besides the questions about strengths and weaknesses, this is another area for which many candidates are unprepared. Therefore, by scoring high on these questions, one can stand out and move ahead of other applicants.

There is more on this topic in Chapter 11 to help you prepare for interview questions, but here is a brief advanced lesson on the use of force. Many colleges only lightly touch on this topic, and many police recruits learn it for the first time in the academy. Again, you need to know what a police officer does in order to know if this job is the right fit for you. If it is something you feel you can do, go for it!

There are different models for the use of force, and we will briefly discuss two of them here. The first is the continuum model, and the second is the Federal Law Enforcement Training Center (FLETC) model. The continuum model tries to match appropriate actions by an officer in response to an offender's behavior. The continuum of force generally contains five to seven levels, which include officer's presence, verbal commands, soft hand techniques, hard hand techniques, less-than-lethal force, and lethal force. Less-than-lethal weapons can sometimes be broken into two different levels, with pepper spray being on a slightly lower level than Tasers, beanbags, and pepper balls. The amount of force an officer uses depends on what level of resistance or threat an offender poses. Officers are always permitted to be "one up" on offenders, but this doesn't mean that an officer is restricted to a certain order, going from level 1 to level 2 to level 3 and so on. An officer can ratchet up several levels all at once if necessary. When an offender is only passively resisting, an officer will normally use soft hand techniques but could step it up if it becomes reasonably necessary to accomplish the task.

William Weigt: Investigator – Peoria Police Department

CJ: What is your current position?

WW: Investigator.

CJ: What are your typical job duties?

WW: I conduct detailed investigations on graffiti suspects and create jackets/group-ings on suspected taggers. I fire all evidence/impound weapons at the Peoria Police Department to get the shell casings for evidentiary purposes to match them to past cases. I am also in charge of the runaway juvenile cases for the city of Peoria.

CJ: How long have you been at your current assignment?

WW: Nine years at this position, 11 years at the Peoria Police Department.

CJ: What other positions have you held prior to this one?

WW: Police officer and police detective.

CJ: You do your police work in a wheelchair. Do you mind discussing what happened?

WW: On December 17, 2005, I was shot in the line of duty while trying to apprehend a homicide suspect. I was moving to a different position after myself and five other officers fired upon the suspect when I was shot in my upper left chest. The bullet missed my bulletproof vest, ricocheted off of a rib and lodged in my T-4/T-5 vertebrae. I fell to the ground and immediately could not move. I was trying to crawl back to cover, but could not move my lower extremities. I cleared over the radio "998-999," which indicates an officer is in a shooting and an officer has been shot. Officer Jason Smith ran to help me out of the line of fire. Jason was dragging me back behind my police vehicle with the assistance of Officer Jeremy Cooper when Officer Chris Dugan stepped in between the sus-pect and us and fired two rounds from his 12-gauge shotgun. Once behind my police vehicle, I laid there holding on to Officer Smith. I told Jason I couldn't move my legs and I was hurt. Jason could not see my wound and had no idea I was bleeding out from the inside and that I had a collapsed lung. I told Jason, "Tell my son to become a man and tell him I love him." Jason said, "You're fine, you just got nicked on the head." I had a scrape on the left side of my face from when I fell. I began to cough up a lot of blood and Jason and Jeremy knew it was more serious. A Maricopa county deputy who was on his way to work stopped to render assistance. His name is Kristen Dever. The other officers put me in the back of Kristen's truck and drove me to a safe place for the paramedics to assess my injury. I was advised there was an entry wound, but no exit wound. I was placed in an ambulance and driven to John C. Lincoln Hospital. I woke up from my coma three days later on December 20, 2005, which was my 31st birthday. I am now paralyzed from my chest down, which is called a complete injury, meaning my spinal cord is completely severed. There is much more to this incident, and I would really like to say "thank you" and express my love for all officers on my shooting scene that morning. Those officers are Jason Smith, Jeremy Cooper, Jeff Carpenter, Chris Dugan, Scott Borsche, and Maricopa County Deputy Kristen Dever.

CJ: Thank you for sharing your story. What are the requirements/qualifications for your current assignment?

WW: For the most part, the same as a police officer.

CJ: What steps did you go through during hiring?

WW: For being a police offer, it was background, physical test, written test, oral board, and psychiatric test, but the investigator spot was given to me. I was the first one, so really no "steps."

CJ: What advice can you offer students who might be interested in pursuing a similar career?

WW: Take it very serious! This job is bigger than one person. It is about being a family, working together, and pro-tecting everybody around you. Be ready for a lot of paperwork, but it is worth it. It is a job that is full of pride—in a good way. Do many ride-alongs. Get your feet wet that way, and pay attention at all times.

The continuum model has been used for years, but it does have some downfalls in modern law enforcement. The U.S. Supreme Court in *Graham v. Conner* (1989) held that force used by police officers is judged upon "objective reasonableness," a standard established by the Fourth Amendment, and incorporates the view of the totality of circumstances. In *Graham*, the court decided, "the test of reasonableness under the Fourth Amendment is not capable of precise definition or mechanical application." However, that is what the use-of-force continuum attempts to do. Many continuum models do not address the concept of the totality of circumstances. Most continuum models are structured in such a way that a specific subject action equates to a specific officer response, regardless of the totality of circumstances known to the officer at the moment force was used. Experienced law enforcement officers know that each use-of-force incident is unique and therefore has a different totality of circumstances. Because many local and state law enforcement agencies use the continuum model, it is important to be familiar with and be able to articulate your knowledge of the agency's use-of-force policy if asked about it in the hiring interview.

The FLETC model is a bit more general and basically follows the guidelines implied (and spelled out) in the Fourth Amendment. All the use-of-force training at FLETC is founded upon the Supreme Court's decisions in *Graham* and in *Tennessee v. Garner* (1985). FLETC focuses on the favorable law enforcement language used by the Supreme Court to teach students what the law tells them they can do, rather than what they can't. FLETC instructors attempt to resolve the various myths regarding the use of force, such as "an officer can never shoot someone in the back," "an officer can never shoot an unarmed person," and "an officer must exhaust all lesser means before using deadly force." Further myths that are dispelled are that "an officer must give a verbal warning before using deadly force," "an officer cannot use deadly force on a suspect wielding an edged weapon until the officer is within 21 feet," and "an officer must be in fear for his or her life before using deadly force." In dispelling these types of myths, students are less likely to err or hesitate during a use-of-force incident (Bostain, 2006).

One stumbling block some applicants run into is the fear of sounding too anxious or too aggressive. Although this is a legitimate concern, sounding too naive or hesitant is usually worse. A good portion of applicants derive many of their opinions about police work from the media, which results in a feeling that police overuse their power. As stated earlier, very little force is actually used in comparison with the overall frequency of citizen contacts, and consequently, there is in fact very little brutality in law enforcement. Although even once is too often for police brutality, the misconceptions regarding the overuse of force can hinder a person from being realistic. The more you can think like a police officer rather than a citizen who has been misled about police work through watching the nightly news, the better you will be at answering use-of-force questions. Could you take someone's life if you had to, cope with the emotional aftermath, and handle all the negative press that goes along with it?

The Polygraph Test

Are you honest enough to be a police officer? Have you committed any crimes that may disqualify you? To be hired by a law enforcement agency, you are expected to be the best of the best. Most large agencies require an applicant to pass a polygraph test. After a thorough background check and polygraph test, a department can feel assured that it has done its best to hire a safe and honest employee. You can examine the basic requirements and disqualifiers for the position of police officer in Chapter 3.

Not all agencies require polygraph tests, but almost all agencies do thorough background investigations. You should check the crime and drug history guidelines of the agency you want to work for. Although most large agencies require polygraph tests, corruption still exists. Because this is always a concern, there is often at least one scenario question in the interview that assesses an applicant's thinking process in the area of ethics. Some sample questions and answers appear in Chapter 11.

Internal Investigations

In police work, you are in the public eye and held to a higher standard. You are considered a police officer 24 hours a day, which means you are held to a higher standard 24 hours a day. Anything you do on your off-duty time is subject to scrutiny from the department and the public. Citizen complaints about unpleasant confrontations with police officers spark investigations from internal affairs. The reality of police work is that the harder working street officers (answering calls for service, writing tickets, and making arrests) will have a higher potential for citizen complaints because of the quantity and category of people they deal with. If a citizen complaint is serious enough, an officer is suspended from work until the accusation is resolved. Often complaints are unfounded and officers are cleared for duty, but the damage caused by the stress (and sometimes media coverage) lingers in the officer's memory, and the investigative report lingers in the officer's personnel file. If an officer is determined to be guilty of wrongdoing, the consequences may be severe because of the higher standard of police officers. This type of stress and other internal political issues can affect an officer's attitude, outlook on life, and overall happiness.

Police officers spend their careers surrounded by victimization, violence, and crime, which includes murders and other cases involving dead bodies, sexual assaults, kidnappings, child molestation, drugs, robberies, and many other experiences of sadness, chaos, and evil. A police officer is vulnerable to injury and death in the line of duty. Because you patrol in a marked car, criminals will usually know you are a police officer before you know they are criminals. Most deaths among police officers take place during arrests and transport, but some officers are murdered just because they are police officers. Faced with all of this, coupled with other miscellaneous external hurdles, police officers have above-average divorce and suicide rates. As hard as it is to get hired by a law enforcement agency, it is not surprising how many officers leave during their academy training or during the first 5 years of service once the reality sets in. Are you the type of person who can remain positive, maintain harmony in your home, and work 40 to 60 hours a week, dealing with some of the most vile people and most depressing experiences? Police work isn't for everyone, but most officers will tell you that it is a very rewarding career with more positives than negatives.

Investigation

The ideal cases are those in which an officer witnesses the crime and makes the arrest at the scene. This is the case with the crime of driving under the influence. Not only are DUIs one of the most prevalent cases a court receives, they also have an extremely high conviction rate—the highest in many jurisdictions. These cases can be a defense attorney's worst nightmare in cities that have traffic/DUI squads. These specialty units receive advanced training and become experts through numerous repetitions of investigation and court appearances.

Other than traffic-related offenses, the average beat officer will witness crimes in progress rarely. The majority of the cases originate from a citizen calling the station and requesting an officer. Often there is a witness who saw the crime take place, but to the attorneys and the jury, it is not considered the same level of proof as if the officer witnessed the crime. The officer's task is to investigate the facts while simultaneously imagining and formulating the court case in his mind and in his notes as he goes along. Officers fresh out of the academy are at a huge disadvantage without any court exposure. It could take a new officer two or three years to have enough court experience to know what he needs to do, ask, say, and document at the onset of the investigation. Too often a case is lost because of something the officer did or didn't do in the first minutes of the investigation. This happens in a variety of ways. Consider this example of how the simplest things can make or break a case:

Officer Davis got dispatched to an attempted kidnapping of a 14-year-old female from a vehicle she was sitting in at a mall. The dispatcher told Officer Davis that several witnesses came to the aid of the victim and that the suspect left the scene in a blue four-door sedan. Upon arrival, Officer Davis decided to immediately get more information about the suspect and vehicle so he could radio the updated description to other officers.

He asked the group to hurry and give him as much descriptive information as they could. The victim and witnesses started giving Officer Davis the suspect and vehicle description, which differed among the group. As Officer Davis tried to formulate a description, the group came to more of a consensus and he was able to narrow it down to a green two-door sedan. He advised other officers and the suspect was quickly located and subsequently arrested. Officer Davis took a statement from the victim and all the witnesses.

At trial, six months later, Officer Davis testified and then got cross-examined by the defense attorney. The attorney asked Officer Davis if he separated the witnesses upon his arrival to the scene in order to prevent them from influencing each other. He asked Officer Davis if he documented what all the witnesses individually described before they came to a final description that was given to other officers. After Officer Davis answered "no" to both questions, he got excused. The defense attorney later called a communications expert to the stand who testified that witness recall is highly inconsistent. He testified that if witnesses listen to each other give accounts of what they saw, it would likely distort their memory.

The defense attorney later narrated a convincing closing argument to the jury. Although the correct suspect was arrested, the jury ended up finding the suspect not guilty. Two of the jurors agreed to talk to the attorneys after the trial. They explained that the officer not separating the witnesses was the most damaging part of the state's case. Although Officer Davis never again made the same mistake, a dangerous felon was released back among the citizens that Officer Davis was paid to protect.

There are numerous rules and standards that govern investigations including the collection of evidence, search and seizure, interview and interrogation, and courtroom behavior. There are plenty of opportunities to muck up a case somewhere along the way. The case doesn't just fall into place as the officer conducts the investigation. The officer has to make it happen through skilled techniques that may include trickery, wit, and critical thinking. The focus of an investigation can be constantly shifting. The case against a suspect can be very strong at one point, but can become weak within minutes as more information is obtained. The skilled investigator knows the right time to make the arrest and set the criminal justice process in motion. Arresting a suspect too quickly can be devastating to a case, and you can't undo it. Lacking celerity can also have severe consequences. Imagine the hit an officer would take from the family, the media, and his own conscience if he delayed arresting a child molester, which ultimately resulted in the victimization of another child. Police officers carry an exorbitant amount of responsibility for exactness and probity. Unlike most jobs, a mistake made in police work isn't met with much clemency, and there is little opportunity for propitiation.

Interviewing and Interrogating

Interviewing and interrogating are important tasks in police work; hence, a recruiter needs to believe that an applicant has these abilities. An interview is an exercise of information gathering. An interrogation is an exercise in persuasion, with the goal being the elicitation of true admissions and hope-fully a true confession. The goals are different, and so are the fundamentals and strategies. A skilled interviewer obtains as much accurate information as possible, which is not just a matter of listening to a story and taking notes. Victims and witnesses need prodding and sometimes need coaxing, especially if they are witnesses against a family member they love. However, the inter-view is not accusatory like an interrogation. A skilled interviewer builds rapport and asks the right questions.

A skilled interviewer is a good communicator, which means he can listen attentively without interrupting, yet can remember what to follow up on for clarifications. With experience, an officer learns to ask about things the victim or witness might not even think is important. There are a variety of factors that dictate an officer's approach. The rules and techniques are different for juveniles in interviews and interrogations. An officer or detective will inter-view a victim of a sexual assault differently than a victim of a delayed theft report being made for insurance purposes.

An interrogation requires special skills. Some officers are far better than others. Interrogation skills are especially crucial for detectives, but having beat officers with sharp interrogation skills is valuable. The assumption is that the person who committed the crime does not want to admit it. In cases where the suspect might be looking at several years in prison or the death penalty, one can imagine the difficulty in gaining a confession, but skilled interrogators get these kinds of confessions all the time. Even if a suspect does not confess to the crime, there are usually several admissions that are made in the interview that can be used in court. Even the smallest admission can make or break a case. An experienced interrogator knows how to solicit those seemingly small statements. An example is a sexual assault suspect. Before the interrogation, the suspect has two choices. He can deny he was the person involved, or in the case of date rape, that penetration ever occurred, or he can admit there was penetration and claim it was consensual. The interrogator wants a full confession, but if the suspect at least admits to consensual pen-etration, it narrows the options that a defense attorney can work with. An admission of penetration with consent would especially hamper the defense if the victim has cuts and bruises and a knife was allegedly used and seized. The interrogator can obtain this type of admission through deception if he chooses. It is easier if there was semen found during the sexual assault exam, but without it, the interrogator can still convince the suspect there is some other kind of evidence. A common ruse is to downplay the importance of obtaining the admission and tell the suspect that you can already prove he was the person who had sex with the victim. Then explain that the only issue left is to figure out if it was consensual. Most suspects take the bait and admit to having consensual sex with the victim.

As discussed earlier, police are allowed to deceive people in appropriate situ-ations. Police officers also get deceived. In fact, some criminals are outstanding deceivers with years of practice. Officers are fact finders, and they need to be able to evaluate statements from citizens for accuracy and truthfulness.

An officer who isn't naturally suspicious of ulterior motives may be easily tricked. Therefore, an applicant who appears too naive and trusting of others might not impress an interviewer.

Interviewers for the hiring of law enforcement positions are generally experienced officers who are very good at what they do. Regardless of specific questions you are asked, the interviewer will continuously be observing and assessing you for numerous traits during the entire interaction. Make sure the interviewer knows that you are not one of the naive ones. If you do not come across as clever, assertive, quick witted, and intelligent, you might not convince the interviewer that you have what it takes.

Report Writing

Skill in written communication is another important element of the model police officer. There is usually some sort of handwritten assignment included in the hiring process. At the hiring stage, the expectations are higher now than they were back in the 1980s, yet we handwrite much less than we did back then. In the early 1980s, before word processing was common and before spell check, officers handwrote reports on a quadruplicate form, with a bottle of Wite-Out and dictionary handy. To pass the written communication test, a candidate needed to write legibly and mostly grammatically correct. In Mesa, Arizona, a high school English teacher was called on to grade the one-page papers for a pass or fail designation. Spelling, grammar, and punctuation errors were marked in red. More than five red marks was a failure. The philosophy was to hire those that already had basic skills and then sharpen their skills through the numerous academy assignments. That way of thinking didn't work out well. Police academies provide a standardized amount of hours dedicated to report writing, but they aren't set up to teach the fundamentals of professional writing. The new philosophy is to hire those with adept writing skills so they are likely to graduate the academy with the ability to write a professional police report upon the very first opportunity.

There is more to writing police reports than the basic mechanics previously discussed. It might seem as straightforward as simply explaining what took place, like updating a personal diary. When a teenage girl goes on a four-hour date and gets her first kiss, her diary entry might look something like this:

Dear Diary,

I kissed Johnny tonight after the movie. It was better than I could have ever imagined. I think I'm in love. He asked me out again. I can't wait.

This short example is accurate as to what happened, but it leaves a lot of questions to the reader. What happened leading up to the kiss? Where did it take place? How long was the kiss? What happened after the kiss? Conversely, if the four hours were covered completely, the entry into the diary could fill up all the pages before it ever got to the part about the kiss. So what should be included when reporting an event? What should be left out?

Knowing what to incorporate into a police report is something a recruit starts to learn in the academy but understands far more clearly once he starts testifying in court. You also find out in court that no matter how much information you put in the report, a defense attorney can still make a jury think you did a poor job of documenting the facts. Getting through the report bashing from the defense attorney often comes down to how good the officer is in testifying in court, which we will discuss in the next section.

Basically, if something is not documented in the police report, it didn't happen. This is true as far as the jury is concerned. There are two common exceptions. First, an officer might disclose undocumented information to the defense attorney prior to trial, usually during a deposition. Once it has been disclosed, it can normally be brought up during direct testimony. Second, the defense attorney might solicit undocumented information during court testimony. An example is when a defense attorney asks a question outside of what is in the report, such as "were you wearing sunglasses when you saw my client swerve?" Once you answer the question, he then asks why such information wasn't in the report. This clever type of ploy makes the jury think the officer purposely left out information that should have been included. Other than these exceptions, if something isn't written in the report, it usually can't be brought up in front of the jury. This doesn't mean other witnesses can't testify to unexpected things that they did or saw, but officers are expected to disclose everything before trial via the police report and a deposition with the attorneys.

Although officers rarely regret writing too much in a report, they have to work within the time frames allotted by their agencies. Unlike the teenage girl writing in her diary about a four-hour date, it is common for an officer to have three or more reports to write at the end of shift. On rare occasions, officers can write the reports in their car between calls for service, but the reports are usually written later at the station with the help of notes and, occasionally, tape recordings and photos.

The officer is closely scrutinized for the amount of time he puts into report writing. If the officer earns too much money by working overtime, it isn't assumed that he is just a really hard worker. The normal assumption is that he is slow at report writing. Consequently, officers generally write the minimal amount of information necessary to get by. Reports that are informational and require no follow-up can be as short as one page. A burglary with evidence, suspects, and arrests can be more than 20 pages, and homicides can require reports of 50–100 pages collectively. With experience, an officer learns what questions to ask, what to investigate, what notes to write, what pictures to take, and how to put it all together professionally several hours later. Don't take English class lightly if you are pursuing a career in law enforcement! If you aren't a good writer, the best time to start improving has already passed. The second best time is now.

Court Testimony

All the hard work put into a case is wasted if the officer can't brave the sapience and craftiness of the defense attorney. The officer must be totally honest in his testimony, but there is much more that goes on in the courtroom and behind the scenes than what the jury realizes. Good court attorneys are psychological consummates. They develop a cornucopia of influential techniques that they use elusively throughout a trial. They get a lot of practice with juries, whereas most street officers might testify in a jury trial once or twice a year. This is one of the reasons why big cases are usually handed off to detectives in the early stages. Detectives can find themselves in court once or twice a month. They get to know the personalities and maneuvers of the attorneys, which helps even the playing field.

Officers that understand the clever and indirect exploits during trial develop their own influential skills and face the challenge with alacrity. The officer is just one witness, but many cases have been lost because the police officer wasn't prepared for the ingenious repartee of the defense attorney. Defense attorneys know that attacking the officer's credibility, work, and/or documentation will more often than not help their case. This is something officers should expect and prepare for. The best way to prepare for your battle with the defense attorney is to know more about the attorney's job and look at it from his point of view. Here is a quick synopsis of what takes place in the attorneys' world.

Attorneys want to win their cases. As they gain experience, they develop their preferred styles and strategies, but just like police officers who face new experiences every day, attorneys face new cases, new witnesses, and new juries. Attorneys therefore must be flexible and willing to react and adjust quickly and cleverly when necessary. Although a trial is very serious to all involved, it is easier to understand some of the clever strategies that take place in the courtroom (and behind the scenes) if you compare it to a game. We will use the game of poker, since it is rich with schadenfreude and universally familiar. The game starts when the prosecuting attorney is dealt a case. He or she will review the case to decide what can be used and what is of little benefit. Instead of cards, the prosecutor has witnesses and physical evidence to work with. Like cards, the witnesses and pieces of evidence are of different strengths, such as an unlikeable victim or a well-respected politician as a witness. The prosecutor can then request further follow-up from the police department in the hope of strengthening the case even more, or the prosecutor can fold and decide that the case isn't worth playing out. Follow-up can include a variety of tasks, such as additional interviews, lab work, or searches. Although similar to a poker game, one difference is that when the prosecutor is ready to play his hand, the defense attorney gets to see a large chunk of it. The defense attorney then develops a strategy to defeat the prosecutor's hand. Part of the strategy a defense attorney uses is to find (or create) weaknesses in the case. This is done mainly through interviews with witnesses, including police officers. An experienced defense attorney approaches interviews with the strategy of creating weaknesses in the case. This is done cleverly and often results in inexperienced police officers giving ammunition to the defense attorney without even realizing it. Defense attorneys delight in any conflicting statements made by officers and any sloppy police work.

Defense attorneys must be just as good actors as are police officers on the street. If there are no mistakes in the interview or no sloppy police work, a defense attorney may talk the defendant into accepting a plea bargain. The defense attorney works hard to minimize the sentence on a plea bargain by pointing out the weakness of the prosecutor's case and providing a short summary of what is predicted to happen if the case goes to trial. Each attorney uses carefully selected words in selling his or her case to the other, hoping to get the opposing side to cower and give up ground. This is one of the opportunities for an attorney to exercise his skills in persuasion. He will also use his cleverness and influencing panache when interviewing witnesses and performing in front of the jury.

A prosecutor might feel very confident in a case and insist that the defendant plea to the charge without any guarantee of a lighter sentence. The defense attorney might riposte by reminding the prosecutor that a particular witness has already changed the story a couple of times and therefore might cause the jury to come back with a not guilty verdict. Just as in a poker game, there is always the unknown of what will happen if the hand is played out, but the players hope others will fold to play it safe.

The trial is where attorneys need their poker faces most. They are playing against each other, and it is the jury they must convince. The prosecutor must convince the jury beyond a reasonable doubt. The defense attorney must provide that reasonable doubt. This is done by the clever use of influential dialogue and creative subtleties. It might appear to a jury that the opposing attorneys are not fond of each other, but in reality most attorneys who oppose each other have mutual respect and can often be seen joking around together when the jury is out of view.

Prosecutors and public defenders work for the government. Public defenders are a necessary part of the judicial system. They are generally more experienced in criminal court than private attorneys. Public defenders get to know prosecutors and judges very well because of the number of hours spent with them in court. Public defenders (and prosecutors) are subjected to more scrutiny than private attorneys. This is not to say that private attorneys are louche. Private attorneys work for a different boss. If a private attorney steps over the line ethically during a trial, his or her boss might never know about it or might not discipline the attorney if it is reported. This is also true with police officers. Unless a prosecutor takes the time to report a police officer that may have acted questionably to his or her sergeant, a dishonest officer can continue unethical practices undetected.

Secrecy is an important element in court proceedings. All the participants in the courtroom (judge, jury, prosecutor, defense attorney, police officers, and witnesses) are bound by confidentiality about certain information at different stages in the court process. This can make the process very difficult at times.

At home, a prosecutor will be unable to discuss a case with the family. A prosecutor may know that a child molester has four prior convictions for child molestation, but she must keep that fact secret from the jury during the trial of a new case. Breaking the court's rules of secrecy can result in a mistrial and disciplinary action. Can you survive in this adversarial arena should you choose a career in law enforcement? Do you already have some of the necessary skills? What are the skills that officers can refine to improve their performance in court? How can officers influence the jury?

One of the most important factors in influencing others is attractiveness. How do you fare? Actually, there is much more to attractiveness than a chiseled figure and picturesque facial features. You can't do much about your height, gender, or race, but attractiveness can be enhanced. This is done through good hygiene, good grooming, makeup, staying in good physical shape, maintaining a professional wardrobe, and exuding confidence. Many agencies require their officers to wear their uniform to court. Detectives are usually required to wear a suit. Homicide and sex crime detectives might find themselves in trials that span two to three weeks. They are encouraged to own at least two suits.

You also need to be cognizant that the colors you wear will have an effect on how others perceive you. For example, dark colors (black, dark gray, and dark blue) are considered power colors and can boost your influential prowess. The color of a necktie is important too. A red tie is too emotionally strong, but a blue tie represents peace and tranquility and is considered the opposite of red. Green is calming and refreshing, and yellow is considered cheerful and an attention getter.

Another important area of influence is using the proper language. An effective testifier knows when to use an active or a passive voice. An example of a passive way to phrase a sentence is "the victim was assaulted by the suspect." The active voice would phrase it "the suspect assaulted the victim." Using an active voice makes statements sound clearer and less wordy. Knowing when to use which type of language is a skill that can be developed with practice. These little tricks of persuasion (attractiveness, wearing the right colors, and using the right language) are all important in your hiring interview, too. Look for opportunities to practice.

The Dangers and Stress of Police Work

After time, many police officers get lackadaisical in their jobs when it comes to officer safety. Those with military or correctional backgrounds are the least likely to experience this injudicious relaxation on the job. Police officers have the privilege of working with law-abiding citizens as well as the criminal element of society. Since officers don't always know who is who, they have to approach almost all situations at a high level of awareness.

In the police world there is an analogy known as the "color clock." The color clock compares colors, similar to those on a traffic signal (but with white substituted for green) with the awareness levels of an officer facing various stimulants. The color clock can be applied to many scenarios, but most citizens aren't routinely preoccupied with personal safety concerns like the police are.

The color white is used to represent a safe, relaxed frame of mind. This is usually the mentality people have when they are at home with family, in church, or engaged in other activities in a safe environment. White represents very low stress. Our bodies need to be in white periodically so as not to release potentially harmful chemicals unnecessarily. Constant stress can lead to harmful effects in the body. Police officers need to learn how to relax at appropriate times because much of their lives are filled with stress and adrenaline rushes.

The color yellow represents a stage of enhanced awareness. Being in yellow prepares a person for what could happen. There are times when a person needs to be in yellow. Anytime a person is vulnerable, such as being outdoors or home alone, she would be wise to do so in yellow. Being in yellow means not having tunnel vision. You are cognizant of all the activity around you. A teenage girl walking home from school in white (thinking about what she will do when she gets home) might not notice a man who just drove past her for the third time. For police officers, it is common to start transitioning into yellow while putting on the uniform. Police officers rarely have the luxury of being in white while on duty.

Red is the fight-or-flight stage when adrenaline is released. Adrenaline is a powerful hormone the body releases in response to excitement and emergency situations. The heart rate increases, the blood vessels contract, and the airways dilate. Speed and strength are increased, and at the same time there is a decrease in the feeling of pain. When a person enters the red zone, it is difficult to rationalize. It is normal for a person to go into panic mode in this stage. This is especially true if a person was in white instead of yellow when the stimulus presented itself. When panic sets in, the body reacts the way it normally does because you have less control of your thinking. This is why it is important to mentally prepare and physically train for what you want your normal response to be. If a person normally screams when a spider appears, this is likely how that person will respond to a kidnap attempt. A popular saying goes like this: It is better to prepare and prevent than to repair and repent. For this reason, law enforcement personnel repetitiously practice their firearms and self-defense tactics to instill the proper, normal reaction during panic mode. Firearms instructors attempt to set up scenarios as realistically as possible, imitating incidents that would likely cause an adrenaline release. It is not uncommon for officers to accidentally fire their weapons during training (sometimes resulting in injuries or fatalities) because of a well-planned course that puts the officers in red. This type of training (done repetitiously) instills a new norm for the officers. In theory, they develop new habits and will therefore react the way they do in training when they are too keyed up to think clearly.

It is extremely difficult to keep a level head when someone jumps from white to red. Perpetrators count on this advantage when they use the element of surprise. Robbers and rapists are thrilled when their victims freeze just like they are commanded to. Officers can't afford to be caught in white while at work. They naturally remain in yellow while in public, especially while on patrol. By being in yellow at the onset of a dangerous experience, less drastic shock to the body is the likely outcome. When correctional officers transfer to police work, they have a huge advantage in the academy over other recruits with little or no experience with life's perils.

The Realities of Working in Criminal Justice

Being realistic and being negative aren't the same thing. Some children start playing peewee football and decide that they want to play in the National Football League (NFL) when they grow up. When they stand on the sidelines during middle school or high school football games and watch the starters play, they begin to get more realistic about their futures. If high school starters are good enough to play for major colleges, they are normally given an eye-opening orientation at the outset of their college careers. In that orientation, they are told that their education is the most important part of their college experience because the odds of playing for the NFL are slim. According to the NFL (2013), in 2012, only 253 college players were drafted to the NFL. Only 256 were drafted in 2011.

Too many students beginning their criminal justice degrees have the goal of working for federal agencies such as the Federal Bureau of Investigation or the U.S. Marshals Service. The reality is that of the 10,000 applicants to the bureau each year, only 500 to 750 are hired (Federal Bureau of Investigation, 2013). Those who are hired as agents rarely reach that rung of the ladder right out of college. Many of those without boosters have worked in law enforcement or the military. They climbed the ladder one step at a time.

Change

According to Thomas Jefferson, "Nothing can stop the man with the right mental attitude from achieving his goal and nothing on earth can help the man with the wrong mental attitude." What is the right mental attitude? Consider these quotations:

- God grant me the serenity to accept the people I cannot change, the courage to change the one I can, and the wisdom to know it's me. (Anonymous)
- When you are through changing, you're through. (Bruce Barton)

- Stubbornness does have its helpful features. You always know what you are going to be thinking tomorrow. (Glen Beaman)
- To exist is to change, to change is to mature, to mature is to go on creating oneself endlessly. (Henri Bergson)
- Those who expect moments of change to be comfortable and free of conflict have not learned their history. (Joan Wallach Scott)
- Continuity gives us roots; change gives us branches, letting us stretch and grow and reach new heights. (Pauline R. Kezer)
- If you would attain to what you are not yet, you must always be displeased by what you are. For where you are pleased with yourself there you have remained. Keep adding, keep walking, keep advancing. (Saint Augustine)
- Our only security is our ability to change. (John Lilly)
- The only man I know who behaves sensibly is my tailor; he takes my measurements anew each time he sees me. The rest go on with their old measurements and expect me to fit them. (George Bernard Shaw)

These are all positive and motivational thoughts, and that is exactly how we should approach our strategies for change. Expect change to be difficult and uncomfortable, similar to dieting to shed 10 to 15 pounds. Do you know what you get if you keep doing what you've always done? If you want to become better at public speaking, speak in public but with a renewed purpose. Approach those things that are out of your comfort zone as practice, but make it perfect practice. If you are one of those students who stand in front of the class and read every word from a PowerPoint presentation in a monotone voice, you will probably be doing the same thing next year. To improve, you must practice doing it the right way, which will likely be uncomfortable. If you are lacking in your written communication skills, take a writing class on the side. Go back and learn those things you missed in middle school and high school when you didn't have the motivation. Remember, criminal justice agencies are also working toward improvement. They want to hire someone who can potentially make them better. Stay focused on that! Are you capable of becoming that person? If your answer is yes, you are correct. If your answer is no, you are correct.

The Search for Happiness

One approach to setting goals is to choose a place where you want to end up and then work as hard as you can to get there. You may never reach your goal, but you will likely make positive strides along the way. An alternative approach is like that of a sophomore pole-vaulter. A pole-vaulter's goal is to beat her personal record. Each time she performs a vault, she is seeking to better herself. She doesn't really risk that insidious feeling of failure because regardless of how she does today, she still holds the record. If she compares herself with the juniors and seniors who vault higher, she is prone to improve, but she might never reach her goal. With "doing your best" as the primary goal, and "being the best you can be" as the long-range goal, there is a high likelihood of success and happiness.

Consider the old saying, "The grass is always greener on the other side of the fence." It only makes sense that someone younger or less fortunate than you is standing at his fence looking into your yard. If you do jump the fence to greener pastures, bask in the success before you look over the next fence and find an even greener hue. Remember, you eventually need to lay down your blanket and enjoy your picnic before it gets dark and the color of the grass doesn't matter anymore.

Summary

Career development is a process. Without some kind of help, one needs to plan on climbing the ladder of success one rung at a time. Expecting to skip rungs of the ladder can potentially result in a feeling of failure and unhappiness. The two factors that affect your happiness most are your relationships and your job. They both have an effect on each other. People tend to like doing what they are good at and excel at things they like to do. Therefore, becoming good at what you choose to do for your job correlates with being happy in your career.

People want choices, but to create choices, you need goals. To reach your goals and expand your choices, you need assets, and the more the better. Some of the most important assets are your talents and skills. You should assess the talents and skills you already have and those you need for the career you are interested in. You then need to be realistic with your goals.

Improving skills and abilities often means stepping outside your comfort zone. Sometimes it involves altering your way of thinking first. The Serenity Prayer, which is used in Alcoholics Anonymous programs, gives perspective to our way of thinking. Most of our skills are improvable with practice. Some skills are more important than others among different careers. You should learn as much as possible about the job you are seeking in order to know what kinds of skills are needed. You should also be realistic about whether a particular dream job is a good fit for you.

One of the skills necessary for police work is being a good actor. Some areas to consider in police work are the ambiguity of the rules, the stress from internal and external factors, and the potential for use of force against citizens and their use of force against you. There are some disqualifiers from police work, such as prior drug use and a criminal history.

Other than traffic-related offenses, the average beat officer will witness crimes in progress rarely. The majority of the cases originate from a citizen calling the station and requesting an officer. Often there is a witness who saw the crime take place, but to the attorneys and the jury, it is not considered the same level of proof as if the officer witnessed the crime. The officer's task is to investigate the facts while simultaneously imagining and formulating the court case in his mind and in his notes as he goes along.

Interviewing and interrogating are important tasks in police work; hence, a recruiter needs to believe that an applicant has these abilities. An interview is an exercise of information gathering. An interrogation is an exercise in persuasion, with the goal being the elicitation of true admissions and hopefully a true confession. The goals are different, and so are the fundamentals and strategies.

Skill in written communication is another important element of the model police officer. There is usually some sort of handwritten assignment included in the hiring process. At the hiring stage, the expectations are higher now than they were back in the 1980s, yet we handwrite much less than we did back then. Knowing what to incorporate into a police report is something a recruit starts to learn in the academy but understands far more clearly once he starts testifying in court. You also find out in court that no matter how much information you put in the report, a defense attorney can still make a jury think you did a poor job of documenting the facts. Basically, if something is not documented in the police report, it didn't happen.

All the hard work put into a case is wasted if the officer can't brave the sapience and craftiness of the defense attorney. The officer must be totally honest in his testimony, but there is much more that goes on in the courtroom and behind the scenes than what the jury realizes. Good court attorneys are psychological consummates. They develop a cornucopia of influential techniques that they use elusively throughout a trial. They get a lot of practice with juries where most street officers might testify in a jury trial once or twice a year. This is one of the reasons why big cases are usually handed off to detectives in the early stages.

The prosecutor and defense attorney use their influential skills to win their cases. They both attempt to persuade the jury to lean their way. Their success ultimately depends on the strength of their cases, but their own litigation skills also come into play. Prosecutors and defense attorneys get more court experience than most other lawyers and are also under very close scrutiny.

Police officers must be mentally and physically ready for incidents that create panic. The "color clock" explains the mental state of a correctional officer throughout the day. White represents a relaxed mental state, such as being at home watching television. Yellow represents an enhanced state of awareness in which tunnel vision goes away and a person is more cognizant of what is going on around her. A correctional officer starts transitioning into yellow as she puts on her uniform to go to work. Red represents a state of panic and adrenaline release, also known as the fight-or-flight response, in which a person faces a potentially dangerous situation. A correctional officer would quickly move to red when attacked by a prisoner or just by hearing a loud alarm go off. It is easier to move to red if a person is already in yellow. Going from white to red will create a greater deal of panic and may make it harder to react appropriately.

You need to be realistic in setting goals. It is unrealistic to expect to go straight from college into your dream career. There may be other steps of the ladder to be achieved first. Change and improvement are always possible, but patience and effort are required. The main things to change are your own perspective and attitude. To be happy, you need to eventually be okay with the color of the grass you stand on and not continue looking over other fences.

DISCUSSION QUESTIONS

1. Do you agree with the statement, "The two factors that affect your happiness most are your relationships and your job"? Why or why not?
2. Do you agree with Campbell's ranked order of assets? What, if anything, would you change?
3. How can a person who is fearful of public speaking become skilled at it?
4. How does it affect your view of police to know that deception is an important part of police work?
5. When is it okay for a police officer to lie?
6. What mental attitude does one need to effect change?
7. Of the two options listed in the section "The Search for Happiness," which approach to setting goals do you most relate to? Why?

REFERENCES

Bostain, J. (2006). Use of force: Are continuums still necessary? *FLETC Journal, 4*(2), 33–37.

Campbell, D. (2007). *If you don't know where you're going, you'll probably end up somewhere else: Finding a career and getting a life.* South Bend, IN: Sorin Books.

Federal Bureau of Investigation. (2013). *Careers.* Retrieved from https://www.fbijobs.gov/index.asp

Graham v. Connor, 490 U.S. 386 (1989).

International Association of Chiefs of Police. (2001). *Police use of force in America 2001.* Retrieved from http://theiacp.org/Portals/0/pdfs/Publications/2001useofforce.pdf

National Football League. (2013). *Draft: History.* Retrieved from http://www.nfl.com/draft/history/fulldraft

Scaramella, G. L., Cox, S. M., & McCamey, W. P. (2010). *Introduction to policing.* Thousand Oaks, CA: Sage.

Tennessee v. Garner, 471 U.S. 1 (1985).

SECTION 2

Pursuing

3

Local and State Law Enforcement

Local law enforcement refers to city and county agencies, which make up 77% of the nation's police employees. Another 14% work in various federal agencies, and only about 9% work for state governments. According to the Bureau of Justice Statistics (Reaves, 2011), local law enforcement consists of approximately 1,133,000 employees with about 765,000 of those being sworn. Being hired initially by a local agency is much likelier than starting a career with a federal agency, mainly because of the number of opportunities available. Being hired by a law enforcement agency is extremely difficult and may seem impossible to some who have already tried, but the opportunities increase if a person is willing to apply where the openings are and not look solely at his or her hometown.

Sworn employees of city agencies are called police officers. Those working for county agencies are called deputies, and sworn state employees are referred to as officers or troopers. Police officers, deputies, and state troopers handle a larger variety of incidents than federal agencies. There are more city codes and state statutes to enforce than federal laws. Additionally, local and state agencies are first responders and thus are at citizens' beck and call for whatever need arises. Federal agencies are more specialized and only some are first responders. Specialization also takes place in state and local agencies, and one can choose to excel and work primarily in a particular area of expertise, such as traffic enforcement, accident investigation, burglary, robbery, child crimes, sex crimes, drug enforcement, special tactics and weapons, and auto theft.

Local Law Enforcement

Police departments range in size from one sworn officer to thousands. The top 10 largest police agencies in the United Sates are listed in Exhibit 3.1. We will use Mesa, Arizona, as a reference for basic hiring and pay scale information, as well as a succinct job description for police officers.[1] This information is similar across the country, including county and state law enforcement. Mesa is the 38th largest city in the United States, with an estimated population of 462,376 in 2015. The estimated median household income in 2015 was $48,136. The full-time police force in 2015 was 1,211 employees, with 782 of those sworn (City of Mesa, 2015).

A police recruit attends the police training academy to learn to perform the responsibilities of an entry-level law enforcement officer, which include interacting with a culturally and socially diverse population; using discretion in solving problems; maintaining public order; preventing crime; enforcing laws and ordinances; conducting investigations; making arrests; issuing summonses, citations, and warnings; and assisting the public. Upon successful completion of academy instruction, a recruit receives further training in the Field Officer Training Program.

The academy is a training course for protective service work in the police department. An employee in this class receives instruction and field training

Exhibit 3.1   Top 10 Largest Police Agencies in the United States

Department	Population	Agency Sworn	Per 1,000	Agency Total	Per 1,000
New York	8,220,196	35,216	4.28	51,480	6.26
Chicago	2,824,434	13,336	4.72	15,436	5.47
Los Angeles	3,870,487	9,504	2.46	12,834	3.32
Philadelphia	1,435,533	6,778	4.72	15,436	5.47
Houston	2,169,544	4,892	2.25	6,317	2.91
Washington, D.C.	588,292	3,913	6.65	4,493	7.64
Phoenix	1,541,698	3,231	2.10	4,379	2.84
Dallas	1,239,104	3,122	2.52	3,739	3.02
Miami-Dade County	1,082,395	3,120	2.88	4,495	4.15
Detroit	860,971	3,049	3.54	3,418	3.97

Source: Reaves (2010).

in the areas of patrol methods, causes of criminality, courtroom procedures, fingerprinting, community relations, and other law enforcement topics to prepare the recruit for a full-time position with the police department. After successful completion of academy instruction and field training, a police recruit is promoted to the class of police officer and performs law enforcement patrol activities in a designated area of the city.

The new rookie officer is assigned to a particular shift with a particular sergeant who assigns the new officer to a specific beat. The new officer's work methods and skills are checked and measured through personal inspections, discussions, and careful reviews of written reports.

Typical police duties involve an element of personal danger. Officers must regularly take action without direct supervision, exercising independent judgment in meeting routine and emergency needs of citizens. Police work requires occasional physical exertion under adverse circumstances, such as foot chases and physical struggles. Officers are subject to rotating shifts, including weekends and holiday work. The minimum qualifications for most large police departments are broken down in Exhibit 3.2.

Exhibit 3.2   Minimum Requirements for Most Large Police Departments

Category	Minimum Requirement	Rationale
Age	Twenty-one years of age upon graduation from the police academy. Usually no upper age limit.	The age at which people are considered mature enough to handle the responsibilities associated with the job.
Height/weight	Generally no minimum standards.	To avoid discrimination, applicants need only to be able to perform the duties of the job. Appearance, however, plays a part in hiring decisions.
Health	Vision: usually must be correctable to 20/20, but some agencies accept 20/50. Hearing: hearing aids are usually allowed to bring hearing into the standard range. Must pass a doctor's physical exam.	Police work is a dangerous and physically demanding job. Police are responsible for their own safety as well as that of others. Agencies hire those who can do every aspect of the job.
Fitness	Varies, but all departments have physical fitness tests with minimum standards to demonstrate that applicants can do ordinary police duties. Tests can include running, jumping, push-ups, sit-ups, stretching, and pulling.	Officers must be able to defend themselves and others, consistently performing at a high level of stress for extensive periods of time. Conditioning can save lives.

(Continued)

Exhibit 3.2   (Continued)

Category	Minimum Requirement	Rationale
Education	High school diploma or General Educational Development (GED) certificate is the minimum, but a college degree in criminal justice is desired.	About 18% of departments require some college at the entry level, but degrees are usually required only for promotions. This issue remains controversial. Having a degree is helpful for hiring considerations, even if it is not required. Studies show that more education generally produces better officers.
Skills and characteristics	Maturity, intelligence, critical thinking, problem solving, high ethical standards, and emotional intelligence. The abilities to read, write, memorize, reason, and communicate.	Some say you must "walk on water" to be hired for police work. Naturally, agencies want the best of the best. Tests and interviews are created to explore these minimum traits.
Background	Investigation includes past employment, medical records, school records, relationships, military records, credit check, driving record, and criminal history.	Ninety-eight percent of agencies perform some level of background check to determine the character of an applicant that isn't apparent through written tests, interviews, and polygraph tests.
Criminal history	No felony convictions. Misdemeanors may not automatically disqualify applicant unless the circumstances warrant disqualification. The majority of large agencies administer polygraph tests. The commission of certain crimes will disqualify an applicant regardless of conviction.	Departments recognize that citizens make mistakes in their younger years, but police also must respect and adhere to the laws of society. Agencies look at the seriousness of crimes committed as well as the amount of crime and the amount of time since crimes were committed.
Drug history	Varies widely. Generally 3 to 5 years since marijuana was used, and it must have been experimental use only. Generally 10 years since harder drugs were used.	As with criminal activity, many citizens experiment with drugs at younger ages. By being more liberal, the candidate pool is increased without necessarily opening up to unsuitable candidates. Agencies perform random drug tests to ensure the continuity of policy adherence.
Psychological health	Generally, candidates must pass an exam or be recommended for employment by an expert designated by the department.	This appraisal of applicants helps identify individuals who may not function well in the police environment. The assessment explores personality disorders, self-management skills, abilities for team functioning, intellectual strength, impact of prior trauma, and anger management.

Because of the confidential and sensitive nature of the information police officers encounter, the successful completion of a background investigation and polygraph test is required. Candidates who are given conditional job offers are also required to pass pre-employment medical exams, psychological test batteries, and drug screening. Because of the safety- and security-sensitive nature of this type of work, officers are generally subject to random alcohol and drug testing from right out of the academy through retirement.

Completion of college-level courses is rarely required but is always desirable. Communication skills, in person and via radio, are essential functions. Police officers mediate disputes and conduct interviews while performing law enforcement patrol activities and investigations. Police officers present testimony and evidence in both civil and criminal court proceedings. They also record information and prepare detailed reports of investigative findings.

Police officers operate patrol vehicles, pursue offenders by patrol vehicle and on foot, stop offenders, subdue resisting offenders using force where appropriate (including deadly force), and arrest offenders. An officer searches persons, places, and things. She seizes and impounds property and evidence, transports persons and property, performs crowd and riot control activities, issues summonses, and maintains proficiency in operating a variety of law enforcement tools, including weapons, vehicles, and computers. A police officer observes criminal behavior and conducts law enforcement investigations, to include the following critical tasks: protecting crime and traffic accident scenes; measuring and diagramming crime and traffic accident scenes; seizing and processing evidence; administering first aid to sick and injured persons for a wide variety of illnesses and injuries; assisting distressed motorists; directing traffic; assisting and referring mentally ill, indigent, and other persons in need; performing evacuations; and moving persons, vehicles, and other property from unsafe locations.

A graduate of the academy will be expected to comprehend and make inferences from written materials including federal and state statutes, city codes and ordinances, and departmental policies and operating procedures to enforce laws. An officer must maintain composure and operational efficiency in high-stress situations and learn job-related material through verbal instruction, observation on the job, structured lectures in a classroom setting, and reading with regard to police procedures and methods, case law, federal and state statutes, and departmental policies and procedures.

An applicant for the police department needs knowledge of general social problems, basic writing skills, and proficiency in the English language. An officer is expected to acquire a working knowledge of police methods, practices, and procedures and apply it to specific situations; learn departmental rules and regulations; acquire a working knowledge of state and city laws and enforce, interpret, and explain the same; learn the geography of the city and the locations of important buildings; acquire a working knowledge of crime patterns and trends in an assigned area; work effectively with all segments of the public; be courteous but firm with people; follow directions; meet specific attendance and scheduling requirements; use good judgment and make effective decisions under pressure; evaluate situations and take appropriate action; observe and recollect details; perform all of the physical requirements of the job; and establish and maintain effective working relationships with other public employees.

The pay scale for police officers in Mesa starts at a salary of $50,960. The top pay for police officers can reach $72,862. Lateral officers are those who are already working as police officers at other agencies and then transfer to different agencies. Their starting pay ranges from $51,524.40 to $69,388.80, depending on experience. Police lieutenants have a pay range of $79,976 to $107,640, while police chiefs' pay ranges from $129,750 to $174,637. Police work, like any full-time government job, offers vacation pay, sick pay, and usually overtime or other forms of compensation.

States have standards and training boards that set the guidelines all law enforcement agencies must adhere to in order to certify their officers. The Arizona Peace Officer Standards and Training Board (AZPOST) establishes the qualifiers and disqualifiers for certification in the state of Arizona. Some basic requirements include age, physical fitness, and the polygraph test. Some of the disqualifiers include drug use and criminal history. To be AZPOST certified, you cannot have used marijuana in the last 3 years and only for experimental purposes, which has been determined not to exceed 20 uses in a lifetime, with no more than five of those uses being at age 21 or older. As far as criminal history, AZPOST looks at a person's conduct rather than the arrest record to determine suitability to be a law enforcement officer. It is the commission of crimes that concerns AZPOST, not convictions only. Commission of crimes demonstrates a willingness or propensity to do illegal things. This shows a lack of respect for the law. Applicants are asked to list all police contacts, whether as suspects, witnesses, or otherwise. Applicants are asked to disclose all undiscovered crimes, including those nobody but the applicants know about. Complete disclosure and truthfulness on these questions is usually more important than what is disclosed. The only absolute disqualifier for certification is the conviction of a felony. Other offenses are reviewed on a case-by-case basis to see how the conduct reflects on the public trust in the profession and the ability of an individual to perform the duties of a law enforcement officer, such as to testify credibly in court. Applicants' answers to all background questions are tested and verified by polygraph tests (Arizona Peace Officer Standards and Training Board, 2013).

As you can see by the multitude of skills required for police work, as well as the disqualifiers, it is no wonder why some claim that you need to "walk on water" to be hired as a police officer. Wait till you see how lengthy and tedious the application is! If you want to work in law enforcement badly enough, all your efforts to get hired will prove worth it. A career in law enforcement is exciting, challenging, and rewarding. Every shift is like a box of chocolates. Unlike in other jobs, instead of continuously checking your watch to see when your workday is over, you will be anxiously checking your watch before work.

There are other types of law enforcement agencies to work for besides the municipal police. We will explore some of these alternative agencies throughout the rest of this chapter. The information in this chapter jumps around to different states to give you a general idea of what might be found in your geographical area, but keep in mind that entering law enforcement may require an applicant to consider moving to where the positions are. Limiting your search to the city or county in which you live might significantly delay your career.

Special Jurisdiction Police

In 2008, about 90,000 full-time personnel, including 57,000 sworn personnel, were employed at more than 1,700 state and local special geographical jurisdiction law enforcement agencies, or had special enforcement or investigative responsibilities. Exhibit 3.3 shows the breakdown of the agencies. We will cover a few of these here in this chapter.

Exhibit 3.3 Special Jurisdiction Law Enforcement Agencies and Full-Time Sworn Personnel by Jurisdiction Type, 2008

Type of special jurisdiction	Agencies	Full-time sworn personnel
Total	1,733	56,968
Public buildings/facilities	**1,126**	**21,418**
4-year university/college	508	10,916
Public School District	250	4,764
2-year college	253	2,648
State government buildings	29	1,138
Medical school/campus	18	747
Public hospital/health facility	48	715
Public housing	13	250
Other state-owned facilities	7	240
Natural resources	**246**	**14,571**
Fish and wildlife conservation	56	5,515
Parks and recreational areas	124	4,989
Multi-function natural resources	16	2,926

(Continued)

Exhibit 3.3   (Continued)

Type of special jurisdiction	Agencies	Full-time sworn personnel
Boating laws	10	461
Environmental laws	7	368
Water resources	18	185
Forest resources	9	65
Levee district	6	62
Transportation systems/facilities	**167**	**11,508**
Airports	103	3,555
Mass transit system/railroad	18	3,214
Transportation—multiple types	5	2,000
Commercial vehicles	12	1,320
Harbor/port facilities	25	876
Bridges/tunnels	4	543
Criminal investigations	**140**	**7,310**
State bureau of investigation	22	3,527
County/city investigations	66	2,006
Fraud investigations	13	636
Fire marshal/arson investigations	21	478
Tax/revenue enforcement	6	177
Other/multiple types	12	486
Special enforcement	**54**	**2,161**
Alcohol/tobacco laws	22	1,280
Agricultural laws	12	387
Narcotics laws	5	233
Gaming laws	10	231
Racing laws	5	30

Note: Excludes agencies employing less than one full-time officer or the equivalent in part timers

Source: Reaves (2011).

Game and Fish Warden

Game warden positions are generally with state agencies. This position offers a challenging career with a wide array of job duties while working with a diverse and abundant wildlife resource. The Wyoming Game and Fish Department currently employs over 60 game wardens, wildlife investigators, game warden trainees, and wildlife technicians all over the state. Wardens in Wyoming act as liaisons between local publics and the department. They enforce fish and wildlife laws, deal with human-wildlife conflicts, and play an active role in managing Wyoming's wildlife. Game wardens receive department housing and a competitive salary with state employment benefits. One of the most rewarding aspects of a warden's job is preventing or solving some of the most egregious wildlife crimes. Wanton destruction (illegally killing a big game animal, often to take only the horns or antlers) is one of those violations. Being able to successfully prosecute violators and keeping them from acting again is extremely gratifying.

Wardens also create big game seasons. An effective big game season can increase opportunities for sportsmen and alleviate game damage problems while keeping animals and their habitats in a healthy condition. Other duties a game warden performs include enforcing game, fish, trapping, and boating laws. To effectively perform these tasks, a warden must spend time in the field. Depending on the circumstances, getting to the field involves the use of trucks, snowmobiles, boats, horses, four-wheelers, or boots. Wardens also collect biological data on the game herds they manage. Wardens often fly over areas in fixed-wing aircraft or helicopters. Other shifts might be spent in a truck looking through binoculars and spotting scopes. Wardens work with landowners to gain access for hunters and fishermen. Landowners may also experience damage to their crops from big game animals or loss of livestock from trophy game animals. It is the warden's duty to respond to these calls, sometimes having to trap the offending lion or bear or chase deer and elk off agricultural land. Responding to calls regarding injured and nuisance wildlife is another important duty. These calls are often in highly visible areas and in the public eye. These situations call for quick, diplomatic, and accurate decision making by the warden.

Nearly a third of a game warden's job is directly related to law enforcement. Another third deals with taking an active role in wildlife management. Wardens collect and analyze biological data for use in managing fish and wildlife populations. A warden is also the public face of the Wyoming Game and Fish Department and is the person most likely to meet and work with the public. Game wardens routinely deal with human-wildlife conflicts and provide vital customer service to their local communities. Game wardens also enjoy the opportunity to work with young students and to give public presentations.

Qualifications include a competitive examination, which is offered each year to qualified applicants with bachelor's degrees in biology, natural resources, or closely related fields. The examination includes a written test of basic wildlife management knowledge, followed by oral interviews and psychological testing of personality profiles. Candidates are ranked throughout the selection process, and jobs are offered as they become available (Wyoming Game and Fish Department, 2013).

Gaming Officer

Nevada tourists can't avoid noticing all the uniformed officers walking the floor at just about every medium to large casino in Las Vegas. These officers aren't actually sworn personnel. These security personnel work privately for individual franchises and may or may not carry firearms. There are, however, sworn law enforcement positions in the gaming industry in Nevada. The Nevada Gaming Control Board Gaming Commission (NGCBGC) offers an array of challenging career opportunities. The board is continuously seeking top caliber professionals with experience and/or education in engineering, computer science, criminal justice, law enforcement, accounting, business administration, auditing, information technology, financial analysis, research, and investigations. There are also many ongoing administrative opportunities.

The NGCBGC provides jobs for enforcers and investigators. An enforcement agent (EA) with the State Gaming Control Board conducts criminal, regulatory, and intelligence investigations. He collects, analyzes, and documents the information obtained and prepares comprehensive reports for the distribution and use of the Gaming Control Board, the Nevada Gaming Commission, and other authorized agencies. EAs arbitrate disputes involving gaming activities, ensure regulatory compliance by gaming licensees, develop and operate informants, and provide instruction and on-the-job training to new agents. In addition, they may act as a first-line supervisor of subordinates, complete assigned special projects and administrative duties, and perform related work as required (Nevada Gaming Control Board Gaming Commission, 2015).

> Qualifications include graduation from an accredited college or university with a bachelor's degree in business administration, public administration, administration of justice, economics, finance, accounting, pre-law, computer science, criminal justice or other applicable degree, or an equivalent combination of education and investigative experience involving white collar crime, narcotics trafficking or money laundering, organized crime, intelligence collection, fraud or closely related experience, and/or professional-level experience in the areas of: accounting, auditing, legal research, business or public administration in a related area or closely related field. Both education and experience can be substituted on a year-for-year basis.

Professional requirements:

- Be a U.S. Citizen
- Be a minimum of 21 years of age
- Possess and maintain a valid Nevada driver's license
- Not have any felony convictions
- Not have any misdemeanor convictions related to controlled substances, theft, moral turpitude, fraud, larceny, or crimes of violence within the last five years
- Not have been convicted of any crime associated with domestic violence
- Not have a DUI conviction within the last five years, or a substantial accumulation of driving violations, indicating disregard for rules and regulations
- Not use or possess illegal narcotics or controlled substances
- Successfully complete a background investigation, which includes personal history, criminal history, driving record, credit rating, and employment references
- Be required to undergo mandatory drug testing prior to appointment and agree to random and reasonable suspicion drug testing as a condition of continued employment
- Be required to take and pass a lie detector (CVSA) and a psychological examination
- Be able to pass a post-offer medical examination by a licensed physician
- Be able to successfully complete a post-offer polygraph examination and psychological evaluation
- Meet the physical fitness requirements established by Peace Officers' Standards and Training
- Be able to obtain certification as a Category I Peace Officer in Nevada within one year of employment
- Successfully complete the Gaming Control Board's Gaming Academy and the Field Training Program
- Adhere to the Board policy prohibiting an employee from gambling or playing any licensed game or gaming device within the State of Nevada
- Be willing and able to qualify, carry and use Board issued, or authorized, firearms in a safe and appropriate manner, and maintain firearm qualification standards as a condition of employment
- Not have any beliefs and/or foundations, which would interfere with the performance (Nevada Gaming Control Board Gaming Commission, 2015)

The salary for an Enforcement Agent is $70,200 (Nevada Gaming Control Board Gaming Commission, 2015).

According to the Nevada Gaming Control Board Gaming Commission (2015), an investigation agent (IA)

Detective Lawrence Rosky: Phoenix Police Department

CJ: What is your current position?

LR: I am a Phoenix Police Department detective assigned to the Gang Enforcement Unit.

CJ: What are your typical job duties?

LR: Being assigned to the Gang Enforcement Unit, the majority of what I do pertains to gang-related issues. However, the activity of gang members crosses over many different areas, so I'm regularly involved with a variety of ever changing investigations and initiatives. Unlike most specially focused detective units within the Phoenix Police Department that deal with only a specific type of crime—such as homicides, robberies, or sexual assaults—gang detectives investigate any such crimes that gang members may commit. My involvement in those efforts could be as simple as targeted enforcement like traffic stops or as elaborate as conducting wiretap investigations.

CJ: How long have you been at your current assignment?

LR: Just under 2 years.

CJ: What other positions have you held prior to this one?

LR: I've been very fortunate to work in several permanent assignments in the 7 years that I have been a police officer. I worked on the Special Assignments Unit (SWAT), as a patrol officer, and as a field training officer. I've also completed several short-term assignments ranging from 1 week to 1 month in various positions. The Phoenix Police Department often allows officers to work temporary assignments so they can augment specialty details and develop skills they can bring back to their permanent assignments.

CJ: What are the requirements/qualifications for your job?

LR: Those assigned to the Gang Enforcement Unit must have at least 3 years of experience and be certified as a detective in order to be eligible for a position on the unit. Once assigned there, detectives are required to investigate gang-related crimes, respond to assist patrol officers with active gang-related crime scenes, conduct suspect interviews, and conduct enforcement and crime suppression strategies in gang neighborhoods. Other responsibilities include instructing other law enforcement personnel and civilians on gang-related issues, attending community meetings, and assisting the Tactical Response Unit and Community Relations Bureau with large public demonstrations and protests. Additionally, most detectives assigned to the Gang Enforcement Unit attend various continuing training opportunities that they individually identify as valuable to their skillsets as investigators and keep them up to date with their constantly evolving responsibilities.

CJ: What steps did you go through during hiring?

LR: The hiring process took approximately 9 months for me. An extensive background check, a polygraph examination, an interview, a physical fitness test, a written test, and a psychological examination were conducted during that time. I then completed a police academy that was conducted roughly 18 hours per week for approximately 9 months. Typically, police officers in Arizona attend training for roughly 40 hours per week for approximately 4 months.

CJ: What advice can you offer students who might be interested in pursuing a similar career?

LR: I would encourage them to thoroughly explore the career. There is a tremendous range of responsibilities in local police agencies. Depending on agency, location, and specific position, one police career could be completely different from the next. Even individuals working within the same assignment can easily have very different work styles and thus very different perspectives to offer. Therefore, don't take the opinion of just a few people when exploring a career in law enforcement.

A ride-along allows a civilian to spend a shift shadowing a police officer to gain a firsthand account of what police officers do on a daily basis. The workload of a police officer can vary greatly from one day to the next, so attending several shifts is important in getting a clear idea of what to expect from a career in law enforcement. Many police agencies will allow civilians to go on several ride-along opportunities for that reason.

Lastly, I would strongly encourage people to consider the reality of the demands of being a police officer. A career in law enforcement means regular exposure to things that are psychologically shocking, can physically stress the human body to great lengths, and cause serious and even deadly physical harm. Therefore, the fortitude of police officers and their personal relationships is routinely tested in ways that are not present in most other careers. By the same token, the personal sacrifices and challenges of a career in law enforcement can be extremely rewarding. There are very few professions that allow someone to be so immersed in humanity. Working as a police officer shines light on a person's greatest personal assets and affords countless opportunities to share them for the benefit of others. While law enforcement might not be for everyone, those who flourish in the environment will be hard pressed to find a career that is more satisfying.

---

investigates applicants for gaming licenses and other transactions or issues requiring Gaming Control Board or Gaming Commission action; may act as field supervisor (team leader - lead agent) of subordinates; collects, analyzes, and documents the information obtained and prepares comprehensive investigative reports on gaming applications for presentation to the Gaming Control Board and Nevada Gaming Commission; may provide on-the-job training, direction, and supervision to subordinates; completes assigned special projects and administrative duties and perform related work as assigned.

The qualifications, requirements, and salary are basically the same as the enforcement agent.

There are other states that allow casino-style gambling but restrict it to small geographic areas or to American Indian reservations. There are currently 30 states with Indian gaming and state gaming agencies. The Arizona legislature passed laws in 1995 expanding the Arizona State Gaming Agency, which became the Arizona Department of Gaming. The department partners with Arizona's Indian tribes to oversee Indian casinos. Gaming in Arizona is governed by the Arizona Tribal-State Gaming Compacts between the state and 21 Arizona tribes.

Arizona employed 104 team members in 2010, including AZPOST-certified law enforcement officers, financial investigators and auditors, certified fraud examiners, slot machine technicians, and administrative staff. The Gaming Vendor Certification Unit (GVCU) determines the suitability of companies and individuals doing business with casinos in Arizona. The GVCU is

comprised of special agents, financial investigators, a compliance auditor, and intake officers. Each company, principals of a gaming company, and key personnel providing gaming products or services must undergo a thorough background investigation. The GVCU certifies all vendors providing financing to tribes for gaming facilities, all management contractors engaged by a tribe to assist in the management or operation of a gaming facility, all manufacturers and distributors of gaming devices, and all companies providing services to casinos in excess of $10,000 in any one month. (Arizona Department of Gaming, 2013a, p. 6)

A special agent's primary function is to conduct investigations to ensure compliance with the Arizona Tribal-State Gaming Compacts, as well as state and federal laws. This includes the following:

- Writing comprehensive reports
- Reviewing regulatory, criminal, and financial documents
- Conducting interviews
- Participating in surveillance and undercover operations
- Preparing search warrant affidavits
- Securing evidence
- Testifying at hearings and in court proceedings

Special agents must possess sufficient knowledge of Arizona criminal code, basic-level computer search skills (to conduct open-source intelligence searches), and the necessary knowledge to prepare criminal intelligence files. Special agents have a starting salary of $50,672.

Financial investigators do not need to be AZPOST certified, but they do need bachelor's degrees in accounting or 5 years of professional financial investigative experience or closely related experience. An advanced degree may substitute for 6 months of the required experience. You will find that many agencies will allow substitutions between education and experience. Financial investigators are paid about the same as special agents. The job description for financial investigators includes conducting forensic financial audits and investigations of all sensitive management position applicants; examining financial and income tax records; conducting in-depth interviews; preparing comprehensive reports of findings; coordinating and conferring with appropriate managers, attorneys general, and tribal entities; presenting testimony in administrative hearings and other courts of law; and acting as the lead investigators in financial investigations (Arizona Department of Gaming, 2013b).

Campus Police

According to the Georgia Institute of Technology, campus police

perform a variety of duties related to the protection of life and property, enforcement of criminal and traffic laws, prevention of crime, preservation of the public peace, apprehension of criminals, and calls for service. [They] perform basic police services in accordance with the missions, goals, and objectives of Georgia Tech Police and in compliance with governing federal and state laws. (Georgia Institute of Technology, Office of Human Resources, 2013)

Here are some major responsibilities of police officers at the Georgia Institute of Technology in Atlanta:

- Engaging in law enforcement patrol functions by foot, bike, or vehicle, including rotating shifts and physically checking the doors and windows of buildings to ensure that they are secure; conducting visual and audio surveillance
- Operating law enforcement vehicles both day and night in emergency situations involving speeds in excess of posted limits in congested traffic and in unsafe road conditions caused by factors such as fog, smoke, rain, ice, and snow
- Effecting arrests, forcibly if necessary, using handcuffs and other restraints, and subduing resisting suspects using maneuvers and weapons, resorting to hands and feet and other approved weapons in self-defense
- Exercising independent judgment in determining when there is reasonable suspicion to detain, when probable cause exists to search and arrest, and when force may be used and to what degree
- Preparing investigative reports, including sketches, using appropriate grammar, symbols, and mathematical computations
- Performing rescue functions at accidents, emergencies, and disasters, including directing traffic for long periods of time; administering emergency medical aid; lifting, dragging, and removing people from dangerous situations; and securing and evacuating people from particular areas
- Mediating disputes and advising citizens of rights and processes
- Gathering information in criminal investigations by interviewing and obtaining the statements of victims, witnesses, suspects, and confidential informers; detecting and collecting evidence and substances that provide the basis of criminal offenses and infractions (Georgia Institute of Technology, Office of Human Resources, 2013)

With a few exceptions, the basic qualifications to work at Georgia Tech are the same as those for municipal agencies. Georgia Tech requires 1 to 3 years of job-related experience. It prefers applicants to have bachelor's degrees, 3 to 5 years working within a police department, and Georgia Peace Officer Standards and Training Council certification.

The selection process for Georgia campus police includes a thorough background check covering education, employment, criminal history, driving history, and credit history; psychological and medical evaluations; drug screening; and successful completion of the police academy entrance examination. The availability to work any day, any shift, and overtime is required. The pay scale for campus police is usually slightly lower than for municipal police (Georgia Institute of Technology, Office of Human Resources, 2013).

Hospital Police Officer

Another law enforcement job seen in many large hospitals is Hospital Police Officer. The Public Safety Career Information Center (2015) notes that this job differs from other peace officer positions by being regularly required to perform law enforcement duties in close proximity to mentally ill and disabled geriatric patients. Their duties include: maintaining law and order on hospital grounds; patrolling and protecting hospital buildings and grounds; checking for unauthorized movement, breaches of security, unsafe conditions, etc.; investigating crimes such as theft, drug possession and sales, assault, rape, arson, etc.; making arrests; testifying in court; enforcing vehicle speed and parking regulations and issuing citations when necessary. Incumbents also monitor patient and visitor activities on hospital grounds; assist nursing personnel in controlling severely combative patients; carry out standard procedures in cases of unauthorized patient absences; provide crisis intervention services to patients regarding incidents such as fights, assaults on staff members, involvement with drugs and alcohol, sexual misconduct, self-inflicted injuries, etc. They transport patients under security as required, and perform other related duties.

Persons appointed as hospital police officers must meet the following requirements.

- Age Limitation: The minimum age of appointment is 21 years of age.
- Driver License Requirement: Possession of a valid driver license of the appropriate class issued by the Department of Motor Vehicles. Applicants who do not possess the license will be admitted to the examination but must secure the license prior to appointment.
- Citizenship Requirement: Pursuant to Government Code Section 1031(a), in order to be a peace officer, a person must be either a U.S. Citizen or be a permanent resident alien who has applied for U.S. Citizenship. Any permanent resident alien who is employed as a peace officer shall be disqualified from holding that position if his/her application for citizenship is denied.
- Felony Disqualifier: as peace officer except as provided under Welfare and Institutions Code, Division 2, Chapter 3, Article 8, Section 1179(b), or Division 2.5, Chapter 1, Article 4, Section 1772(b). Except as provided for by these statutes, persons convicted of a felony are not eligible to compete for, or be appointed to, positions in these classes.
- Employment Background Investigation: Pursuant to Government Code Section 1031, prior to appointment, persons successful in peace officer examinations shall be required to undergo a thorough law enforcement level background investigation to include criminal history check, references, and financial stability. Persons unsuccessful in the background investigation cannot be appointed as peace officers.
- Medical Examination and Psychological Screening Requirement: Pursuant to Government Code Section 1031(f), persons successful in peace officer examinations are required to successfully pass a thorough medical and psychological screening prior to appointment date.

Persons unsuccessful in the medical and psychological screening cannot be appointed as peace officers.

- Drug Testing Requirement: Applicants for positions in these classes are required to pass a drug-screening test.

Massachusetts General Hospital (2015) provides this information for its hospital police activities:

The Operations Division at Massachusetts General Hospital is responsible for providing day-to-day protective services to the Mass General Community. Operations staff includes security officers, special police officers, supervisors and managers who, in addition to providing patrol and crime prevention services, also respond to various types of emergencies, employee, patient and visitor needs, reports of criminal activity, and requests for assistance. Services offered by the Operations Division include:

- Access Control
  - Monitor security systems
  - Frequent patrols of buildings, garages, and outside areas (vehicle, bicycle, foot)
  - Facilitate employee and visitor access
- Emergency Response
  - Code Blue/medical assistance
  - Code Red/evacuation
  - Code Pink
  - Code Black
  - Code Disaster
  - Code Silver
  - Hazardous materials incidents
- Crime Prevention Services
  - Computer/laptop lockdown
  - ALERT program (Awareness Lets Everyone Reduce Theft)
- Community Policing
  - Threat/risk assessment
  - Liaison services
  - Personnel escorts
- Infant Protection Program
- Training and Educational Seminars
- Hospital Policy and Procedure Compliance
- Staff Assistance
  - Patient standby/restraint
  - Removal of unauthorized persons
  - Eloped patient searches
  - Patient valuables assistance
- Security Detail Coverage

A beneficial entry on a résumé for a police or security position at a hospital is specialized training in the National Incident Management System. This type of training is free, online, and offers a certificate for your portfolio. You can access this free training at http://training.fema.gov/IS/NIMS.aspx. There is more information about this training and certificate in Chapter 10.

Diversity Issues

There will probably always be those who think law enforcement agencies hire minorities and women mainly to be fair or to send the right message, but the truth is police agencies need representation from minorities and women. Police departments learned this a long time ago. There will still be biases, just as at any type of job, but most Caucasian male police officers in contemporary law enforcement never witnessed the worst of the past. The presence of minorities and women in police work is the new norm. Diversity is advantageous in any job but especially in law enforcement. As with the blind men and the elephant (Chapter 1), the more opinions and life experiences an agency can draw from, the better the outcome will be. If you are the right kind of person to work in law enforcement, you will be able to get through the hurdles that minorities and women still face.

Police departments wisely persuade minorities and women to work in hiring units in the hope of encouraging skeptics to apply. Having a diverse recruiting staff at job fairs presents the proper image for police departments and allows women and minorities to ask questions about equality, harassment, and bias issues. Minorities and women in hiring units are also part of the interviewing team for applicants. It is wise for minorities and women to look into the atmosphere of the departments they are applying to. If you can feel good about the attitude of a department, you will go into an interview with a better mind-set. Remember, you want to show your personality. Try to eliminate any doubts and thoughts you don't need in the interview.

Summary

There are law enforcement opportunities in various capacities, which include municipal, county, state, and federal agencies. The largest concentration of law enforcement employees is at the municipal and county levels, which are also referred to as local law enforcement. Local and state law enforcement offers a greater variety of work experiences than federal agencies. To work as a police officer, you need to meet the minimum requirements established by your state's standards and training board for police officers. The requirements and expectations for police work are enormous. The hiring process is very tedious for applicants and expensive for agencies.

Another area of employment in law enforcement is with the various special jurisdiction agencies. One type is the state fish and game departments.

A position with game and fish offers a challenging career with a wide array of jobs. The Wyoming Game and Fish Department currently employs over 60 game wardens, wildlife investigators, game warden trainees, and wildlife technicians all over the state. One of the most rewarding aspects of a warden's job is preventing or solving some of the most egregious wildlife crimes. Nearly a third of a game warden's job is directly related to law enforcement. Another third deals with taking an active role in wildlife management. Qualifications include passing a competitive examination, which is offered each year to qualified applicants with bachelor's degrees in biology, natural resources, or closely related fields.

There are currently 30 states with Indian and state gaming agencies. One position for gaming agencies is special agent, whose primary function is conducting investigations to ensure compliance with the agreements between tribes and states, as well as state and federal laws. Another position is financial investigator, whose duties include conducting forensic financial audits and investigations of all sensitive management position applicants; performing examinations of financial and income tax records; conducting in-depth interviews; preparing comprehensive reports of findings; coordinating and conferring with appropriate managers, attorneys general, and tribal entities; presenting testimony in administrative hearings and other courts of law; and acting as lead investigator in financial investigations.

Many universities employ campus police who perform a variety of duties related to the protection of life and property, enforcement of criminal and traffic laws, prevention of crime, preservation of the public peace, apprehension of criminals, and calls for service. Some of the basic qualifications to work at Georgia Tech include a high school diploma or GED certificate, 1 to 3 years of job-related experience, a valid Georgia driver's license, and a skill set that includes excellent verbal and written communications, honesty, the ability to take action quickly, independent and sound judgment, an ability to prepare reports, and initiative in applying work methods.

Another law enforcement job seen in many large hospitals is hospital police officer. This job differs from other peace officer positions by being regularly required to perform law enforcement duties in close proximity to mentally ill and disabled geriatric patients.

Minorities and women are needed in law enforcement. Agencies often encourage women and minorities to work in recruiting. Recruiters work at job fairs answering questions, and they also interview applicants.

DISCUSSION QUESTIONS

1. Do you feel that the educational requirements for police officers are too lenient? Why or why not?

2. Are there any requirements for law enforcement you don't agree with? Explain.

3. Law enforcement is one of the only professions that routinely administers polygraph tests to applicants. Do you feel that this is unfair? Why or why not? How about police employees who are not sworn?

4. Do you feel that law enforcement needs to be diverse, hiring more minorities and women? Why or why not?

5. What particular jobs are interesting to you? Why?

6. In states where marijuana is legal, do you feel that police departments should weaken or eliminate their drug policies and allow officers to use the substance? Why or why not?

NOTE

1.   Throughout the book (primarily in Chapters 3 through 9), information is provided on specific employment opportunities with local, state, and federal agencies, as well as public and private institutions. Citations refer the reader to the general careers or employment pages at these entities' websites, but job postings change frequently, so the reader shouldn't necessarily expect to find that the jobs described are presently available. The intent is to provide a sense of the requirements and realities of the various positions described.

REFERENCES

Arizona Department of Gaming. (2013a). *2013 annual report*. Retrieved from https://gaming .az.gov/sites/default/files/Y13DeptFR.pdf

Arizona Department of Gaming. (2013b). *Human resources & employment opportunities*. Retrieved from http://www.azgaming.gov/content/hr

Arizona Peace Officer Standards and Training Board. (2013). *Home page*. Retrieved from http:// www.azpost.state.az.us/

City of Mesa. (2015). *Demographics*. Retrieved from http://www.mesaaz.gov/business/economic-development/business-environment/demographics

Georgia Institute of Technology, Office of Human Resources. (2013). *Careers@Tech*. Retrieved from http://careers.gatech.edu

Massachusetts General Hospital. (2015). Retrieved from http://www.massgeneral.org/police/about/ operations/default.aspx

Nevada Gaming Control Board Gaming Commission. (2015). *Home*. Retrieved from http://gaming .nv.gov/

Public Safety Career Information Center. (2015) Retrieved from http://www.publicsafetyinfo.org/ index.php/law-enforcement.

Reaves, B. A. (2010, December). *Local law enforcement, 2007*. Retrieved from http://www.bjs.gov/ content/pub/pdf/lpd07.pdf

Reaves, B. A. (2011, July). *Census of state and local law enforcement agencies, 2008*. Retrieved from http://www.bjs.gov/content/pub/pdf/csllea08.pdf

Wyoming Game and Fish Department. (2013). *Game and Fish career home*. Retrieved from http:// wgfd.wyo.gov/gameandfishjobs/frmCareerDetails.aspx

4

Crime Lab

Introduction

Having a witness to a crime is valuable for the successful prosecution of a case. Gaining a confession from a suspect is another key component. However, neither of these on its own is good enough to convict a defendant of a crime. The days of routinely convicting innocent people have been over for quite some time. As we develop more technology and discover better methods of manipulating evidence, more is expected. Today, the successful prosecution of a case depends largely on physical evidence that is properly collected, tested, and presented.

DNA (deoxyribonucleic acid) technology has become one of the most effective forensic tools law enforcement uses to convict suspects of certain crimes. DNA can be found in blood, semen, hair, saliva, sweat, skin cells, vomit, tears, earwax, and feces. A drop of blood the size of a pinhead is enough to identify a suspect. Because such small samples can be used, crime scenes must be cautiously searched and the evidence properly collected to preserve any evidence available. Once collected, the materials must be properly tested. A record of all those who have handled the evidence must be documented. If comparisons are successful, the evidence must then be presented in court along with testimony from those who took part in each step of the process. The jury would need to be educated by the expert witnesses so that they would understand what the evidence corroborates, proves, or disproves.

Fingerprints remain among the most common and consistent means for identifying suspects. They are infallible, because the crucial features never change, barring any surgeries, injuries, or diseases. A lot of fingerprinting technology has been computerized, including a national computerized system that allows identity matches to be completed in minutes. However, the use of powders, sprays, tape, ink, and paper continues to be a necessary part of fingerprint collection and identification. The fingerprint expert who sits at a desk with a magnifying glass and fingerprint cards continues to be an essential employee at many law enforcement agencies.

Until technology advances its methods, there will be a need for compound microscopes, comparison microscopes, stereoscopic microscopes, polarizing microscopes, microspectrophotometers, and scanning electron microscopes. Vials, test tubes, syringes, catheters, electrocardiographs, blood gas analyzers, ophthalmoscopes, chromatographs, endoscopes, and ultracentrifuges will remain important tools in forensic work as well. Until scientists work miracles in the area of robotics, there will always be a need for humans to operate the equipment, perform necessary tasks, and testify in court.

The television show *CSI* may mislead viewers somewhat on the realities of forensics and crime scene work. Nevertheless, the actual present-day capabilities of what can be accomplished at a crime scene and in the lab are astounding. Like a family sitting at a table assembling a 500-piece puzzle, crime scene technicians (CSTs) and other forensic experts are part of the criminal justice family, contributing vital pieces to the successful outcomes of multifaceted cases.

Forensics is the use of science and technology to investigate and establish facts in criminal or civil courts of law. There is a variety of criminal justice–related positions in forensics, including criminalist, pathologist or biologist, computer forensics specialist, CST, forensic nurse examiner, toxicologist, entomologist, accident reconstructionist, odontologist, anthropologist, and psychiatrist. Some jobs, such as medical examiner, require expertise in more than one of these areas of science.

The criminal justice system comprises several separate entities working together for a common purpose. The more each component knows about the other working parts, the better the overall quality of the output. Detectives need to know what prosecutors require to prosecute cases. Prosecutors need to know the protocols of police work so that they can intelligently formulate their questions during trials. First responders, detectives, crime scene techs, and prosecutors need to understand the procedures involved in lab work to know what to look for, where to find it, how to preserve it, how and when to collect it, how to package it, and how to store it. CSTs need to understand the rules of evidence, how to work a crime scene, and how to testify properly in court. Because of the wealth of knowledge needed to be effective in criminal justice jobs, there is more than one path to get there. Working in a forensics-related field is no exception; there are numerous avenues one can take. As with any other job, the more you have on your résumé, the likelier you are to get an interview.

Throughout the rest of this chapter, we will look at some of the forensic jobs one can strive for, including the qualifications, requirements, and salaries. We will explore job descriptions and requirements at various agencies to encompass a broad spectrum of information. You can search government job websites periodically for additional information and available positions. We will also discuss some of the preparations that can be done now to brighten your résumé and portfolio.

Crime Scene Technician

CSTs are almost always civilian positions. CSTs perform a variety of analytical examinations. They process crime scenes using chemicals, light source enhancement, and other methods. They reconstruct crime scenes, preserving marks or impressions made by shoes, tires, or other objects with plaster or moulage casts. They sketch and draw details of crime scenes; collect and package evidence for presentation in court; prepare reports or presentations of findings, methods, and techniques used to support conclusions; and complete photograph referrals, blood draws, photographs, and prints of dead persons at the morgue.

CSTs are responsible for executing competent forensic processing during calls for service. Often calls develop into complex investigations involving high-profile matters and sensitive information. CSTs gather and ensure the integrity of physical evidence or subsequent scientific evaluation for court presentation. They sometimes conduct laboratory examinations of physical evidence using a variety of forensic applications and instrumentation. CSTs prepare detailed investigative and supplemental case reports and communicate with follow-up investigators regarding observations and processing actions. They also identify, collect, preserve, package, and present biological evidence, latent fingerprints, tire impressions, shoe impressions, tool marks, and other physical evidence. They can act as liaisons among crime laboratories, investigators, prosecutors, and defense attorneys, and confer with experts in relevant specialties as necessary. This position also requires court testimony about work performed.

An applicant for the position of CST generally needs to be 21 years of age; have a bachelor's degree in natural science, forensics, or a related field; and have 5 years of evidential or crime scene experience. However, some agencies around the country make available volunteer programs in which no degree or experience is required. This type of program offers the opportunity to gain the experience that so many agencies require. Forensic laboratory experience can also be substituted for the required bachelor's degree. A polygraph test, agency proficiency test, and interview process constitute the normal protocol for applicants seeking this position. The pay scale for CSTs is approximately $28,000 to $48,000.

Forensic Scientist

Forensic scientists work with law enforcement at the federal and state levels and in large cities. Smaller agencies that can't afford their own crime labs contract with other cities or their state labs. To be a forensic scientist with the Illinois State Police, you need an undergraduate degree in forensic science or one of the natural sciences. Commonly recognized natural sciences include disciplines such as agricultural science, animal science, biochemistry, botany, biology, chemistry, medical technology, geology, preliminary medicine, physics, and zoology. Trainees get paid while learning their new profession.

A new hire with the Illinois State Police would be trained in one of several specialties, which include forensic biology and DNA, drug chemistry, latent prints, firearms and tool marks, microscopy, questioned documents, forensic toxicology, and trace evidence. Forensic scientist trainees receive

Matt Richardson: Crime Scene Specialist – Phoenix Police Department

CJ: What is your current position?

MR: I am a Crime Scene Specialist III (CSS) for the Phoenix Police Department

CJ: What are your typical job duties?

MR: My main function is to utilize the latest forensic techniques for detection, documentation, and preservation of physical evidence at crime scenes. At Phoenix PD, a crime scene could be defined anywhere from simple injury photos to a multiple homicide. Evidence could consist of any of the following: notes, photographs, sketches, fingerprints, blood (DNA), hair/fibers, shoe/tire impressions, weapons of all types, and all other tangible items (beer cans, ammunition, cell phones, etc.). After the scene has been thoroughly documented and the evidence preserved, I am responsible for preparing detailed reports and diagrams relating the work I did for the incident. My experience as a Level III also requires that I train probationary CSSs in the skills needed for this career.

CJ: How long have you been at your current assignment?

MR: I have been a crime scene specialist for 11 years.

CJ: What other positions have you held prior to this one?

MR: I was a laboratory technician in the Controlled Substances section for a year prior to becoming a CSS. Before that, I worked as a materials coordinator for MD Helicopters in Mesa, Arizona.

CJ: What are the requirements/qualifications for your job?

MR: The minimum requirement to become a Crime Scene Specialist I is an associate level degree in criminal justice, chemistry, or a related field, or a year of experience in crime scene processing. For a Crime Scene Specialist III, I am required to maintain a certification with the International Association for Identification and recertify every five years. However, other education, experience, and abilities required to perform the basic duties can be substituted.

CJ: What steps did you go through during hiring?

MR: I had to attend an oral interview that I was invited to, and pass a basic physical agility test. I had to pass an extensive background investigation, which was based off a large packet of forms that I was required to complete fully and accurately. I also had to pass a polygraph test, which was very unnerving. After being hired I attended an in-house academy that introduced me to the skills needed to perform the essential duties of the job. I worked to complete an extensive training outline of required readings, demonstrations, and mock casework. My training also included cross training with the other eight laboratory sections in our facility. After which I was assigned to a senior CSS who took me to real scenes and honed my skills further until I was deemed ready to go solo.

CJ: What advice can you offer students who might be interested in pursuing a similar career?

MR: Be a law-abiding citizen and contribute to the community in positive ways. Don't break the law or participate in illegal drug activity. It's much harder, if not impossible, to get a job within a law enforcement agency when you do.

Tell the truth, and the whole truth, during your interviews and background investigations. If you are caught smudging the facts your hiring process will likely cease.

Try to obtain more than the minimum requirements. When we open a position, several hundred people apply. Most of those have 4+ year degrees and some type of related experience. Your competition is tough! Try volunteering for a police agency, hospital, or your local university security/police force. Jobs/internships within a laboratory type setting are also a plus.

This job can have the potential for a high turnover rate. The novelty of it wears off quickly and stress levels can be overwhelming at times. We deal with extremes constantly, e.g., violence, weather, disease, legal battles, bugs, animal brutality, anti–law enforcement sentiment, and fatigue to name a few. Be prepared for that. Don't just choose this career because it is glamorized on television. Know what level of commitment you are being asked to do.

If you are looking to get into the analytical side of things you will need a hard science degree. Chemistry, biology, forensics, mathematics, physics, or something along those lines. Social degrees will not allow you to advance into positions such as forensic biology, trace, firearms examiner, toxicology, controlled substances, etc., regardless of the amount of experience you have.

comprehensive instruction in the use of the most advanced scientific technology and procedures for analyzing evidence. The length of training programs varies with the forensic disciplines. The length of a person's training will depend on his or her ability to progress through a program. The average training times tend to be as follows:

Forensic biology: 18 months (stain identification for 5 months, DNA for 13 months)

Documents: 36 months

Drug chemistry: 12 months

Firearms and tool marks: 24 months

Latent prints: 24 months

Microscopy: 18 months

Toxicology: 18 months

Trace chemistry: 23 months (instruments and arson for 14 months, glass for 4 months, explosives for 4 months, and paints and polymers for 1 month)

In Illinois, under normal circumstances and if there are no major quality issues, a trainee would be promoted to a Level I forensic scientist after 1 year. Trainees are paid in the range of $44,424 to $64,560. An applicant must undergo a written exam and score an A. The next phase is an interview, and the last phase is a background check. The pay scale for forensic scientists ranges from $44,424 as a trainee to $96,804 as a Level III scientist (Illinois State Police, Division of Forensic Services, Forensic Sciences Command, 2013).

Medical Examiner

As a medical examiner in Maricopa County, Arizona, you would perform autopsies to determine the cause and manner of death. You would review items related to autopsies, such as hospital charts, medicolegal death investigator reports, law enforcement agency reports, and postmortem results. You would also investigate unnatural deaths by performing scene investigations, gathering information, and responding to hospitals. You would serve as an expert witness in depositions, grand jury sessions, trials, and conferences with attorneys. You would also provide expert witness capabilities for all forensic criminal and civil actions associated with cases investigated and any other forensic needs within Maricopa County. You would participate in conferences with family members, law enforcement representatives, attorneys, and other individuals to provide information on investigations and autopsies. You would train personnel such as forensic technicians, investigators, photographers, and others assisting in autopsies. You would also be expected to provide assistance and guidance to organ donor centers and participate in mass fatality planning, training, and other relevant exercises as needed. You would possibly be asked to present lectures for students, officers, and the general community. You may need to provide information to citizens, groups, the news media, and the general public. You would write scientific papers and presentation materials, attend seminars and lectures for continuing education in forensic medicine, and provide training and observation opportunities to selected students during autopsy examinations.

Some of the qualifications for medical examiner in Maricopa County include graduation from an accredited school of medicine and possession of a current license to practice medicine in the state of Arizona as required by the Arizona Department of Professional Regulations. You would need to display knowledge of the principles and practices of forensic pathology and the laws, rules, and regulations governing forensic services. You would need the ability to operate a personal computer, including experience with Microsoft Office programs. You would need to be able to communicate effectively orally and in writing. You would need to establish and maintain a positive working relationship with members of law enforcement agencies, as well as prosecuting and defense attorneys, and to conduct research in forensic pathology. You must be board certified in anatomic or clinical pathology and in forensic pathology by the American Board of Pathology.

The hiring process for Maricopa County medical examiner involves an online application, after which the agency fills positions as needed through interviews, background checks, and polygraph tests. As part of the online application process, you are required to answer these four questions:

1. Are you currently licensed to practice medicine in the State of Arizona?

2. Do you have experience performing autopsies?

3. Are you certified in forensic pathology by the American Board of Pathology?

4. This position may require the ability to work on-call, weekends, and holidays, as needed. Are you able to work these shifts/days?

The salary range for medical examiner is $152,194 to $173,659 (Maricopa County Human Resources, 2013).

Investigative Technician

The position of investigative technician in San Diego, California, is a job within the Trial Support Services Unit within the Bureau of Investigation, allocated only to the district attorney's office. Investigative technicians provide audiovisual, fingerprint, and graphic design support for the district attorney's staff. This position is law enforcement related; investigative technicians perform criminal investigations of alleged violations of criminal and civil laws. If you were hired as an investigative technician in San Diego, you would perform the following essential functions:

- Create court exhibits, such as photo boards, maps, and timelines
- Photograph crime scenes, lineups, and other items of evidence
- Edit, duplicate, convert, and enhance audio and/or video recordings and files
- Provide testimony in court
- Consult with attorneys concerning the production and presentation of evidence
- Operate photographic, audiovisual, computerized, and trial presentation software in producing trial exhibits
- Videotape and document courtroom proceedings, lineups, and crime scene activities
- Provide courteous, high-quality service to members of the public by personally responding to requests for service or making appropriate referrals
- Record, categorize, and file rolled, inked, and electronic 10-print fingerprint cards
- Compare and classify fingerprints using recognized techniques, reprinting suspects if necessary, and establishing or eliminating the identity of specific individuals by visually inspecting, examining, and matching inked or electronic fingerprints

Some of the knowledge base and skills you would need for a position such as this include knowledge of operating and using computers and computer-aided design systems; skills in investigating methods and techniques, including the collection and preservation of data, presentation methods, and techniques for court appearances; understanding chain-of-evidence procedures; comprehension of basic photographic film processing and procedures, including the operation and use of photographic, audiovisual, and computer equipment; and expertise with audio and video equipment, fingerprinting, closed-circuit television systems, and video and digital-image compression techniques to maintain evidence integrity.

All agencies look for employees who communicate effectively, are knowledgeable workers, are customer focused, value and respect others, have the drive to excel, are good at teamwork and collaboration, are open to continuous learning, demonstrate ethical behavior, and are supportive of change.

The desirable education for this position includes an associate's degree from an accredited U.S. college or university or a certified foreign studies equivalency in evidence technology or a related field from an accredited institution or a federal, state, or local agency. You also need 1 year of full-time work experience comparing and identifying fingerprints to determine the prints' usability in the areas of civil and criminal investigations and providing technical investigative support to law enforcement personnel, attorneys, or other investigative personnel, which must have included designing and producing a variety of exhibits presented in court. An alternative to an associate's degree would be 3 years of full-time work experience.

San Diego performs a thorough background check as part of the hiring process. You must have a reputation for honesty and trustworthiness. Misdemeanor or felony convictions could be disqualifiers depending on type, number, severity, and how recent they are. The annual salary for this position ranges from $53,082 to $64,542 (County of San Diego, 2013).

Criminalist

DNA Analyst

The position of DNA analyst is a technical and advanced professional-level laboratory position in a specialized field of biology involving work with DNA evidence from cases. Working in this position in Charlotte, North Carolina, involves the application of laboratory techniques, materials, equipment, and instruments used in various physical and chemical analyses of evidence obtained at crime scenes or elsewhere and the presentation of findings for investigative and prosecution purposes. The work is performed in accordance with standardized laboratory methods and controls to ensure accurate and verifiable analyses of specimens. If you had this position in Charlotte, you would be required to conduct complex analyses requiring subjective opinions. You would need the ability to work with minimal instructions and the ability to use complex instrumentation. Your work would be performed with considerable independence under the general direction of a supervisor. Because of the nature and complexity of DNA casework, you would need to meet the minimum requirements, which are the following:

- A bachelor's degree in biology or a related science with coursework including biochemistry, genetics, molecular biology, and statistics
- Three years of experience in forensic biology or DNA casework as a Level II criminalist or higher in an accredited crime laboratory
- Knowledge of laboratory techniques used in body fluid identification and location of trace evidence
- Knowledge of the methods used in collecting and preserving physical evidence and presenting such evidence in court as an expert witness

- Knowledge of the background and theories supporting the testing procedures used in the identification of body fluids and location of trace evidence
- Knowledge of laboratory safety and quality assurance
- Ability to communicate effectively with detectives and attorneys

Final candidates must pass a pre-employment drug-screening test. During the selection process, candidates may be asked to take a skills test and participate in other assessments. Candidates may also be required to pass a physical exam, polygraph exam, other skill evaluations, and a background check. Criminal conviction checks are required on final internal and external candidates applying for positions with the city (City of Charlotte & Mecklenburg County, 2013).

This position in Charlotte is a grant-funded position that pays an annual salary of $60,000 to $63,000. There are a variety of grant-funded positions in the criminal justice domain, but there are also risks associated with grant funding. There is no guarantee that funding will continue after the initial term is over. The amount and length of a grant depend on how much money the government has to allocate and how much money was dedicated to the particular program. Criminal justice grants normally become available when the government opts to spend money in an area of concern or dire need, such as domestic violence, community policing, or forensic nursing for sexual assaults. The grant opportunity is advertised, and a deadline is set for applications. Agencies that meet the qualifications will submit grant applications, which are quite lengthy and cumbersome. There can be anywhere from 20 to 40 different applications turned in for one grant allocation. The amount of money the government distributes for a particular grant could be anywhere from $0.5 million to $2 million or $3 million. After grant requests are reviewed, money is disbursed to the programs that look best on paper. Often the agencies with the best grant writers are the ones that get funded. If the funded programs function appropriately and the economy remains strong, the government may choose to continue its support. Some cities will take over the funding of valuable programs if grants terminate, but too often when grant funding ends, the job ends.

Toxicologist

As a toxicologist, you would analyze blood and urine evidence using established procedures and guidelines, keep precise records, and develop scientific conclusions. You would comply with discovery orders, participate in laboratory projects, and complete tasks as assigned by your supervisor. You would observe and participate in training for police cadets regarding testing. You would need to properly maintain the records and prepare sectional standard operation procedures for maintaining accreditation. You would need to provide technical assistance to police officers and assist district attorneys, other law enforcement agencies, and civic groups. You would also provide testimony at district and county court proceedings.

Houston, Texas, requires its toxicologists to have bachelor's degrees in chemistry, criminalistics, biology, physics, or related fields, with a minimum of 30 hours of chemistry, but no experience is required. Houston also administers a skill assessment evaluation. If you are considered for employment, you are required to pass a background check and a polygraph test. Applications are submitted online at the city's website. The salary for a toxicologist in Houston ranges from $33,358 to $68,900 (The City of Houston, 2013).

Forensic Nurse Examiner

A forensic nurse examiner at Tacoma General Hospital in Tacoma, Washington, is responsible for providing assessment, screening, treatment, and forensic evidence collection for adolescent and adult victims of sexual assault. This position requires substantial specialized knowledge, judgment, and skills based on the principles of biological, physiological, behavioral, and sociological sciences. This position requires critical thinking skills in making decisions regarding patient care. An applicant would need to have the knowledge necessary to integrate the available standards, resources, and data.

Forensic nurses are also hired by law enforcement agencies around the country that are large enough to fund their own advocacy centers. Victims of sexual assault are taken straight to advocacy centers and receive forensic exams in private instead of going to hospital emergency rooms and competing with others for time. Forensic nurse examiners working for law enforcement agencies specialize in sexual assault and child molestation investigations. Some agencies contract with forensic nurses and have them on call when needed. Often the government offers grants for sexual assault nurse examiners (SANEs), which help smaller agencies set up systems for victims of sexual assault to receive better treatment than the typical hospital experience.

At Tacoma General Hospital, forensic nurse examiner experience is not required. There, Multi-Care offers a 5-day core SANE training course to selected applicants. The 40-hour training (all in person, with no online component) meets the International Association of Forensic Nurses advanced certification requirement to be able to take the advanced certification exam. Forensic nurse examiners travel to nine emergency rooms throughout Pierce and South King counties. SANEs in Tacoma work around the clock to provide medical forensic evaluations to patients needing care following an act of sexual violence. Patient examination experience is required. External applicants will also be required to attend 2 weeks of system orientation prior to SANE training.

The job at Tacoma General Hospital requires you to have a Washington registered nursing license as well as 2 years' experience in a family, women's health, maternal and child, or emergency health care setting as a nurse and experience in crisis management and/or advanced psychosocial nursing. The salary for the job of forensic nurse varies depending on experience, credentials, location, and whether it is a grant position. A forensic nurse can make anywhere from $50,000 to $120,000 (Tacoma General Hospital, 2015).

Forensic Psychiatrist Specialist

A forensic psychiatrist specialist in Boston, Massachusetts, conducts court-ordered evaluations and risk assessments for individuals in court or in community settings and for patients within mental health facilities. Court clinic duties include providing direct service to individuals with mental illnesses or substance use disorders who become involved with the courts or criminal justice system. These duties include conducting court-ordered forensic evaluations of pretrial or adjudicated defendants. The duties also include conducting court-ordered statutory evaluations pertaining to involuntary commitment to mental health or substance abuse inpatient systems, assessing mental status, and answering dispositional questions. As a forensic psychiatrist specialist, you would provide the court with nonstatutory evaluations and with clinical consultation and conduct risk assessments and forensic reviews of individuals with mental illnesses and others who have significant histories of violent behavior or other problematic risk-related behavior. You would conduct assessments of drug-involved individuals and perform other duties as required.

If you worked in Boston as a forensic psychiatrist specialist, you would provide timely court-, community-, and hospital-based evaluations for competency to stand trial and criminal responsibility. You would conduct forensic risk assessments and other forensic consultations as requested by Department of Mental Health (DMH) Forensic Mental Health Services. You would provide testimony as requested by the court or DMH in the role of expert witness and in conjunction with evaluations conducted for the purpose of providing assessments and evaluations concerning clients facing judicial proceedings. You would provide consultation to the court, probation officers, and community providers who are involved with clients at other agencies. You would conduct on-site inspections of Department of Correction segregation units and specified correctional mental health units as a surveyor on a DMH interdisciplinary team and provide follow-up and on-site monitoring visits when requested by the assistant commissioner of forensic services.

To apply, you must have at least 3 years of residency training in a recognized program in general psychiatry and at least 3 years of full-time, or equivalent part-time, professional experience in the field of psychiatry. You could substitute 1 year of residency training in a specialized area of psychiatry, such as psychopharmacology or psychoneurology, for the third year of residency training in general psychiatry and the 3 years of professional experience in the field of psychiatry. You would need a valid registration as a physician under the Massachusetts Board of Registration in Medicine. Some preferred qualifications for this position include the following:

- Completion of an approved fellowship in forensic psychiatry and/or certification in forensic psychiatry by the American Board of Psychiatry and Neurology
- Ability to conduct court-ordered forensic evaluations and risk management assessments

- Considerable knowledge of types and symptoms of mental, emotional, and substance abuse disorders
- Ability to recognize symptoms of mental, emotional, and substance abuse disorders; interact with people who are experiencing varying levels of distress and dysfunction; and analyze psychological data, draw conclusions, and make appropriate recommendations
- Ability to gather information through observing and questioning individuals and by examining records and documents
- Ability to exercise discretion in handling confidential information and maintaining accurate records
- Ability to complete computer-based data collection forms and possession of the degree of computer literacy required for completing reports
- Knowledge of psychopharmacology, medical conditions, and behavioral therapeutic techniques and familiarity with theories of psychotherapy and counseling, as well as an understanding of current treatment approaches available for individuals with serious mental illnesses, including severe personality disorders
- Knowledge of and ability to explain the provisions of laws, rules, regulations, policies, procedures, guidelines, and standards governing assigned activities to individuals, families, and other community providers
- Knowledge of human services, juvenile justice, and criminal justice systems
- Ability to work under considerable time pressure, to work on multiple tasks at one time, and to produce high-quality reports according to applicable standards and guidelines
- Ability to complete high-quality written forensic reports and evaluations and testify in court
- Ability to be appointed as a designated forensic psychiatrist supervisor or eligibility to become a designated forensic psychiatrist supervisor within 2 years of the date of hire

The salary for forensic psychiatrist specialists ranges from $138,580 to $225,608 annually (Commonwealth of Massachusetts, Human Resources Division, 2013).

Forensic Interviewer

The position of forensic interviewer is common in law enforcement and advocacy centers. Forensic interviewers generally have the responsibility of interviewing children and adolescents ages 2 through 17 and vulnerable adults who are alleged to be victims of or eyewitnesses to abuse or violence. An experienced forensic interviewer uses research-based interview protocols and techniques in a developmentally appropriate manner to elicit factual information.

An example of an agency that employs a forensic interviewer is Childhelp in Phoenix, Arizona, a leading national nonprofit organization dedicated to helping at-risk children and victims of child abuse and neglect. Childhelp focuses on advocacy, prevention, treatment, and community outreach. Childhelp's programs and services also include residential treatment services, children's advocacy centers, therapeutic foster care, group homes, and child abuse prevention, education, and training. The essential responsibilities of forensic interviewers at Childhelp are as follows:

- Schedule and coordinate joint forensic interviews of alleged child, adolescent, and vulnerable adult abuse victims with multidisciplinary team members
- Conduct forensic interviews of alleged victims and witnesses of abuse on behalf of multidisciplinary team members
- Maintain and update case files, case lists, video logbooks, and statistical tracking
- Provide written documentation pertaining to interviews conducted for case review purposes
- Participate in weekly case reviews, including coordinating case review information with multidisciplinary team members
- Participate in defense interviews
- Testify in civil and criminal court proceedings regarding general interview processes, techniques, and interviews regarding individual cases as appropriate and requested
- Remain current on research involving forensic interviewing and abuse investigations
- Participate in monthly interview program peer review sessions, providing training regarding interview protocols and child developmental levels
- Consult with members of a multidisciplinary team as requested or deemed necessary

Minimum requirements at Childhelp include the following (Childhelp, 2013):

- A master's degree in social services or other related fields
- Five years' experience working in a multidisciplinary environment with child protective services, law enforcement, and human services
- Ability to communicate effectively with children and adolescents, ranging in age from 2 to 17 years, to solicit sensitive case information pertaining to abuse or eyewitness accounts of abuse
- Fluency in both English and Spanish (preferred but not required)
- Academic training or practical experience in developmental stages of children and the dynamics and effects of intra- and extra-familial child abuse
- Familiarity with and a disposition toward the multidisciplinary team approach regarding the investigation and prosecution of child abuse cases

- Ability to communicate effectively in writing and orally to a variety of individuals and groups

Women are normally preferred as forensic interviewers, but you might not see that elsewhere in print. Forensic interviewers may be needed with adult victims, but they primarily interview children about sexual molestation and physical abuse. Although some children will open up to a skilled male interviewer without too much apprehension, more often than not, it was a male perpetrator who harmed the child. There may be a lack of trust, which is a huge stumbling block. Women also play a nurturing role in children's eyes, which aids in building rapport.

There is more to interviewing children than being friendly. A trained interviewer knows how to build rapport, how to ask questions, and how to interpret a child's answers and body language. Building rapport with children can be challenging. Children usually know why they are being interviewed and may have their defenses up. If the perpetrator is a family member, a child might be afraid of having to face the abuser again. You must be careful not to make promises you can't keep. You can't give children treats or gifts prior to an interview, because a defense attorney will use that information to convince a jury that the child was influenced to say what the interviewer wanted to hear. The key is to know about the development of children at all stages.

Once rapport has been established, a skilled interviewer will transition into the fact-finding portion of the interview with questions that are as nonleading as possible. An example of a leading question is "Did he touch you in your private area?" A nonleading question would be "What happened?" A skilled interviewer knows how to listen without interrupting, so as not to disturb the steady flow of a narrative. A trained forensic interviewer knows how to go back and clarify statements that may seem unclear to a prosecutor and jury. An expert interviewer is constantly aware of a child's choice of words and body language. One of the signs of a true statement is when a child's narrative is complete and includes information that happened before, during, and after the incident. A pretender will usually not offer any more information than necessary, resulting in shorter answers.

To become a forensic interviewer, you can take one of several routes. One path would be to earn a degree in child psychology, with a minor in criminal justice. Another option is to become a police officer, transfer to detective work in the area of child crimes, attend all available trainings offered by forensic interviewers, and get a degree in child psychology. You could also consider working or volunteering for child protective services or a domestic violence shelter to add child interviewing and group work experience to your résumé. Once you have some training, experience, and credentials, you can seek opportunities for further experience in your quest to become an expert.

Forensic interviewers are often paid very well, depending on credentials, experience, location, and whether the positions are grant funded. Those working in police departments earn about as much as lieutenants. Salaries can range from $45,000 to $90,000. Forensic interviewers can also work under contracts with several agencies at a time. They may set up offices with interview rooms that are wired for video recording (hidden) and decorated in a child-friendly manner. If you went this route, you would work under an appointment system and bill the department on the basis of the interview time and any follow-up court testimony. This type of setup is perfect for someone who doesn't want to work full-time or wants to work extra jobs.

Forensic Entomologist

Academic institutions typically employ forensic entomologists, but they can provide valuable information and work with law enforcement, medical examiners, and coroners in establishing a portion of the postmortem interval (PMI). Entomologists are experts at determining the ages of insects on human remains. Such information can be extremely valuable when law enforcement investigators are attempting to establish a time frame to support or refute suspect or witness statements.

Approximately 8,000 women and men work as professional entomologists in the United States, which includes teaching, working as extension entomologists, raising bees, enforcing quarantines and regulations, performing insect survey work, consulting on integrated pest management topics, selling insecticides, controlling pests, and conducting research on insect classification, taxonomy, biology, ecology, behavior, and control. A great number of entomologists work in some aspect of economic or applied entomology that deals with the control of harmful insects.

Many police agencies, coroners, medical examiners, and federal agencies throughout the United States are now relying on forensic entomologists to assist in answering vital questions concerning death investigations. Although forensic entomologists are often called upon by attorneys, law enforcement agencies, and medical examiners to analyze entomological evidence, few are employed full time by law enforcement agencies. Many board-certified forensic entomologists are employed by institutions of higher education.

The specific area of entomology called upon by law enforcement is medicocriminal forensic entomology. It is generally criminal in nature, focusing on the insects that colonize human tissues in the PMI. It has been assumed that forensic entomologists estimate the PMI. However, forensic entomologists actually estimate the ages of the insects developing on human or animal remains and therefore actually estimate the time of colonization. This is the time at which eggs or larvae are deposited on the remains. The adult arrival time is also added to the time of colonization, and thus a forensic entomologist can derive the time since colonization of the remains. More specifically, forensic entomologists often determine the minimum time since colonization.

Medicocriminal entomology is a powerful tool for forensic scientists, medical examiners, coroners, and law enforcement. It has been used for the following purposes:

- Estimating a portion of the PMI
- Establishing the geographic location of death
- Associating the victim and suspect with each other and with the scene
- Identifying possible sites of trauma
- Acquiring alternative toxicological samples
- Providing alternative DNA samples
- Resolving traffic accidents resulting from panic due to stinging insects in an automobile
- Resolving aircraft incidents in which entomological evidence was found to be a contributing factor
- Identifying criminal misuse of insects that are induced to bite or feed upon a victim
- Resolving child neglect and elder abuse cases

The requirements to be a forensic entomologist are as follows:

- A master's degree or doctorate in entomology
- Graduate coursework with a specialization and area of concentration in the forensic application of entomology
- Five years of relevant case experience
- Five case exemplars to submit to the American Board of Forensic Entomology
- Ability to score 80% or higher on a written examination
- Ability to score 80% or higher on a practical examination and case workup on a mock case

If you are interested in becoming a forensic entomologist, you may consider a degree in biology or zoology. Finding an undergraduate degree in entomology would be difficult. You may find employment at a large law enforcement agency at which you would also take on other responsibilities depending on the needs and your expertise. Entry-level salaries can be as low as $29,000 per year, but experienced forensic entomologists working in government jobs can make more than $70,000 annually (North Carolina Association for Biomedical Research, 2013).

Diversity in Forensic Jobs

Negative issues for women and minorities in the forensic field are almost nonexistent, or at least no different than for other jobs outside the criminal justice realm. Unlike in law enforcement, there are approximately equal numbers of women and men in forensic careers. Equally ubiquitous are opportunities for women and men in obtaining the education and experience necessary for most forensic jobs.

Summary

Forensics is the use of science and technology to investigate and establish facts in criminal or civil courts of law. As technology develops and better methods of manipulating evidence are discovered, more is expected. Today, the successful prosecution of a case depends largely on physical evidence that is properly collected, tested, and presented. DNA technology has become one of the most effective forensic tools law enforcement uses to convict suspects of certain crimes. DNA can be found in blood, semen, hair, saliva, sweat, skins cells, vomit, tears, earwax, and feces. Fingerprints remain among the most common and consistent means of identifying suspects. They are infallible because the features never change, barring any surgeries, injuries, or diseases.

The criminal justice system comprises several separate entities working together for a common purpose. The more each component knows about the other working parts, the better the overall quality of the output. Some of the prominent forensic jobs in the criminal justice system include CST, forensic scientist, medical examiner, investigative technician, DNA analyst, toxicologist, forensic nurse examiner, forensic psychiatrist specialist, forensic interviewer, and forensic entomologist.

There is a specific need for women as forensic interviewers because this position deals primarily with children. Children often respond to women more easily than to men. The position of forensic interviewer requires less schooling than some of the other positions in the field of forensics and pays very well. Women and minorities are more prevalent in the forensic field as a whole.

DISCUSSION QUESTIONS

1. Many jobs in the forensic world require experience. How can a person get the minimum experience if other similar jobs also require it? Explain.

2. Agencies such as Childhelp that work closely with child victims generally prefer their forensic interviewers to be women. Should this type of job bias be allowed? Explain.

3. What job in the forensic arena sounds most interesting and enjoyable to you? Why?

4. What job in forensics appears to be the most difficult to attain? Why?

5. At one time, we didn't have the DNA capabilities we now enjoy. Nonetheless, our courts flourished with trials, and criminals were convicted by juries. As technologies have been invented and improved, expectations have also been raised. Do you feel that it is fair for prosecutors to be expected to provide more and better evidence than in the past? Why or why not?

REFERENCES

Childhelp. (2013). *Employment opportunities*. Retrieved from http://www.childhelp-usa.com/pages/employment

City of Charlotte & Mecklenburg County. (2013). *Human resources: Job posting information*. Retrieved from https://cltjobs.ci.charlotte.nc.us

The City of Houston. (2013). *Jobs*. Retrieved from http://www.houstontx.gov/jobs/

Commonwealth of Massachusetts, Human Resources Division. (2013). *Home page*. Retrieved from https://jobs.hrd.state.ma.us

County of San Diego. (2013). *Job postings*. Retrieved from http://agency.governmentjobs.com/sdcounty

Illinois State Police, Division of Forensic Services, Forensic Sciences Command. (2013). *Employment*. Retrieved from http://www.isp.state.il.us/Forensics/html/Employment.html

Maricopa County Human Resources. (2013). *Home page*. Retrieved from http://agency.government-jobs.com/maricopa/default.cfm

North Carolina Association for Biomedical Research. (2013). *Bioscience careers: Entomologist*. Retrieved from http://www.aboutbioscience.org/careers/entomologist

Tacoma General Hospital. (2015). *Forensic nurse examiner*. Retrieved from http://www.indeed.com/job/Forensic-Nurse-Examiner-at-Tacoma-General-Hospital-in-Tacoma,-WA-48463502e6496126

5

Victim Services

The Crime Victims' Rights Act of 2004 forced many changes in the criminal justice system. The onus was put on all city and state governments to ensure that victims receive the rights promised them by the legislation. These rights included the following:

- The right to notification
- The right not to be excluded from proceedings
- The right to protection from the accused
- The right to speak at criminal justice proceedings
- The right to restitution
- The right to consult with the prosecuting attorney
- The right to proceedings free from unreasonable delay
- The right to be treated with fairness and respect for the victim's dignity and privacy

In reading these rights that are now mandated, you may be surprised that they weren't already awarded to victims. Why weren't these amenities offered to victims all along? Before the economy crashed in 2007, some would have answered that it was a lack of money and resources. However, since 2007, we have seen agencies work with less because they have to. Police departments and courts have had to rethink and alter how they accomplish their everyday tasks. If anything good came out of the budget collapse, it was these forced improvements. Better victim services are just one of many transformations in recent years. Some of the new victim responsibilities were given to police departments, and some were given to the courts.

It should be pointed out that the deficit of efficient services for victims wasn't due to a lack of concern on the part of police and courts. It is difficult to change paradigms in any occupation, but it is especially hard in law enforcement. While assistant chiefs and captains were dealing with departmental issues, police chiefs handled outside political issues, which included pleading with city management for more manpower. Justifying a need for patrol officers was always much easier than selling new programs, such as victim services. Had administrators of police departments recognized the need for better treatment of victims, the idea of trying to change officers' approach to their job would have been a huge undertaking, if even possible. Worrying about victims of crime isn't what many police officers signed up for (prior to 2004). Even today, the victim-focused mentality isn't found among all police employees, but more and more hiring units are looking for just that type of mind-set.

There have been huge changes in intimate partner violence laws all across the country, and many veteran officers have had to be taught new procedures for handling domestic disputes. In the early 1980s, an officer would have to ask the victim of domestic violence if she (or he) would prosecute the perpetrator. Often the victim would be afraid to follow through because of fear of the perpetrator or lack of trust in the criminal justice system. Frequently, a victim would tell the on-scene officer that she (or he) just wanted the offender to leave for the night. The officer would make the offender leave but would sometimes make the victim feel bad for wasting his time. The offender would leave, the officer would leave, the offender would return, the victim would receive more bruises, and the police would never know.

The crime victims' movement intensified during the mid-1980s, and many agencies received funding to facilitate better treatment of victims. The Victims of Crime Act (VOCA) of 1984 was the catalyst. Over $1 billion has been spent on victim assistance programs since the start of VOCA funding. This funding has come from numerous contributors besides the government. Many community leaders have also stepped up and persisted in keeping the vision alive. Instead of the crime victims' movement being just a temporary fad, it has become one of the most successful and supported movements in recent history. Today, thanks to 30 years of perpetual change and improvement, we have witnessed the emergence of enhanced victim-centered protocols and the creation of new jobs associated with victim advocacy.

Today, many victim advocacy positions are funded by state and federal grants, but city governments remain accountable to support the programs. Police departments and courts look for victim services personnel who are grant savvy. Many victim services specialists are self-supportive, writing their own grant requests to retain their positions in the agencies for which they work. City governments sometimes have to budget for victim services positions when grant funding isn't available. We will explore some positions at a range of agencies around the country to give general examples of job descriptions and requirements.

Victim Advocate and Related Positions

A civilian position that has surfaced at many police departments in the past few decades is crime victim advocate. To work for the Farmington Police Department in New Mexico as a crime victim advocate, you would perform a variety of administrative and professional public safety assistance work in planning, coordinating, and directing services for victims of violent crimes. Many agencies employ advocates for victims of all crimes. A significant aspect of the work in Farmington involves public contact with adult and child victims of violent crime, law enforcement staff, and community groups. Advocates work under the general supervision of a designated detective lieutenant. Advocates perform advocacy duties for victims within the criminal justice system. They are responsible for the development, administration, and evaluation of the victim program and serve as spokespersons and liaisons with other law enforcement staff, allied professional agencies, community groups, and the community at large to carry out the purpose of the program. Advocates conduct public speaking presentations for the general public; training for allied professionals; and updates and training for law enforcement staff, victim advocate staff, and program volunteers, and they monitor case management, which includes analyzing reports, contacting victims, developing action plans with victims, and monitoring case progression through the judicial system. Farmington requires a minimum of a bachelor's degree in criminal justice, social science, or a related field (a master's degree is preferred) and 3 years' experience in victim assistance programs or other nonprofit victim-oriented programs. Farmington requires 1 year's experience working with the criminal justice system and 1 year's experience in grant writing or a satisfactory equivalent combination of experience and training. All applicants must provide enough information for a thorough background check. Considerable knowledge of and experience with strategic planning, program development, personnel management, and grants and budgets are also preferred. Farmington requires working knowledge of the adult and juvenile criminal justice system, good knowledge of victimology and crisis intervention techniques, the ability to prepare reports, and the ability to effectively communicate in both oral and written form (City of Farmington, 2013).

Because victim advocates are often paid by grants, the victim advocate or victim services supervisor is usually responsible for writing the grants. Having grant-writing experience is not always vital for advocate positions, but it can propel you ahead of other candidates for practically any position in government work for which grant writing is a preferred skill. Grant-writing training is offered all over the country. You can go online and find an affordable training course in your area, which will offer a certificate upon completion. In some areas, you can find training for as little as $100. Once you receive your certificate, you can list "grant writing certified" on your résumé. The ideal situation for a victim advocate is a job in which the city sponsors the position and includes all the usual benefits, such as sick pay, vacation time, and health insurance. The pay for most advocacy jobs ranges from $24,000 to $44,000.

Men don't routinely conduct victim advocacy, but there are some advantages to having men involved in the work. Victims of theft or burglary rarely need as much intervention as those of family deaths, sexual assault, or domestic violence, but in many government agencies, victim advocacy is available for victims of all types of crimes. Most advocacy work is short term.

Advocates help victims get through the initial crises and refer victims to counselors if necessary, but they seldom perform counseling themselves.

Advocacy is significant in domestic violence cases. Victims of domestic violence stay in abusive relationships for a variety of reasons. Some of the top reasons are fear, economic dependency, belief that the abuser will change, isolation, cultural influences, immigration status, religion, low self-esteem, and the benefit of children. Advocates play a multifaceted role with these types of victims. Advocates educate victims to help them understand their abusers better and learn what resources are available. They develop safety plans with victims. Advocates find shelter for victims and help them acquire financial help to travel and eat. Advocates become liaisons between victims and the criminal justice system to help ensure that their cases are investigated properly and that abusers receive prompt consequences. Advocates accompany victims to court to obtain orders of protection and then follow through with the police to make sure the orders are served.

Law enforcement and attorneys benefit by having someone take the victim by the hand. If a victim retains confidence in the criminal justice system, it is likelier that she will follow through with her part in a case. Even though a victim no longer needs to say "I'll prosecute," a case is unlikely to be successful if the victim refuses to testify in court.

There are 56 state coalitions and the National Coalition Against Domestic Violence that target domestic violence prevention. You can find a list of the state coalitions and their contact information at http://www.ncadv.org/learn/state-coalitions. These coalitions work closely with the state governments from which they often receive much of their funding. The Arizona Coalition Against Domestic Violence (AzCADV) was organized in 1980. It was formed so that professionals and concerned citizens statewide could unite, increase public awareness about the issue of domestic violence, enhance the safety of and services for domestic violence victims, and reduce the incidence of domestic violence in Arizona families. AzCADV is based in Phoenix and has significant statewide presence. It is a nongovernmental, nonprofit membership organization that works with more than 170 formal members and allies to carry out its mission and objectives (Arizona Coalition Against Domestic Violence, 2013).

Those working within the realm of AzCADV include victim advocates, legal advocates, system advocates, and trainers. AzCADV hosts a number of volunteer opportunities to bring concerned leaders, citizens, and communities together to solve some of the most pressing issues facing domestic violence victims and the domestic violence community. Some of the volunteer opportunities are with the Legislative Advisory Committee, Legal Committee, Domestic Violence Programs Committee, Women of Color Committee, and SHARE Survivors Advisory Committee (Arizona Coalition Against Domestic Violence, 2013).

There are similar volunteer opportunities in all 56 state programs. Volunteering with a domestic violence coalition would add a great bullet point to your résumé. Some coalitions have volunteers doing the bulk of the work. The

Nebraska Domestic Violence Sexual Assault Coalition is a statewide advocacy organization committed to the prevention and elimination of sexual and domestic violence. Its aim is to enhance safety and justice for victims of domestic violence and sexual assault by supporting and building upon the services provided by the network of local programs. For its first 10 years, the coalition was a volunteer organization with no paid staff and no office. In 1987, the coalition received funds from the Department of Social Services to open an office and hire a staff person (Nebraska Domestic Violence Sexual Assault Coalition, 2013).

The Oregon Coalition Against Domestic and Sexual Violence is a statewide nonprofit corporation composed of 45 member programs. It offers support services to providers and community partners, including systems advocacy; development and distribution of funds, information, referrals, and technical assistance; training and education; and shaping public policy around intimate partner violence, sexual assault, and stalking. The coalition was formed to support efforts at passing legislation important to the antiviolence movement, such as the landmark Oregon Abuse Prevention Act and the Rape in Marriage Law. The coalition was incorporated in 1978 and continues to strengthen support systems in favor of victims of domestic and sexual violence.

With some advocacy experience, you could transition into other positions within a coalition or its partner organizations. One example is the position of social media and events coordinator for the Oregon Coalition Against Domestic and Sexual Violence. This individual provides a wide array of event, administrative, technical, and office coordination. This position is responsible for the overall coordination of the agency's regional conferences, annual conference, technology infrastructure, integration of software applications, and training regarding technology use. The minimum qualifications for the position of social media and event coordinator include the following:

- An understanding of and agreement with the coalition's mission statement and philosophy regarding the elimination of sexual violence, empowerment, inclusiveness, and social change
- Two to 5 years' experience working with domestic or sexual violence survivors
- Three years of experience providing internal technology support
- Proficiency in database and website administration
- Demonstrated understanding of social media activities and use
- Very high attention to detail and excellent verbal and written communication skills
- An associate's degree in computer systems administration or the equivalent of education and experience
- Ability to travel statewide on some overnight and weekend trips

The position of social media and event coordinator pays between $36,000 and $40,000 (Oregon Coalition Against Domestic and Sexual Violence, 2013).

The Tennessee Coalition to End Domestic and Sexual Violence is a state-wide nonprofit organization that provides training, technical assistance, policy work, and legal services to victims of domestic violence, sexual assault, stalking, and trafficking. The coalition employs a sexual assault victim advocate for its sexual assault legal clinic. The goal of the clinic is to provide comprehensive and holistic legal representation in civil matters for victims of sexual assault. The funding for these services allows the coalition to provide representation to clients in 34 counties. The sexual assault victim advocate for the Tennessee coalition is responsible for assisting the staff attorneys in representing sexual assault victims. Specific duties include the following:

- Conducting intake for referred clients and performing safety needs assessments
- Making referrals for resources needed to increase victim safety
- Working directly with sexual assault programs to obtain documents necessary for legal representation
- Assisting in collecting and managing data related to clients

The qualifications and desired qualities for this position include knowledge of and experience with sexual assault victims, excellent communication skills, fluency in languages other than English, cultural knowledge, familiarity with Microsoft Word, and the ability to work with people from diverse backgrounds. As with most advocate positions, the salary is between $30,000 and $44,000 (Tennessee Coalition to End Domestic and Sexual Violence, 2013).

The position of prevention specialist exists at the Florida Coalition Against Domestic Violence. Working for the Florida coalition in this position, you would provide training and technical assistance to Florida's 42 certified domestic violence centers and allied partners. You would need knowledge of the root causes of violence against women and oppressed groups, proven training experience, an ability to multitask, and a consistent employment history. You would need extensive knowledge of primary prevention for domestic violence; experience planning, implementing, and evaluating prevention programs; experience working with youth and engaging youth leadership; experience with the coordinated community response to domestic violence; and a proven history of successful organizing for social change. You would need a high school diploma or equivalency and 4 years' relevant experience, or a bachelor's degree in a related field and 3 years' relevant experience.

Another position with the Florida coalition is statewide domestic violence hotline advocate. In this job you would provide crisis intervention, information, referral, and ongoing advocacy to survivors of domestic violence who call Florida's toll-free statewide domestic violence hotline. When not answering the hotline, you would provide administrative support for the program department, build upon the existing hotline resources, review hotline data, assist with developing hotline trainings and corresponding curricula, and support the direct supervisor with other duties and assignments. To be a statewide domestic violence hotline advocate, you would need to possess a high school diploma or equivalent and have 4 years' relevant experience, or a bachelor's degree in a related field and 3 years' relevant experience. As a hotline advocate, you must have extensive knowledge of the dynamics of domestic violence and a history of successful advocacy on behalf of survivors. Experience working at a certified domestic violence center is preferred (Florida Coalition Against Domestic Violence, 2013).

The Washington Coalition of Sexual Assault Programs employs training specialists, a common position in most states. Training specialists develop, implement, evaluate, and facilitate training and events related to the continuum of sexual violence and sexual assault services. Washington prefers employees from historically marginalized communities (Washington Coalition of Sexual Assault Programs, 2013).

Generally, a training position requires the same skills as an advocacy position. Individuals who can present in front of large groups are also sought. Job interviews for training positions usually involve giving a short presentation in front of the staff to demonstrate your abilities. Spanish fluency is a plus for any advocacy position but especially for trainers. Often a grant will specify that the employee hired under the grant be bilingual.

The National Resource Center on Domestic Violence, located in Washington, D.C., employs training and resource development specialists, who are responsible for coordinating domestic violence training, specialized technical assistance, and resource development on a wide range of subjects and issues that intersect with domestic violence dynamics, prevalence, intervention, prevention, and public awareness. The training, technical assistance, and resource development are guided by high-quality research, analysis, information, and resources on domestic violence and are provided to individuals and local, state, tribal, and federal entities throughout the United States.

A training and resource development specialist requires a bachelor's degree or equivalent from an accredited 4-year college or university and a minimum of 5 years' experience in work directly pertaining to domestic violence, social justice, systems advocacy, or social change or any equivalent combination of education and experience. Direct domestic violence service experience is strongly preferred. For this position, you would need to demonstrate knowledge and experience of planning, developing, and implementing technical assistance and training specifically related to domestic violence. You would need to assess the development and delivery of resources, consultation and services, and follow-up and evaluation (National Resource Center on Domestic Violence, 2013).

Victim advocates are also employed in courts and prosecutors' offices. As a court victim advocate specialist in Brighton, Colorado, you would provide information, assistance, and support to victims, witnesses, and deputy district attorneys in cases filed for prosecution in district, county, and juvenile court divisions. You would provide information to victims and witnesses regarding the functions and role of the Victim Witness Services Unit in the district attorney's office and of victims' rights as set forth in Colorado statutes. You would

Shelly Ward: Victim Services – Mesa Police Department

CJ: What is your current position?

SW: Victim Services Administrator.

CJ: What are your typical job duties?

SW: Coordinating, administering, and managing all functions of the Victim Services Unit for the Mesa Police Department. Direct supervision of five full time staff (three victim advocates, two victim notification clerks), and coordination of volunteers (office assistants, interns, and Victim Assistance Program (VAP) volunteers). I provide direct victim assistance to crime victims, assist with victim compensation, orders of protection/injunctions against harassment, navigation of the criminal justice system, referrals to community service agencies, and assistance in exercising statutory rights. In addition, I manage victims' rights program (VRP) and Victims of Crime Act (VOCA) grants, represent the Mesa Family Advocacy Center at community meetings, and develop policies related to the delivery of victim rights and services to ensure that the Mesa Police Department is in compliance with victims' rights legislation. I develop curriculum and conduct training sessions for employees and volunteers. In addition, I review cases, prepare grant requests, compile monthly, quarterly, and annual reports in compliance with grant and department requirements. I'm subject to emergency call out during off duty hours to respond to crisis situations.

CJ: How long have you been at your current assignment?

SW: Five months.

CJ: What other positions have you held prior to this one?

SW: Victim Advocate—City of Mesa Prosecutors Office, Quality Assurance Administrator—Blue Cross Blue Shield of AZ.

CJ: What are the requirements/qualifications for your job?

SW: Any combination of training, education, and experience equivalent to graduation from an accredited college or university with a bachelor's degree in social work, sociology, psychology, or closely related field, a minimum of 4 years experience in counseling, social work, or crisis intervention including at least one year of supervisory/managerial experience.

CJ: What steps did you go through during hiring?

SW: After the initial panel interview I was required to complete a background check, fingerprint card, polygraph examination, and psychological examination.

CJ: What advice can you offer students who might be interested in pursuing a similar career?

SW: Volunteer!! The best way to learn about victim advocacy is to provide service through volunteering with agencies that provide victim services or crisis intervention. There are a number of agencies that provide service to victims such as shelters, advocacy centers, educational outreach, and law enforcement agencies that typically have a volunteer program. Educate yourself! Many agencies offer free training on topics like domestic violence, sexual assault, and crime (e.g., Arizona Coalition to End Sexual and Domestic Violence). Listen, listen, listen! Be present for the victim—it's not our job to fix the victim. We are there to provide support, encouragement, education, and tools to empower the victim to help himself or herself walk through their situation.

provide practical explanation of Adams County and Broomfield County court-room procedures to victims and witnesses, including general criminal justice processes and definitions of legal terminology. You would provide referrals and information regarding the availability of crisis intervention services, victim compensation funds, victim assistance, legal assistance, immigration and financial assistance resources, mental health resources, and social services. You would initiate and respond to in-person, telephone, and written contact with victims and witnesses to provide factual, accurate, and timely case-related information. You would assist victims and witnesses with payment of mileage and witness fees. You would need to attend and participate in training opportunities that are directly related to unit services and maintain statistical data regarding services provided to victims and witnesses.

The requirements to be hired in Brighton include a bachelor's degree in human services or a related field and 2 years' experience working with victims of crime in a criminal justice or community-based service program, and it is preferred that applicants have National Organization for Victim Assistance or Colorado Organization for Victim Assistance advocate certification. Spanish fluency is another requirement for this position, which is common for many advocacy jobs. This job pays a salary of $40,704 (Brighton, Colorado, Human Resources, 2013).

Some agencies partner with the courts and receive funding from the government and other donors from the community. One such nonprofit organization is Edwin Gould Services for Children and Family (EGSCF), which is located in Brooklyn, New York. As a provider of services to battered women defendants, EGSCF partnered with the Center for Court Innovation to develop a project at the Midtown Community Court (MCC) providing on-site, intensive services to people arrested for prostitution and other offenders, sensitive to this population's experience of trauma, including domestic violence, sexual assault, and transgender and homophobic violence. The MCC is a public-private partnership and a project of the Fund for the City of New York. Its mission is to respond constructively to quality-of-life crimes and to work to prevent further crimes before they occur. It accomplishes these goals by sentencing persons arrested for misdemeanors in the court's catchment area to a range of community service and social service sentences, including drug treatment, job training, and counseling. As an advocate for this organization, your responsibilities would include the following:

- Completing intake and psychosocial assessments and keeping accurate records
- Providing individual counseling and case management to both mandated and voluntary clients
- Facilitating therapeutic groups for women, transgender individuals, and men and developing the group curricula
- Developing and conducting training for court stakeholders
- Developing a directory of resources for program participants
- Drafting court compliance memoranda

- Providing statistical and narrative reports covering services provided on a monthly basis
- Attending casework supervision and clinical training at MCC
- Participating in weekly case conferences, clinics, and staff meetings at MCC

Qualifications and skills that are required for this job include the following:

- A bachelor's degree in social work or a related field
- Experience working with victims of trauma, including domestic violence and sexual assault
- Experience working within the criminal justice system and understanding of mandated programs
- Experience working with the lesbian, gay, bisexual, and transgender communities
- Spanish fluency (preferred)
- Knowledge and understanding of trauma, specifically domestic violence and sexual assault

The salary for an advocate at MCC ranges from $35,000 to $40,000 (Edwin Gould Services for Children and Families, 2013).

The Arizona Attorney General's Office, Criminal Division, Office of Victim Services has a position for an advocate program specialist. This individual performs casework, human services, and administrative duties of moderate difficulty. An advocate program specialist assists victims through the complex criminal justice system, providing quality crime victim services—including both mandated and nonmandated services—as cases progress through the judicial pretrial or post-conviction process, handling often high-profile and complex cases such as multiple-victim white-collar crimes, elder exploitation, and death penalty cases. Casework includes victims' rights notification activities, monitoring and advocating for compliance with court orders for restitution, and the promotion of victims' interest and participation in the criminal justice progress. Advocate program specialists provide services in the form of crisis counseling, intervention, and follow-up services to victims, such as referrals to community agencies for assistance, court orientation and escort, and personal and legal advocacy. Advocates implement program policies and procedures, operate manuals and protocols, and serve as resources on victims' rights issues. They facilitate attorney-victim meetings and serve as liaisons between victims and prosecutors, courts, the criminal justice system, and community agencies statewide. They are also responsible for the completion and accurate case documentation of activities and services; assisting in the selection, training, and monitoring of volunteer interns; providing coverage for other advocates; and completing periodic assignments from the advocate program manager and the director of the Office of Victim Services. Ideal candidates have bachelor's degrees from accredited universities with an emphasis on social science and/or extensive experience in victim services or a related field (Arizona Attorney General, 2013).

Courts also have positions for volunteers and interns in victim services, such as the court-appointed special advocate (CASA) in Hawaii. Formerly known as the volunteer guardian ad litem program, the CASA program employs trained volunteers who are appointed by the court to represent the best interests of children in child abuse or neglect cases, in and out of court. CASA volunteers must be at least 20 years old and able to spend between 4 and 25 hours a month serving as fact finders, advocates, and monitors for children in need. The judiciary provides free training and staff support for all volunteers (Hawaii State Judiciary, 2013).

Albany, New York, has a court advocate volunteer program at the Albany County Crime Victim and Sexual Violence Center. The center is a therapy, counseling, advocacy, and referral service for victims of crime. It is located in downtown Albany and is currently staffed by a director, three New York State–licensed therapists (one of whom specializes in child therapy), four crime victim caseworkers, a prevention educator, a volunteer coordinator, and two support staff. In addition, it maintains a 24-hour hotline for victims and survivors of sexual assault.

The center has been an autonomous department of Albany County government since 1975 and adheres to the philosophy of client-centered treatment. The center is charged by the Albany County Legislature to provide trained counselors for all victims, regardless of their intention of making a police report or prosecuting. Court advocate volunteers identify and speak to victims of crimes when those victims attend the arraignments of their offenders. Volunteers are expected to provide emotional support for victims, as well as be able to answer questions clients may have about the criminal justice system. In addition, volunteers will assist victims in applying for compensation for monetary losses resulting from crimes through the New York State Office of Victim Services. Volunteers must be familiar with the categories of compensation available, and they fill out these applications with victims while in court. These forms, along with the new client form, intake form, and follow-up form, are completed and submitted to the administrative aide.

All potential court advocate volunteers complete applications provided by the Crime Victim and Sexual Violence Center. Each applicant is interviewed by a member of the professional staff, and then references are checked prior to acceptance into the program. The center provides training sessions for all volunteers on victimization and the criminal justice system. Training is divided into modules, which consist of online studies, quizzes, and group role-playing experiences with the center's professional staff. Topics include legal courts and police, victims of crime, domestic violence, offenders, family and civil court, and an advocate's role and forms.

Upon completion of 15 hours of training, volunteers arrange to shadow staff members in court on several occasions. The volunteers are assigned to specific courts when the staff and the volunteers both feel confident in the volunteers' ability to work unsupervised. Supervision is provided as needed by a center caseworker. In addition, court advocate volunteers are required to complete an additional 35 hours of the U.S. Office for Victims of Crime training required to become certified as a crime victim service provider. This training is done in conjunction with court advocacy placement. The center welcomes all persons 19 years of age and older as court advocate volunteers (Albany County Crime Victim and Sexual Violence Center, 2013).

The courts in Augusta, Georgia, have a victim advocate position. Advocates provide direct services and information to victims of misdemeanor crimes within the guidelines of the Criminal Justice Coordinating Council, local government, and department policies. Advocates report to the chief assistant solicitor general, the domestic violence prosecuting attorney, the victim-witness manager, or another designated person, and they work with governmental and victim-related agencies, crime victims, and the public to provide administrative support. The principal duties of court advocates include the following:

- Attending court sessions and assisting in providing crime victims with information regarding victims' rights pursuant to Crime Bill Act of 1995
- Assisting in notification procedures for victims regarding the criminal justice process
- Working as liaisons among victims, social services, and government agencies
- Assisting victims of domestic violence with victim compensation forms
- Assisting in documenting data of victim contacts and notices, recording court dispositions, and maintaining data for monthly and yearly reports
- Responding to requests for information from officials, employees, other staff members, the public, and other individuals
- Preparing grant and funding proposals and statistical reports to meet grant requirements
- Interviewing victims
- Serving as resources to subordinate personnel

The requirements for education and skills include the following:

- A bachelor's degree in psychology or social work
- At least 5 years in a similar position or sufficient experience to perform principal duties and responsibilities, usually associated with the completion of an apprenticeship or internship
- Considerable knowledge of Georgia laws pertaining to misdemeanors and victims' advocacy
- Familiarity with county and departmental rules and regulations and the criminal justice system
- Proficiency in implementing program activities, interpersonal relations, public speaking, and time management

This position pays between $31,283 and $49,783 (Augusta, Georgia, 2013).

There are also opportunities to work at private shelters and victim service facilities. These agencies are connected to the overall network of victim services throughout their states. The majority are nonprofit agencies that receive funding from the government and numerous private partners. One such facility is Harbor House in New Philadelphia, Ohio, which is a domestic violence shelter and substance abuse halfway house serving Tuscarawas and Carroll counties in Ohio. As a division of Personal & Family Counseling Services of Tuscarawas Valley, Inc. (an affiliate organization of Ohio Guidestone), Harbor House is dedicated to serving both victims of domestic violence and their children, as well as women who are recovering from substance abuse.

Harbor House has a position for residential advocate (RA), who provides direct client support by monitoring the household and supervising a client's activities, in addition to crisis intervention. RAs help clients adjust to shared family living while being responsible for their safety and well-being. RAs monitor medications, complete necessary paperwork, answer the crisis line, and assess callers' appropriateness for admission into the program. To work as an RA, you would need an associate's degree or enrollment in college with a major in sociology, psychology, or criminal justice (or a related field) and to have completed a minimum of 12 hours of course work in your major field or have work or life experience. Four months to 1 year of applicable employment experience at a residential facility is strongly preferred (Personal and Family Counseling Services of Tuscarawas County, 2013).

There is a position for sexual assault/abuse advocate at The Nord Center in Lorain, Ohio. This is a full-time employee who reports to the Children's Advocacy Center and Lorain Crisis Resource Center coordinator. This individual has the general responsibility for providing direct services to survivors and secondary survivors of sexual assault and abuse. This includes during exams, forensic interviews, scheduled appointments, and the 24-hour hotline and on-call schedule. Sexual assault/abuse advocates are responsible for providing services that meet the needs of survivors (both children and adults), constituents, and the community in compliance with program standards.

The minimum requirements for this position in Ohio include a bachelor's degree in social work or a related field. An associate's degree in social work or a related field may be considered with previous experience working with children and adults who have experienced sexual assault and abuse. You would need to be able to work well under pressure and demonstrate good time management and organizational skills for this position. Certification through the Ohio Advocate Network is preferred. Previous crisis intervention and diversity training is desired. The necessity for travel requires that the employee possess a valid driver's license, have proof of automobile insurance, and have use of a personal vehicle. Favorable references or evaluations are also required (The Nord Center, 2013).

Hospitals also employ victim services personnel. White Plains Hospital in New York has a position for a clinical social worker, who provides social work services to patients and families, including obtaining, analyzing, and evaluating data relating to medical and psychosocial programs. Clinical social workers formulate and carry out treatment plans and initiate and follow through in a cooperative effort with other members of home care interdisciplinary teams to enable patients to be maintained safely in the community or discharged to appropriate facilities. The requirements for education and skills include the following:

- A master's degree in social work from a school of social work accredited by the Council on Social Work Education
- Licensed master social worker or licensed clinical social worker approval from the State Education Department of the University of the State of New York
- Two years' experience in an acute care hospital or related setting (White Plains Hospital, 2013)

The Grady Health System in Atlanta, Georgia, has a position for victim/witness advocate (VWA). VWAs work directly with sexually assaulted patients, primarily in emergency rooms, women's urgent care centers, and rape crisis centers. VWAs work closely with the center's manager to coordinate services for victims in the hospital and in the courtroom; serve as liaisons with police, the courts, and district attorneys regarding sexual assault case management; and provide community education in Fulton and DeKalb counties. The qualifications for the position of VWA are a bachelor's degree in counseling, social work, criminal justice, or a related area and a minimum of 1 year of related experience. For this job, you must have skills and experience to work effectively with the police, the courts, community agencies, hospital staff, volunteers, center staff, patients, and their families. You must also have skills to effectively handle persons under emotional stress and be able to problem solve (Grady Health System, 2013).

At any given time, you can find 200 to 300 job openings (online) for advocate-type positions around the country. Regardless of the state you live in, there is an abundance of volunteer opportunities, internships, and paid positions. Common requirements for a paid position are education and experience. Often the educational preferences fall within the areas of sociology, psychology, and criminal justice. You have some control of your minor and major, but obtaining experience working with victims is dependent largely on what opportunities are available and what fits your schedule. It is easy to tell yourself that you are too busy to squeeze in any time to volunteer somewhere. It is sometimes just a matter of priorities. The key is to search out openings and grab the first opportunities that come along. The first agency you volunteer for is another step on the ladder and another bullet point on your résumé. You can keep looking for new and better breaks while you are doing your best where you are. Just remember that each agency you work at is another reference for a background check. Make each experience a positive one.

If criminal justice is currently your major, consider psychology or sociology as your minor. These fields can open up more doors than just criminal justice alone. As you saw with some of the job descriptions in this chapter, it is often necessary to have some knowledge of criminal justice as well as victimology or social work. Having a dual plan may bump you ahead of others for internships as well.

A remarkable master's degree that is relevant for all social work is in community counseling. This is a difficult 60-hour program with a 600-hour internship obligation. With this master's degree, you can test to become nationally certified as a counselor. You may decide to go on and become licensed, but just the degree and certification will satisfy the requirements for almost any social work position.

Diversity in Victim Services

Naturally, victim services is a woman's ambit. Fortunately, minorities are adequately represented as well. Although rare for most professions, the labor force and supervision in social work are predominantly female. Is there a place for men in this type of work? Absolutely! This is especially true in the area of domestic violence. An important goal of intervention and counseling is to empower victims. Many women suffer years of brainwashing from their male counterparts (and vice versa). Combining a male counselor with a female counselor can open up an opportunity for the male counselor to model proper relational etiquette. Although not necessary, men can assist skilled female counselors in restoring hope to battered, defeated survivors.

It is refreshing to women when men join the battle to advocate for women's rights. There are organizations for men against violence against women all over the country. Male patrol officers and detectives working in areas such as domestic violence, sexual assault, and crimes against children can also have a huge impact on victims' road to recovery by receiving some training from experienced victim service specialists and improving their skills.

In some parts of the United States, particularly in California, Arizona, New Mexico, and Texas, there is an extra need for Hispanic and American Indian organizations and advocates. The Arizona governor's office spends millions of dollars annually to support domestic violence and sexual assault prevention programs. Some grants are specifically for improving services in underrepresented communities. Spanish fluency is a valuable asset for those who choose victim services as their career.

Summary

Since the enactment of the Crime Victims' Rights Act of 2004, there have been a number of forced changes in the criminal justice system. The treatment of victims has improved thanks to these revisions. Police agencies and courts have created new positions, such as victim advocates, to carry out the imposed modifications. There have also been huge changes in intimate partner violence laws all across the country since the early 1980s. These laws have improved the way victims are treated, specifically in domestic violence investigations.

Victim advocacy positions are available in police departments, courts, private agencies, and hospitals. There are opportunities for volunteering, internships, part-time positions, and full-time careers. With experience, one can work in related positions in supervision or support. Volunteering is a great way to gain experience and another eye-catcher on the résumé. Many positions are grant funded, making grant-writing experience a big plus on the résumé as well.

Common degrees for victim assistance work are in sociology, psychology, and criminal justice. A notable master's degree to consider is in community counseling, which requires a 600-hour internship. Along with this degree, one can obtain a national certification.

Victim services is a career represented predominantly by women, and it is well represented by minorities as well. There is a need for Spanish speakers, especially in California, Arizona, New Mexico, and Texas.

DISCUSSION QUESTIONS

1. Why did it take legislation such as the Crime Victims' Rights Act of 2004 to compel police departments and courts to improve their treatment of victims of domestic violence?
2. What are some pros and cons of grant-funded positions?
3. What are some pros and cons to having men involved in victim services?
4. Should all officers receive mandatory academy training from victim services specialists? Should they receive more in-service training after the academy? Explain.

REFERENCES

Albany County Crime Victim and Sexual Violence Center. (2013). *Become a volunteer*. Retrieved from http://www.albanycounty.com/Government/Departments/CrimeVictimandSexualViolence Center/CVSVCVolunteer.aspx

Arizona Attorney General. (2013). *Employment*. Retrieved from https://www.azag.gov/employment

Arizona Coalition Against Domestic Violence. (2013). *Home page*. Retrieved from http://www .azcadv.org

Augusta, Georgia. (2013). *Career opportunities*. Retrieved from http://agency.governmentjobs.com/ augustaga/default.cfm

Brighton, Colorado, Human Resources. (2013). *Home page*. Retrieved from http://www.brightonco .gov/249/Human-Resources

City of Farmington. (2013). *Employment: Current open positions*. Retrieved from http://www.fmtn .org/city_government/human_resources/44/current_job_openings.html

Edwin Gould Services for Children and Families. (2013). *Job opportunities*. Retrieved from http:// www.egscf.org/get-involved/careers?

Florida Coalition Against Domestic Violence. (2013). *Employment opportunities at FCADV*. Retrieved from http://www.fcadv.org/node/10

Grady Health System. (2013). *Careers*. Retrieved from http://grady.ttcportals.com/#

Hawai'i State Judiciary. (2013). *Family court volunteer opportunities*. Retrieved from http://www.courts.state.hi.us/courts/family/family_court_volunteer_opportunities.html

National Resource Center on Domestic Violence. (2013). *Home page*. Retrieved from http://www.nrcdv.org

Nebraska Domestic Violence Sexual Assault Coalition. (2013). *Employment and volunteer opportunities*. Retrieved from http://ndvsac.org/get-involved/employment-and-volunteer-opportunities/

The Nord Center. (2013). *Employment opportunities*. Retrieved from https://www.nordcenter.org/careers/?

Oregon Coalition Against Domestic and Sexual Violence. (2013). *Current job listings*. Retrieved from http://ocadsv.org/take-action/jobs?

Personal and Family Counseling Services of Tuscarawas County. (2013). *PFCS employment*. Retrieved from http://www.personal-family-counseling.com/employment-opportunities?

Tennessee Coalition to End Domestic and Sexual Violence. (2013). *Career opportunities*. Retrieved from http://tncoalition.org/#/career-opportunities.html

Washington Coalition of Sexual Assault Programs. (2013). *Job opportunities*. Retrieved from http://www.wcsap.org/job-opportunities

White Plains Hospital. (2013). *Careers*. Retrieved from http://www.wphospital.org/Careers/Search-Jobs-and-Apply-Online

6

Other Non-Sworn Positions

Introduction

Serving as a sworn peace officer is not appealing to everyone. A civilian career in law enforcement is a viable alternative. Civilian (non-sworn) positions can be found in abundance at all law enforcement agencies. With a few exceptions, civilian jobs require less training and pay less money than the sworn positions, but these jobs offer a fantastic opportunity to give back to the community in the law enforcement field.

Some common civilian jobs within the realm of law enforcement include crime analyst, communications, police aide, records clerk, property/evidence clerk, supplies/equipment/fleet management (SEF), animal control officer, detention/jail officer (see Chapter 7), crime prevention/community outreach specialist, forensic technician (see Chapter 4), information technology specialist, intelligence analyst, parking enforcement officer, public information officer, and victim service providers/advocate (see Chapter 5). In this chapter we will look at a description of these jobs as well as the requirements, qualifications, necessary skills, relevant hiring information, and salaries.

Crime Analyst

Crime analysts assist law enforcement agencies in translating massive amounts of data into useable information about crime patterns and trends, which ultimately helps to improve the efficiency of manpower deployment. They help predict when and where a crime may occur and identify potential suspects. An analyst's role is didactic, tactical, strategic, and administrative.

Although the potential wasn't fully realized, crime analysis became an integral part of policing with the development of the Metropolitan Police Department by Robert Peel in 1829. It wasn't until the 1970s that departments in the United States began changing their attitudes, accepting and trying new ideas. In the 1990s, law enforcement in the United States made an impressive shift toward proactive thinking and started to capitalize on crime analysis. In the last two decades (in medium to large police departments), hundreds of new crime analysis programs have been integrated all over the country.

A crime analyst does the bulk of the work in an office environment, but also spends time in the field. They work closely with all law enforcement professionals, which may include accompanying investigators at crime scenes and team briefings. They need to be critical thinkers and skilled at information and mapping technology. They need to have expert ability to communicate their findings to staff members, using charts and graphs. During a typical day, a crime analyst might perform any of these activities:

- Accumulate and maintain databases on criminal activity
- Evaluate crime trends and prepare maps, graphs, and charts to assist in defining their results.
- Gather and manipulate information for officers and staff members on demand
- Produce statistics on a variety of data including crimes, arrests, and calls for service.
- Operate data mining or other intricate IT techniques to profile and predict criminal behavior.

Most agencies hiring crime analysts require a bachelor's degree. It can usually be in criminal justice, psychology, sociology, or criminology. The degree needs to heavily include public administration, probability and statistics, research methodology, and computer applications. Some jurisdictions may require the crime analyst to be a sworn law enforcement officer, and some may require certification at the state level.

Skills in statistical analysis and research analysis have the greatest impact on the starting salary for a crime analyst, which averages about $40,620. Reports vary, but in 2015 the median salary was approximately $79,870 according to O*Net online (2015). Those having skills in CAD and statistical mapping will have a significant advantage in this field.

Communications

In emergency situations, citizens often call 911 to request help from the police, fire department, or other emergency medical technicians. As a dispatcher, you would collect applicable information, such as the name of the caller, the details of the situation, and the address. Using high-tech communications equipment, you would then assess the location of emergency medical teams and police officers and dispatch the appropriate unit or team. You might need to provide medical information to the caller until emergency help arrives. Your goal in emergency situations would be to stay on the line with the caller, gathering necessary information while keeping the caller calm and safe.

A dispatcher works in a high-stress, fast-paced environment. A delay or improper response can place the caller in higher risk of danger. Callers are often excited and frightened and may not give accurate information without some skilled prompting. The caller may be abusive or angry, and you would need to be able to stay in control of the situation. As a dispatcher, you would use computers and telephones while communicating with emergency response personnel on two-way radios. Monitoring computer screens for long periods of time can be tedious and could cause back pain and eyestrain. As a dispatcher you might be subjected to rotating shifts and alternative work schedules.

To be a dispatcher for the town of Gilbert, Arizona, you would need to have 3 years' experience with a police agency for their lateral program or you can enter a non-lateral position, which pays less to start. Gilbert considers the ideal candidate to possess the ability to deal with critical situations under pressure, quickly, and effectively. They are looking for someone who is proficient at processing information from multiple sources simultaneously while determining the most appropriate course of action. The education requirements for the position are a high school diploma or GED. You would need to possess and maintain a valid Arizona Criminal Justice Terminal Operator Certification or be able to obtain one within 6 months of hire. You would need to be available to work days, evenings, nights, weekends, and holidays on a rotating schedule. You would be required to pass an extensive screening process that includes a polygraph examination, background investigation, drug screen, and medical and psychological evaluations. Starting pay for the lateral position could be as high as $28.57 per hour depending on experience (Town of Gilbert, Arizona, 2015).

The town of Gilbert utilizes an online application system that includes a questionnaire to be filled out by the applicant. These are the questions:

1. Items 1–10 reference general requirements for candidates of all civilian positions in the Gilbert Police Department. The last three questions reference your education, work history and availability. Please answer all questions truthfully and completely. Are you at least eighteen (18) years of age?
   Yes
   No

2. Do you have a high school diploma or GED?
   Yes
   No

3. Have you been convicted of a felony or any offense that would be a felony if committed in Arizona?
   Yes
   No

4. Were you dishonorably discharged from the United States Armed Forces?
   Yes
   No

5. Have you sold, produced, cultivated or transported marijuana for sale?
   Yes
   No

6. Have you sold, produced, cultivated, or transported for sale any other dangerous drugs or narcotics?
   Yes
   No

7. Have you used marijuana for any purpose within the past eighteen (18) months?
   Yes
   No

8. Have you used marijuana while employed with a law enforcement agency?
   Yes
   No

9. Do you have a pattern of abuse of prescription medication or illegal use of dangerous drugs or narcotics within the past seven (7) years?
   Yes
   No

10. Have you been convicted of or adjudged to have violated traffic regulations that would equal eight (8) or more points within the past thirty-six (36) months?
    Yes
    No

11. Do you have at least one year of customer service work experience?
    Yes
    No

12. Do you have at least three years of full-time experience working within a police agency, dispatching police officers and related resources in response to 911 emergency calls for service?
    Yes
    No

13. Are you able and willing to work days, evenings, nights, weekends and holidays on a rotating schedule?
    Yes
    No

14. If offered employment by the Town of Gilbert, you would be required to pass an extensive police background investigation, to include the following: a polygraph examination; personal and business reference checking; a credit report; investigation into traffic, civil and criminal offenses and drug usage. If offered employment, would you submit to a police background investigation?
Yes
No

15. The following question is strictly confidential and will not be made part of your application for employment. Preference Status per Arizona Revised Statute 38-492 (select all that apply):
a. Veteran
b. Disabled Veteran
c. Veteran Spouse/Surviving Spouse
d. Disabled Person
(Town of Gilbert, Arizona, 2015)

Police Aide

In some agencies, a police aide (PA), driving a marked police car, is dispatched to particular types of calls for service. An aide conducts investigations and writes reports for a variety of calls not requiring a police officer's presence. It is common to use police aides for minor vehicle collisions and criminal incidents without suspect information. Some agencies utilize aides in clerical duties that include typing and filing police forms, such as accident reports, evidence cards, arrest records, or schedules. Additionally, aides post information to police records manually or using typewriter or computer; disseminate information to the public over the phone or in person concerning missing persons, arrests, or other police related business; and receive and record physical evidence seized at crime scenes by police officers and detectives.

A PA in Albuquerque, New Mexico, assists officers on patrol with traffic accidents, misdemeanor offenses, delivery of paperwork, parking enforcement and many other duties and responsibilities. The PA program allows PAs to learn about the Albuquerque Police Department's policies and procedures prior to entering the police academy as a police cadet. If you are hired as a PA in Albuquerque, you will earn $13.91 per hour after graduating from an academy taught by police academy certified instructors. Two years as a PA will waive the college/military requirement for police officer/cadet. The requirements to work as a PA in Albuquerque include:

- Must be 18 years of age
- Must have a valid driver's license
- Must be a United States citizen
- Must have a high school diploma or equivalent (GED)
- No misdemeanor convictions within the last 3 years

- 18- to 20-year-olds must not have used a misdemeanor illegal drug (i.e., marijuana) within the last 6 months. Twenty-one years or older must not have used a misdemeanor illegal drug (i.e., marijuana) in the last 3 years.
- An applicant cannot have been convicted of a domestic violence act.
- No DWIs within the last 5 years, whether from an administrative sanction by a Motor Vehicle Department, a criminal conviction, or a military disciplinary action
- No multiple DWIs within the last 10 years whether from an administrative sanction by a Motor Vehicle Department, a criminal conviction or a military disciplinary action
- No felony convictions
- Any financial accounts referred to collections, written, or charged off will be reviewed on a case-by-case basis and may be cause for disqualification. (City of Albuquerque Police Department, 2015)

There is also a physical fitness test that includes:

- Number of push-ups in 1 minute: *minimum 15 repetitions*
- 1.5-mile run: 15:54 (minutes:seconds)
- 300-meter run: 71 seconds
- Number of sit-ups in 1 minute: *minimum 27 repetitions*

If you were to go through the hiring process, you would encounter these steps:

1. Application/interest card

2. City entrance exam

3. PIQ

4. Physical fitness test

5. Nelson Denny exam

6. Personal history statement

7. Written psychological exam

8. Background investigation

9. Polygraph exam

10. Psychological interview

11. Chief's selection board

12. City of Albuquerque employment application

13. Medical exam/drug screen (City of Albuquerque Police Department, 2015)

Records Clerk

Notwithstanding the abundance of paperless technologies, police departments still need assistance with data entry, processing citations, document scanning, maintaining alarm permit files, assisting the public and police employees with records requests, and everything else associated with records management. Records clerk is an administrative support position responsible for clerical, technical, and customer service work involving the maintenance, intake, processing, dissemination, and retention of police records. These are some of the specific job duties:

- Process criminal reports, fingerprint cards, photographs, returned checks, false alarms, and other miscellaneous information
- Process notices or arrest affidavits for transmittal to other governmental agencies requiring said information
- Process uniform traffic citations for transmittal to the clerk's office and Department of Motor Vehicles
- Perform computer entry of daily reports in a timely manner; process daily accident, incident, and arrest reports
- Handle customer requests from citizens, insurance companies, law enforcement agencies, and criminal justice personnel relative to the location and dissemination of official police records consistent with applicable state and/or federal law and departmental policy
- Receive, issue receipts, and process monies for report copies, parking tickets, and record services
- Prepare, file, and distribute criminal reports as required; provide releasable information
- Enter information into and maintain accuracy of the police department's computerized records system
- Enter information into and retrieve information from the [National Crime Information Center/Florida Crime Information Center] system
- Prepare and scan documents as part of the records retention program required by the state (Government Jobs, 2015a)

The education requirement for records clerks in Lakeland, Florida, is a high school graduation or GED. Prior experience in a confidential work environment or police department is preferred. Essential skills include the ability to multi-task (amid interruptions), communicate effectively both orally and in writing, and type at least 40 words per minute. A good candidate needs to demonstrate knowledge of Microsoft Office Suite. Lakeland requires their clerks to have knowledge of general office procedures; working skill in performing duties with minimal supervision; working skill in maintaining accurate files and records; considerable interpersonal skills to deal effectively and professionally with a diverse group of internal and external customers, which may include irate and mentally disturbed persons; ability to read and write

Sandra Garay: Emergency Dispatcher – Maricopa County Sheriff's Office

CJ: What is your current position?

SG: My current position is Emergency Dispatcher.

CJ: What are your typical job duties?

SG: My job duties are answering 911/nonemergency lines and entering calls for service. Additionally, I dispatch responding units to these calls for service within MCSO jurisdiction, also answer hotlines from other agencies requesting assistance. As a dispatcher, I ensure all the units on my channel/frequency are accounted for, dispatched to the correct location, and given all important and safety information within a call for service that he or she is responding to, all while running subjects for warrants, stolen vehicles, and valid documentation.

CJ: How long have you been at your current assignment?

SG: I have been in this position for approximately 17 months. This included 10 months of on-the-job training, including a two-week academy.

CJ: What other positions have you held prior to this one?

SG: Prior to this, I worked as a paralegal for approximately 6 years, in both criminal and immigration law.

CJ: What are the requirements/qualifications for your job?

SG: Must have a high school diploma or GED, customer service/clerical experience, ability to type at minimum 42 words per minute.

CJ: What steps did you go through during hiring?

SG: I applied via the county website, took a written test (reading, math, and grammar), typing test, and attended a panel interview. Additionally, I had to pass an extensive background check, polygraph exam, and psychological evaluation. I had to submit records for all schools attended, including original diplomas/degrees. The complete process took about 4 months; however, I applied approximately 5 months prior to being called for an interview.

CJ: What advice can you offer students who might be interested in pursuing a similar career?

SG: I would advise prospective students to research the position and maybe sit in at a communications center to get a feel for how things are and the type of work we do. I love my job and enjoy it daily. Even though it is very rewarding, it can also be very stressful. I would suggest that prospective applicants know ahead of the time and understand that they will be the calm voice behind the storm and the guiding eyes and ears to every unit out in the field.

at a level required to complete forms, proof correspondence, and enter data into computer terminal; ability to perform basic math; ability to file and retrieve materials from established alphabetic or numeric filing system; ability to learn new software programs (Government Jobs, 2015a).

Additional knowledge, skills, and abilities needed to work for Lakeland, Florida, include:

- Knowledge of business English, spelling, and punctuation; office practices and procedures including various computer software applications
- Knowledge of state and federal laws relating to records management and the dissemination of public and private information
- Skill in operating computers and standard office equipment
- Ability to make arithmetic computations and tabulations rapidly and accurately
- Ability to readily acquire and make minor decisions from working knowledge of applicable regulations and related division policies and procedures
- Ability to maintain confidentiality of sensitive and exempt of criminal justice information
- Ability to communicate with the public, employees, and officials tactfully and courteously and to establish and maintain harmonious working relationships with other employees
- Ability to solve problems logically and expeditiously
- Ability to prepare and maintain correspondence, reports, records and to perform routine office management details without referral to a supervisor
- Ability to prioritize work to meet time constraints (Government Jobs, 2015a)

The application is submitted online for the position in Lakeland. Upon acceptance of the application, you would be notified of a testing date for the Police Records Clerk Knowledge Test. This a test of knowledge and skills related to the basic duties of the job. Once the test is passed, your qualifications and test scores would be reviewed to determine if you would be invited to an interview. The interview process consists of a structured panel interview that is scored by experts using the Police Records Clerk Competency Model. If you were to be chosen for employment, you would need to pass a polygraph examination, medical examination, drug screening, and background investigation. If hired, you would begin the in-house training and familiarization of the positional duties. You would be on probationary status for 1 year. You would be required to obtain a state notary certification within 12 months of employment. The salary for this position is $14.83 to $22.24 hourly if hired as a part-time clerk. Salaries are higher for full-time clerks (Government Jobs, 2015a).

Those with disabilities find working in records a satisfying career. It isn't overly demanding, and although you have individual tasks to perform, you work closely with a team of coworkers. While performing in the records department, you would be required to sit, talk, hear, walk, use hands to finger motions, handle and feel objects, tools, or controls, and reach with hands and arms. You would occasionally lift or move objects up to 25 pounds. As far as vision requirements, you need to have close vision and the ability to adjust focus (Government Jobs, 2015a).

Property/Evidence Management

Agencies use civilian personnel to manage and organize equipment, uniforms, and supplies, and to be safe keepers of crime scene evidence, found property, and other seized goods. Large departments normally divide these responsibilities, but if you work for medium or smaller sized departments, you may handle both. Agencies differ in the title of these positions, but it is important to distinguish evidence handling from the job of overseeing supplies, equipment, and fleet.

The property and evidence control function provides for control and security of recovered, seized, and evidentiary property, as well as lost, found, or abandoned property in the possession of the police department. This position is of critical importance as it supports investigations, helps to guarantee successful prosecution at criminal and civil trials, facilitates the timely return of property to its rightful owners, and establishes the agency's reputation as being worthy of the public's confidence and trust. Law enforcement agencies, faced with the necessity to develop and maintain strict measures for the receipt, handling, security, and disposition of property, seek employees of high character and intelligence.

Working with criminal evidence carries with it the responsibility to protect the chain of custody and to be able to testify in court of how you managed to do it. To maintain the chain of custody, evidence must be preserved from the time it is collected to the time it is presented in court. To prove that evidence has remained intact, prosecutors need all those who handled the evidence to testify

- that the evidence presented in court is the same evidence they collected or received,
- to the date and time the evidence was received and transferred to another person, and
- that there was no undocumented examination or tampering with the item while it was in custody.

The way a police agency demonstrates the proper chain of custody is through a standard protocol of documenting packaging, marking, and handling. We will use a sexual assault investigation to demonstrate how this works and how difficult it is to maintain a chain of custody. The dispatcher will receive a call of a sexual assault and will dispatch an officer to the victim/

witness location. If the dispatcher ascertains that the sexual assault occurred at a different location, another officer will be sent to that location to preserve the scene. The officer arriving where the victim is will ask the victim for basic details and prevent her from using the restroom or changing clothes. If it is determined that a sexual assault occurred, a detective is usually called out to take over the investigation. Because the victim is in possession of evidence, such as blood, semen, hair, and saliva, the officer must remain with her until responsibility for the evidence is turned over to another member of the police department.

The officer will usually transport the victim to the hospital to have an examination done for the purpose of obtaining evidence (which may include colposcopy pictures in child cases). When the detective arrives at the hospital, the officer may leave, but his report must document the time he first took possession of the evidence (the victim) and the time he turned it over to the detective. The doctor will perform a standard sexual assault exam according to the training and standards of the county. Hospitals generally store sexual assault kits stocked with swabs, vials, envelopes, and anything else the county attorney requires. The doctor turns the kit over to the detective or, in the case of many mid- to large-size agencies, a crime scene technician who is well trained in the collection and preservation of evidence. The detective or crime scene technician will also collect the clothes worn by the victim.

At the scene of the offense, the first arriving officer will remain there until relieved by another officer or the detective. This could take 4 to 8 hours if a search warrant is needed. Once the search warrant is signed, the detective will show up to the scene of the crime with a sergeant, one or two other detectives, a crime scene technician, and possibly a photographer. The scene is processed and the seized items are placed into paper bags and marked with the date, time, location, finder's name, packager's name, and a description of the item. Although there are often three to four people looking around for evidence, the normal procedure is for one person to do all the packaging and for that person to also transport the evidence to the evidence lockers at the police station. Doing it this way makes the court testimony less cumbersome. All those involved in the finding or packaging of evidence writes a report that documents the dates and times of every relevant action they took.

If there is any missing link in the chain of custody, evidence will likely be deemed inadmissible in court. Before the evidence ever reaches the evidence clerk, it has already been in the custody of several other people who will write a report and will possibly be called upon to testify in court. Once at the police station, the evidence is separated into different categories. The clothes and bed sheets will either be frozen immediately, or dried first and then frozen. The blood vials will be refrigerated. Other miscellaneous items might be put in temporary lockers to allow the detective and attorneys to view the evidence again before locking it up for trial.

As an evidence clerk in this scenario, you would place your information on each packaged item before placing it in locked storage. Each package would already be signed or initialed by as many as two or three people, generally over the seal to help prove the package has not been opened by anyone else. Your intake of the items would be documented in the computer, ready for you to add updates each time the evidence is handled by anyone but you. Until the items are securely locked, you wouldn't be able to walk away from them to use the restroom or to eat lunch. Your releasing and reaccepting of some of the evidence might occur three or four more times before trial. At some point the crime lab will take custody of the clothes, sheets, blood, and the remainder of the sexual assault kit when they are ready to perform their tests. They will make a new cut in the package and when done, will seal the new opening and initial across the seam. You will again take custody of the items and update the computer in preparation for your court testimony.

Finally, a detective would come and collect all the items for court. You wouldn't see the items again until you are handed a package in court and asked if it is the same evidence you were in possession of. You would look at your documentations and your standard signature across the seal and be able to testify to the jury that the evidence is in fact the same evidence and that it has not been tampered with since you last had it.

This scenario involves one case, but an evidence clerk can check in evidence from 25 to 50 cases each day. In order to avoid needing a warehouse that could house a 747, the evidence clerk needs to continuously dispose of property that is no longer needed. This is done in several ways. Some property just needs to be returned to the victim or suspect once a case and appeals are completely finished. Some property is initially received for destruction, so it just needs to be disposed of according to department regulations. There is also found property that is usually held for a set amount of time to allow an owner to come forward. If not claimed, it is thrown out, auctioned off, or used for various law enforcement purposes.

To work as an evidence clerk in Columbia, South Carolina, you would need to be a graduate from high school or vocational school or have a GED with some work experience in receiving, labeling, logging in, packaging, and storing evidence. You would be completing logs and forms, preparing notifications for property owners, preparing evidence for destruction or disposal as directed, conducting routine inventory of evidence and property, transporting evidence, picking up evidence, preparing property for public sale, and making auction arrangements. To be selected you must be able to type 30 corrected words per minute. You would need a valid South Carolina Class D driver's license and have an acceptable driving record. You would need knowledge of personal computer equipment with skills in the use of Microsoft Office and regular data entry. The salary in Columbia is $24,784 to $32,219 annually (City of Columbia Police Department, 2015).

_____ **Supplies/Equipment/Fleet Management**

Law enforcement agencies use a variety of equipment to perform their daily tasks. Supplies are generally kept in a room at the police station or off site in a warehouse if more room is needed. Agencies generally hire a supervisor over the supplies, equipment, and fleet (SEF) and as many clerks as needed to ensure the department operates efficiently. Some of the items that would be under the direction of SEF would include guns, uniforms, office supplies, vehicles, badges, recorders and tapes, cameras and film, phones, report forms, copy paper, computers, file cabinets, desks, radios, and GPS systems.

In Victoria, Texas, the SEF clerk performs the following duties (City of Victoria Police Department, 2015):

- Keeps track of city false alarms daily and send information to Finance each month
- Assists with coordinating off-duty work assignments and the off-duty schedule
- Orders uniforms for all licensed personnel and assists with writing bid specs
- Assists with getting new officers uniformed and equipped
- Coordinates with training for new officers and changes out current officers as needed
- Assists with managing departmental inventory and maintaining accurate inventory records for each division
- Maintains monthly reports for each section in the support services division
- Assists in the updating of the Departmental General Orders and Procedures, ensures that employees acknowledge changes, and maintains hard copy of the orders
- Assists with running licenses plate information from abandoned vehicle reports and sends out certified letters to all individuals that own the abandoned vehicles
- Completes and submits Sexual Assault Exam Reports to be sent off for reimbursement

To work in SEF for the Pinellas County Sheriff's Office in Florida, your duties would be to

- gather and maintain strict control over items to be auctioned and disposed of according to state statutes;
- conduct annual fixed asset inventories throughout the year;
- submit reports of inventory results;
- maintain all inventory records electronically as well as manually;
- record, tag, or engrave all assets before distribution;

- deliver equipment and supplies to all locations within the Sheriff's Office;
- measure current and new employees, fit for uniforms, and notify buyer of all items needed;
- fill requisitions for uniform items utilizing established procedures;
- receive, unpack, and inspect stock items for conformity with specifications;
- store parts and supplies in accordance with established inventory procedures;
- utilize the computer to enter required information for record keeping, correspondence, reports, and inquiry;
- maintain the location of fixed asset property in the computer system;
- monitor and work with inmate workers; and
- participate in Sheriff's Office recruitment and community relation activities as directed. (Pinellas County Sheriff's Office, 2015)

The basic qualifications to be a SEF clerk in Pinellas County include a high school diploma or GED, 3 years of related experience, a score of 80% on a computer literacy test, a score of 80% on a Microsoft Office Professional test, and possession of a valid driver's license. Other requirements include knowledge of the state laws and Sheriff's Office rules and regulations concerning property control and distribution, knowledge of inventory control procedures and modern office practices concerning record keeping and inventory control, knowledge of various database and research software required to efficiently perform the essential functions and job duties, and ability to perform all functions of the job classification without posing a direct threat to the health or safety of other individuals in the workplace. The pay range is $30,600 to $48,960 (Pinellas County Sheriff's Office, 2015).

Animal Control

People who become police officers generally enjoy the prospect of encountering something new and different with every case. They welcome a challenge, and they gain satisfaction by helping people with their problems. However, there are certain types of calls for service that police officers dread, such as the animal calls. Knowledge of the proper care of animals is not tested in the police hiring process and not taught as part of the police academy curriculum. Animal cages and control poles aren't part of the equipment in the trunk of patrol cars.

Patrol officers appreciate it when there are animal control officers on duty, which is not always around the clock. Many agencies have their animal control officers working during the day and swing shift but leave the animal calls to the patrol officers between midnight and 6:00 AM. For this reason, the animal control officers expect to arrive at work in the morning to find animals locked up and ready for them to process.

Animal control officers working for the City of Emporia, Kansas, perform duties related to the impounding and containment of stray, injured, or nuisance animals, both domestic and wild. They enforce all city ordinances related to animal control, respond to public complaints, and perform other related duties as assigned. They perform their duties independently in accordance with existing city laws and departmental procedures.

To be hired in Emporia you would need knowledge of basic animal care and knowledge of (and experience working with) various breeds of dogs and cats. It would be preferred if you had some veterinary training. You would be expected to perform routine heavy manual labor in all weather conditions. You would need the ability to communicate in a courteous manner, to work effectively with other employees, supervisors, and the public, and the ability to understand and follow oral and written instructions. You would need to be at least 18 years old and be willing to relocate to Lyon County upon employment. You are required to have a high school diploma or GED; possess a valid Kansas driver's license; and pass a physical exam, drug/alcohol screening, and background check upon any conditional offer of employment. The pay for this position is $12.50 per hour (Monster, 2015).

Crime Prevention/Community Outreach

Although predominantly reactive since its inception, law enforcement has gradually introduced some proactive crime prevention programs in the last four decades that have altered that paradigm. These types of programs are difficult to sell to the city management because they require money and manpower yet don't offer any kind of benefit to the city that is immediate, empirical, or measurable. Naturally, these programs are the first to be disbanded when the city has to make budget cuts. It is easier to justify a proactive crime prevention program if it is tied in with community relation objectives. Some common examples include school resource officers, community policing, Neighborhood Watch, Drug Abuse Resistance Education (DARE), and Gang Action Interagency Network (G.A.I.N.). Police departments generally organize a crime prevention unit that becomes the catalyst for these programs and many more as the budget allows. With some exceptions, crime prevention units are entirely staffed by civilians, under the supervision of a police sergeant or lieutenant.

To be a crime prevention officer in Palmdale, California, you would perform the following duties:

- Develop, organize, and present public outreach activities and programs related to crime prevention and emergency preparedness; serve as a liaison among the community, city departments, and the Sheriff's Department
- Make recommendations regarding crime prevention through environmental design to residents, apartment managers/owners, and businesses

- Oversee and implement the Business Watch program to educate businesses about crime awareness, prevention, and safety issues related to recent criminal activity
- Prepare and make in-person presentations to retail and commercial businesses, business organizations, employers, and employees on issues such as workplace safety, customer safety, and prevention of common business or retail-related crimes
- Oversee and implement the Neighborhood/Apartment Watch programs to educate citizens about crime awareness, prevention, safety and reporting issues; prepare and make in-person presentation to citizens, neighborhood groups, and others on such issues as personal safety, child abuse, burglary, drug abuse, juvenile delinquency, and dispute resolution
- Propose ordinance revisions or new ordinances to address crime or disorder issues in the community
- Meet with community members to resolve neighborhood disputes, grievances, and other related social problems
- Oversee and implement the graffiti abatement and restitution program, work with internal and external agency staff as required, and produce records and documentation to support restitution orders
- Provide technical assistance related to emergency preparedness/management preparation and implementation activities, including coordination of required staff training
- Review residential and/or commercial development applications; conduct site checks, and make safety recommendations to planning staff; meet with affected city departments, the Sheriff's Department, and development applicants to resolve security issues
- Develop, prepare, or make available a variety of informational materials, such as brochures, handouts, newsletter articles, and audiovisual presentations related to crime prevention awareness; prepare text for the city's website related to crime prevention information; prepare press releases and public service announcements for distribution to a variety of media outlets
- May prepare grant applications related to crime prevention program elements, monitor grant activities and approve payments within authorized limits, and provide input to budget recommendations
- Identify potential crime problems and initiate actions to implement preventive measures; research new topics and legislation related to crime prevention and emergency preparedness
- Build and maintain positive working relationships with coworkers, other city employees, and the public using principles of good customer service (City of Palmdale Police Department, 2015)

You can qualify to work for Palmdale with any combination of experience and training that would provide the required knowledge and abilities to do the job. An acceptable way to obtain the required knowledge and abilities would be one year of responsible clerical or technical support experience in a law enforcement agency or related field and an associate's degree in any field. Palmdale would require you to have knowledge of basic techniques of crime prevention and community policing services, methods and techniques of delivering customer service, English usage, spelling, grammar, and punctuation, modern office methods and equipment, including use of personal computers and related applications, and principles of basic arithmetic and mathematical calculations (City of Palmdale Police Department, 2015).

Additionally, Palmdale would expect you to have the ability to assist in the coordination, design, maintenance, and presentation of program elements related to crime prevention activities; intermittently review documents related to program operations; observe, identify, and problem solve crime prevention operational issues and procedures; and understand, interpret, and explain a variety of crime prevention program policies and procedures. In this job, you would be expected to sit at desk and/or stand for long periods of time; occasionally bend and twist to reach office equipment; participate in site visits that may include walking, standing, bending, and climbing; perform simple grasping and fine manipulation; write or use a keyboard to communicate through written means; run errands; lift or carry weight of 20 pounds or less; make effective public presentations related to program activities; write clear, understandable, and concise reports; prepare business correspondence; learn the organization, procedures, and operating details of assigned responsibilities; develop and present crime prevention programs; make security evaluations and related recommendations; identify potential safety/security problems and initiate action for preventive and corrective measures; operate a variety of modern office equipment such as electronic calculators, facsimile machines, and copiers; and use computer software programs including word processing, spreadsheet, and data base applications. The pay for crime prevention officer is $39,720.00 to $50,700.00 annually (City of Palmdale Police Department, 2015).

Information Technology Specialists

Technological advances with police equipment such as in-car mobile data terminals (MDTs), digital video, computerized mapping, and wireless communication have spawned a significant need for qualified IT professionals in police agencies. Much of the available high-tech equipment is a luxury, but law enforcement unequivocally depends on communication and computer systems to fulfill the core operations. A crash in the system, albeit even for a short time, can decrease officer and citizen safety, allow dangerous criminals to elude an arrest, and increase the risks of civil liability. Police departments need a strong IT unit that can quickly respond to the daily technological needs.

In Corona, California, the police department's information technology technician (IT tech) serves as a liaison between the city's IT department and the police department. If selected for an IT tech position, you would provide support to users at the police department and your assignments would focus primarily on law enforcement related hardware and software systems. To apply for a position at Corona, you would need to attach transcripts and/or certifications for IT-related course work from an accredited college or trade school in computer science, data processing, computer information systems, or information management. As an IT technician in Corona you would be paid $17.40 to $21.24 hourly and as your job assignment you would

- respond to user requests and provide technical assistance on PC systems, hardware, software, and standard applications;
- provide help desk information and support, determine cause of problem, offer temporary solutions if problem cannot be resolved within an appropriate timeframe, and distribute training manuals and documentation to assist users in resolving problems;
- assist users on standard software applications; demonstrate methods and techniques for advanced uses of software packages in developing such materials as color overheads, presentation graphics, desktop publishing materials, complex tables, charts, and databases; provide one-on-one assistance in learning application basics and resolving problems;
- install and maintain specialized software, including but not limited to performing setup functions, developing associated file structures, report formats, and input forms, ensuring file security, performing data entry to populate associated databases, and documenting procedures;
- work with department staff to diagnose and solve software and data-related problems;
- install, sets up or relocate, configure, troubleshoot, and support PC hardware/software;
- install and configure software upgrades;
- perform tuning of operating systems to enhance PC performance;
- install and configure network interfaces and Internet connections;
- diagnose network cable and configuration problems; and
- install, configure, and troubleshoot all computer peripheral systems and equipment, including, but not limited to printers, scanners, digital cameras, PDAs, and other equipment. (Government Jobs, 2015b)

Intelligence Analysts

What is the difference between criminal analysis and intelligence analysis? This question was easier to answer prior to the impressive surge of crime analysis in the 1990s. The answer really lies within the goals of the agency

Jacqueline McClanahan: Crime Analyst – Mesa Police Department

CJ: What is your current position?

JM: Crime Analyst.

CJ: What are your typical job duties?

JM: Analyze the past 24 hours of Uniform Crime Reporting (UCR) calls and create a daily briefing packet based on the information discovered. This packet includes a daily map and a gang activity map. It also includes a significant trends page and weekly mission page. I brief the commander and lieutenants on the information every morning. I provide recommendations as to where patrol, gang detectives, and undercover units should be deployed. I analyze police reports and look for possible crime trends. I perform additional research in order to prepare a crime bulletin for distribution to command staff, officers, the fusion center, and outside agencies. I gather intelligence information provided to me by detectives and build link analysis charts, flow charts, time lines, or phone toll analysis. I prepare weekly Computerized Statistics and Accountability Model (COMPSTAT) reports for the chief of police and district commander. I attend monthly COMPSTAT meetings and brief the chief on issues occurring in my assigned district. I work closely with the crime prevention officer to prepare information for community and business meetings. I analyze prior year UCR data to determine if a spike in activity may occur during the same time of the current year. I fulfill statistical requests from the chief, city council, media relations, and command staff at the district. I work on projects for patrol officers, detectives, and criminal intelligence officers. As senior analyst, I train all the new crime analysts and crime analysts' technicians, instruct at the police academy training the new recruits on crime and intelligence analysis, and create and maintain numerous databases related to crime analysis information.

CJ: How long have you been at your current assignment?

JM: Sixteen years.

CJ: What other positions have you held prior to this one?

JM: Prior to this I worked for the Seattle Police Department. I was a sworn officer for 13 years. Four years of that I was assigned as a detective to the crime analysis unit. I spent 5 years working the street and responding to 911 calls. I was on the community police team for a year and then did 2 years as a DARE officer.

CJ: What are the requirements/qualifications for your job?

JM: Any combination of training, education, or experience equivalent to graduation from an accredited college or university with a bachelor's degree and one year of progressively responsible experience performing data analysis.

CJ: What steps did you go through during the hiring?

JM: Background check, polygraph test, psych test, a written test for the position, and a practical test for the position.

CJ: What advice can you offer students who might be interested in pursuing a similar career?

JM: Volunteer or intern for a crime analysis unit. Get your foot in the door and start at an entry-level position. Most crime analyst positions are very specialized and higher levels. Try to get in as a crime analysis tech or as a crime analysis aide. If you don't qualify for something like that, go into records or dispatch just to get your foot in the door and then you can get training, shadowing an analyst, or other opportunities. Many times the jobs will open up internally first.

that employs them. Some agencies don't distinguish between the two and thus handle all the intelligence work with one unit. Those that do employ two separate units would describe criminal intelligence analysis as primarily an investigative process, in which the mission is to capture and convict offenders. Crime analysis would be described as primarily a problem-solving process with a mission to deter and reduce crime. Some agencies utilize sworn officers to work in the intelligence unit, but more and more agencies are seeking experienced civilians to perform the tasks.

In general, intelligence analysis focuses on the gathering and distribution of information about organizations, schemes, and conspiracies. Intelligence analysts work closely with detectives and undercover teams to hunt for heads of criminal organizations. They follow the flow of money and monitor relationships and activities. They combine the data with personal information about the participants and hand it off to the proper operations teams to follow up with stakeouts, stings, and arrests.

Intelligence units generally hold all the special licenses and permissions from federal agencies and phone companies. Undercover officers and some other detectives need to carry a fake driver's license. The intelligence unit usually manages that program by providing the training and obtaining the credentials. There is also a need for certain detectives to have a free pass for obtaining nonconfidential phone call information in a hurry without having to wait for a warrant. The intelligence unit manages that program by training the selected employees and issuing them a code. The intelligence unit monitors those with special permissions to assure their authorities are not misused. Working in intelligence is a perfect spot for retired military and law enforcement personnel.

According to INTERPOL, the central tasks of intelligence analysis are to

- help officials, senior law enforcers, policy makers, and decision makers to deal more effectively with uncertainty and new challenges,
- provide timely warning of threats, and
- support operational activities and complex investigations. (INTERPOL, 2015)

At INTERPOL, intelligence analysis is divided into operational and strategic analysis.

Although the fundamental skills are similar, the two categories differ with regard to the level of detail and the type of client for whom the products are designed. Operational analysis aspires to achieve a specific law enforcement outcome, such as an arrest, seizure, forfeiture, or the disruption of a criminal group. The analytical support includes identifying links between suspects, and their involvement in crimes and criminal activity, identifying key investigative or information gaps, and preparing profiles of known or suspected criminals.

Strategic analysis aims to inform higher-level decision makers. The objective is to provide warnings of threats and to support senior decision makers to deal with emerging criminal issues, which may include allocating resources to various types of crime or increasing training in a particular crime-fighting technique. Strategic analysis includes the identification of modus operandi, crime trends and patterns, emerging threats, and the potential impact of external factors such as technology, demographics, or economics on crime (INTERPOL, 2015).

The FBI's intelligence analysts are in the forefront of national security. They collect bits of information to form refined views on issues of public safety and national security by

- utilizing language, cultural, and historical knowledge to combat international threats by working within specifically defined geographical and/or functional areas;
- discovering domestic threats by leveraging local and national intelligence databases, analyzing intelligence collected in the field offices, and developing fact-based conclusions and intelligence reports; and
- shaping intelligence policies by maintaining extensive networks and partnering with local, national, and international contacts within the intelligence and law enforcement communities and leverage it to prepare briefings, reports, and communications for senior FBI executives and other intelligence community and law enforcement entities. (Federal Bureau of Investigation, 2015)

The FBI has three career tracks for intelligence analysts: tactical, collection/reporting, and strategic. Although each career track is different, all are built on the intelligence cycle: planning, collection, exploitation and analysis, and dissemination and reporting. The tactical track is embedded on investigative squads and units in the field or at headquarters to provide support on active cases. They assess and communicate real-time analytic judgments regarding specific threats and intelligence gaps, understand emerging threats to enhance domain knowledge and exploit collection opportunities, and bridge operational squads by identifying collection opportunities and gaps and helping to assure timely and accurate reporting of intelligence.

The collection/reporting track works to understand, assess, and corroborate intelligence. They enhance FBI collection capabilities, disseminate raw intelligence against priority collection requirements and intelligence gaps, report raw intelligence in a timely manner through various forms of media, documents, and general information to determine patterns, and identify human and technical source collection opportunities.

The strategic track consolidates comprehensive information into strategic analytic products that contextualize intelligence and enhance each division's understanding of threats, gaps, and vulnerabilities. They perform domain analysis to articulate the existence of a threat in the area of responsibility, perform enterprise-wide strategic analyses, and conduct studies to identify threats and trends (Federal Bureau of Investigation, 2015).

Periodically, positions open in local police departments, but the units are usually small and rarely have turnover. To work for Sangamon County,

Illinois, as a Criminal Intelligence Analyst I, you would perform criminal intelligence casework in the Sex Offender Registration Unit. You would perform a variety of intelligence, analytical, reporting, and charting techniques as assigned by higher-level analysts or your supervisor. You would prepare and document investigative recommendations and reports of analyses. Additionally, you would serve as a special unit member on strategic study projects under higher-level analysts or supervisor. You would compile, analyze, and disseminate data collected on subjects, and provide direct support statewide to criminal justice agencies (Government Jobs, 2015c).

To work for Sangamon County, you would need the knowledge, skill, and mental development equivalent to the completion of 4 years of college, preferably with course work in philosophy, behavioral sciences, and law enforcement. Sangamon County requires one year of professional criminal investigative experience or completion of an agency approved training course. They require you to have working knowledge in computers as utilized in criminal investigation analysis. You also need elementary knowledge of state, federal, and local criminal laws and regulations as they relate to the criminal investigative process. You would need strong communication skills and the ability to construct court exhibits, create criminal intelligence charts, and testify in court as an expert witness with proper courtroom demeanor. The pay is $4,291.00 to $6,452.00 monthly (Government Jobs, 2015c).

Parking Enforcement

Most parking enforcement jobs are independent of police departments. Those outside of police departments report directly to a governmental agency such as the Department of Transportation or Public Safety. Qualifications with those agencies are typically less demanding than police departments. Outside of the police department, a position as a parking enforcement officer is usually obtained through a civil service employment program. It is considered a law enforcement position. Candidates only need to meet a few minimum requirements such as possession of a high school diploma and a driver's license. A two-year or four-year degree is always helpful but not required. Local or state police departments have additional qualifications such as U.S. citizenship and no felony convictions. They will likely require a background check, a polygraph exam, medical exam, psychological exam, and physical test.

Parking enforcement officers receive training in the law and are granted authority to issue citations, tow and impound vehicles, and order drivers to move their vehicles when blocking traffic. They operate confidential computerized systems so they can obtain records on vehicles and thus contact owners about information or actions regarding their vehicle. They must be capable of responding to hostile or irate individuals while performing their duties, which makes it necessary to include physical tests as part of the hiring process. Typical duties for parking enforcement include:

1. Patrol areas in vehicles or on foot

2. Conduct vehicle searches using tag or license information

3. Issue tickets to improperly parked vehicles

4. Check meters for expiration of time limits

5. Place large signs or boots on vehicles that have far exceeded parking limits

6. Collect coins from parking meters

7. Alert repair crews to damaged or missing meters

8. Enforce animal control laws

9. Alert police, fire, or medical personnel to emergency situations (Lawenforcementedu.net, 2015)

The U.S. Bureau of Labor Statistics reported that parking enforcement officers earned an average annual salary of $37,750 in 2014. The top 10% of parking enforcement officers received average salaries of $56,200. The top five states with the highest employment were California, Massachusetts, New York, Illinois, and Pennsylvania. The largest employers of parking enforcement officers were as follows:

Organization	Employees	Average Salary
Local government	7,000	$39,130
Colleges, universities, professional schools	1,070	$28,310
State government	260	$43,850
Junior colleges	60	$37,530

Source: U.S. Department of Labor, Bureau of Labor Statistics (2015)

An example of a police department job as a parking enforcement officer is with Westerville, Ohio. Under the direction of a police supervisor, you would be responsible for enforcing all local and state parking laws within the City of Westerville. Your primary responsibility would be parking enforcement and security in the business district, but you would perform other duties as needed and assigned. Your work would be performed within the guidelines of division general orders with some discretion in the enforcement of local and state parking laws. Your performance would be reviewed daily by a corporal and would be reflected on your annual performance evaluations. Westerville's part-time position pays $16.34 to $19.62 hourly. As a parking enforcement officer in Westerville you would perform these duties:

- Enforce all local and state parking laws
- Respond to emergency calls for assistance; provide care and treatment to citizens and prisoners
- Assist in criminal and accident investigations
- Perform traffic enforcement duties as necessary with concentration on parking violations
- Perform routine security inspections
- Complete detailed written reports; effective oral communication
- Patrol community on foot or in police cars (Government Jobs, 2015d)

To work for Westerville as a parking enforcement officer you would need knowledge of federal, state, and city laws related to law enforcement, division policies and procedures, and emergency medical care. You would need effective oral and written communications skills and the ability to maintain accurate records and prepare meaningful reports, to recognize unusual or threatening conditions, to work a variety of shift assignments, and to work unusual hours and flex shift assignments. The requirements for this position include

- Ohio Peace Officer Training Academy (OPOTA) certification,
- high school diploma or GED,
- must be at least 21 years of age,
- both eyes must be correctable to 20/20 vision and no color blindness,
- must possess a valid state of Ohio motor vehicle operator's license free from excessive violations,
- must meet division standards for physical fitness, and
- maintains all required certifications. (Government Jobs, 2015d)

Public Information Officers

The media can be relentless when it comes to informing the public about law enforcement developments. It is fitting for police departments to let the media get their information directly from the police department rather than from some third party source. However, with stark histories of dangerous and violent encounters, most police employees fret at the thought of being interviewed by a reporter. Of those who are fearless in front of a camera, only about 4 hours were dedicated for media training in their 21-week academy curriculum. And of course, there are also those peculiar police employees that coworkers hope never get in front of the camera.

The public judges the whole police department based on the one or two officers they come into contact with, or hear about or see in the media. Thus, the position of public information officer (PIO) is arguably one of the most important positions in a police department and must be filled by someone with boundless skills. A consummate PIO can keep young overzealous reporters in check while gathering credible information that can be released to the public. If the department doesn't have a PIO on top of things, the media will be out gathering information from bystanders at the scene who are profuse with partial and tainted information (Johnston, 2016).

The hiring, selection, and placement of the PIO are critical decisions. The ideal PIO that can help an agency disseminate its message, facilitate better interaction among the agency, the media, and the public, and can help put police administrators at ease. A full-time PIO is necessary for large agencies, whereas for small to midsize departments such a luxury might be unattainable. However, it is necessary for all agencies of every size to have one or more trained employees to work with the media. The answer for many departments is to utilize civilians for this position.

According to *Police Chief Magazine* (Morley & Jacobsen, 2007), when choosing a PIO, administrators should consider an individual's ties to the community. The PIO should promote the agency's value and mission statement. It is a good foundation to have a strong background in police operations, but the PIO does not have to come from the ranks of sworn personnel. Candidates should be seen as trustworthy and possess good public speaking and report writing skills. Although it is not imperative that the PIO have formal education in journalism, academic and professional experience in the field would help PIOs survive through some challenging times.

To work for the Maricopa County Sheriff's Office (MCSO) in Arizona, you would perform the following duties:

- Work directly with administrative staff to develop and implement policies and strategies related to internal and external communications, public relations, marketing, community relations, and public information
- Direct the activities of the public relations detail and manage effective relationships with all news media
- Develop mechanisms and strategies to facilitate communication between the police chief, city manager, and police employees regarding progress toward organizational goals, changes, and achievements
- Write management reports from analysis of research or investigation
- Represent the department in various dealings with the public or other agencies
- Communicate with and advise other departmental staff on service requests, problems, or issues relating to area of responsibility
- Plan and compose news stories, articles, speeches, radio and television scripts, bulletins, and various periodic and special purpose reports
- Coordinate special events such as open house programs, displays, and exhibits

- Produce general video and slide productions
- Answer written and telephone inquiries regarding police department activities
- Maintain regular and reliable attendance
- Demonstrate superior seamless customer service, integrity, and commitment to innovation, efficiency, and fiscally responsible activity
- Provide effective and efficient liaison efforts with City of Maricopa Public Information Officer (City of Maricopa, 2015)

The minimum requirements for this position at MCSO are 3 years' experience in public relations, journalism, or a related field, and previous public sector and government television broadcast functions, operations, and content experience. You must possess a valid Arizona driver's license at time of appointment and maintain a satisfactory driving record. You would be subject to meeting established polygraph and background standards. You would be required to use personal or city vehicles on city business. You need a bachelor's degree in journalism, public relations, advertising, or a related field, and prior law enforcement or police public information officer experience. Any equivalent combination of education, training, and experience, which provides the requisite knowledge, skills, and abilities for this job, may be substituted for evaluation at the discretion of city management (City of Maricopa, 2015).

Summary

A civilian career in law enforcement is a viable alternative to a sworn position. Civilian (non-sworn) positions can be found in abundance at all law enforcement agencies. With a few exceptions, civilian jobs require less training and pay less money than the sworn positions, but these jobs offer a fantastic opportunity to give back to the community in the law enforcement field. Some common civilian jobs within the realm of law enforcement include crime analyst, communications, police aide, records clerk, property/evidence clerk, supplies/equipment/fleet management (SEF), animal control officer, detention/jail officer (see Chapter 7), crime prevention/community outreach specialist, forensic technician (see Chapter 4), information technology specialist, intelligence analyst, parking enforcement officer, public information officer, and victim service providers/advocates (see Chapter 5).

Crime analysts assist law enforcement agencies in translating massive amounts of data into useable information about crime patterns and trends, which ultimately helps to improve the efficiency of manpower deployment. They help predict when and where a crime may occur and identify potential suspects. An analyst's role is didactic, tactical, strategic, and administrative.

A dispatcher works in a high-stress, fast-paced environment. A delay or improper response can place the caller in higher risk of danger. Callers are often excited and frightened and may not give accurate information without some skilled prompting. The caller may be abusive or angry, and you would need to be able to stay in control of the situation. As a dispatcher, you would use computers and telephones while communicating with emergency response personnel on two-way radios. Monitoring computer screens for long periods of time can be tedious and could cause back pain and eyestrain. As a dispatcher you might be subjected to rotating shifts and alternative work schedules.

A police aide, driving a marked police car, is dispatched to particular types of calls for service. An aide conducts investigations and writes reports for a variety of calls not requiring a police officer's presence. It is common to use police aides for minor vehicle collisions and criminal incidents without suspect information. Some agencies utilize aides in clerical duties that include typing and filing police forms, such as accident reports, evidence cards, arrest records, or schedules. Additionally, aides post information to police records, manually or using a typewriter or computer, disseminate information to the public, over the phone or in person, concerning missing persons, arrests, or other police related business, and receive and record physical evidence seized at crime scenes by police officers and detectives.

Notwithstanding the abundance of paperless technologies, police departments still need assistance with data entry, processing citations, document scanning, maintaining alarm permit files, assisting the public and police employees with records requests, and everything else associated with records management. Records clerk is an administrative support position responsible for clerical, technical, and customer service work involving the maintenance, intake, processing, dissemination, and retention of police records.

The property and evidence control function provides for control and security of recovered, seized, and evidentiary property, as well as lost, found, or abandoned property in the possession of the police department. This position is of critical importance as it supports investigations, helps to guarantee successful prosecution at criminal/civil trials, facilitates the timely return of property to its rightful owners, and establishes the agency's reputation as being worthy of the public's confidence and trust. Law enforcement agencies, faced with the necessity to develop and maintain strict measures for the receipt, handling, security, and disposition of property, seek employees of high character and intelligence.

Law enforcement agencies use a variety of equipment to perform their daily tasks. Supplies are generally kept in a room at the police station or off site in a warehouse if more room is needed. Agencies generally hire a supervisor over the supplies, equipment, and fleet (SEF) and as many clerks as needed to ensure the department operates efficiently. Some of the items that would be under the direction of SEF would include guns, uniforms, office supplies, vehicles, badges, recorders and tapes, cameras and film, phones, report forms, copy paper, computers, file cabinets, desks, radios, and GPS systems.

People who become police officers generally enjoy the prospect of encountering something new and different with every case. They welcome a challenge, and they gain satisfaction by helping people with their problems. However, there are certain types of calls for service that police officers dread, such as the animal calls. Knowledge of the proper care of animals is not tested in the police hiring process and not taught as part of the police academy curriculum. Animal cages and control poles aren't part of the equipment in the trunk of patrol cars. Patrol officers appreciate it when there are animal control officers on duty, which is not always around the clock.

Although predominantly reactive since its inception, law enforcement has gradually introduced some proactive crime prevention programs in the last four decades that have altered that paradigm. These types of programs are difficult to sell to the city management because they require money and manpower yet don't offer any kind of benefit to the city that is immediate, empirical, or measurable. Naturally, these programs are the first to be disbanded when the city has to make budget cuts. It is easier to justify a proactive crime prevention program if it is tied in with community relation objectives. Some common examples include school resource officers, community policing, Neighborhood Watch, DARE, and G.A.I.N. Police departments generally organize a crime prevention unit that becomes the catalyst for these programs and many more as the budget allows. With some exceptions, crime prevention units are entirely staffed by civilians under the supervision of a police sergeant or lieutenant.

Technological advances with police equipment such as in-car mobile data terminals, digital video, computerized mapping, and wireless communication have spawned a significant need for qualified IT professionals in police agencies. Much of the available high-tech equipment is a luxury, but law enforcement unequivocally depends on communication and computer systems to fulfill the core operations. A crash in the system, albeit even for a short time, can decrease officer and citizen safety, allow dangerous criminals to elude an arrest, and increase the risks of civil liability. Police departments need a strong IT unit that can quickly respond to the daily technological needs.

Intelligence analysis is primarily an investigative process, in which the mission is to capture and convict offenders. Crime analysis would be described as primarily a problem-solving process with a mission to deter and reduce crime. Some agencies utilize sworn officers to work in the intelligence unit, but more and more agencies are seeking experienced civilians to perform the tasks. In general, intelligence analysis focuses on the gathering and distribution of information about organizations, schemes, and conspiracies. Intelligence analysts work closely with detectives and undercover teams to hunt for heads of criminal organizations. They follow the flow of money and monitor relationships and activities. They combine the data with personal information about the participants and hand it off to the proper operations teams to follow up with stakeouts, stings, and arrests.

Parking enforcement officers receive training in the law and are granted authority to issue citations, tow and impound vehicles, and order drivers to move their vehicles when blocking traffic. They operate confidential computerized systems so they can obtain records on vehicles and thus contact owners about information or actions regarding their vehicle. They must be capable of responding to hostile or irate individuals while performing their duties, which makes it necessary to include physical tests as part of the hiring process.

The public judges the whole police department based on the one or two officers they come into contact with, or hear about or see in the media. Thus, the position of public information officer is arguably one of the most important positions in a police department and must be filled by someone with boundless skills. A consummate PIO can keep young overzealous reporters in check while gathering credible information that can be released to the public. If the department doesn't have a PIO on top of things, the media will be out gathering information from bystanders at the scene who are profuse with partial and tainted information.

DISCUSSION QUESTIONS

1. What is the difference between crime analysis and intelligence analysis?

2. What is the difference between an evidence clerk and a supply clerk?

3. Are there any of the civilian positions that doesn't need to require a polygraph as part of the hiring process?

4. What type of a person would make an ideal PIO? In your answer, consider factors such as race, gender, age, and physical characteristics.

5. Do you agree with the statement that the public judges the whole police department based on the one or two officers they come into contact with? Why or why not?

REFERENCES

City of Albuquerque Police Department. (2015). *Police service aide*. Retrieved from http://apdonline.com/police-service-aide.aspx

City of Columbia Police Department. (2015). *Evidence & property clerk*. Retrieved from http://www.columbiasc.net/jobs/0/331

City of Maricopa. (2015). *Public affairs specialist*. Retrieved from http://www.maricopa-az.gov/web/job-descriptions/519-police-public-affairs-specialist

City of Palmdale Police Department. (2015). *Crime prevention officer*. Retrieved from http://agency.governmentjobs.com/palmdale/default.cfm?action=viewclassspec&ClassSpecID=94818

City of Victoria Police Department. (2015). *Police department job descriptions.* Retrieved from http://www.victoriatx.org/departments/police/recruitment-training/police-department-job-descriptions

Federal Bureau of Investigation. (2015). *Intelligence analysts.* Retrieved from https://www.fbijobs.gov/intelligence-analysts

Government Jobs. (2015a). *Police records clerk.* Retrieved from https://www.governmentjobs.com/jobs/946500/police-records-clerk

Government Jobs. (2015b). *Information technology technician.* Retrieved from https://www.governmentjobs.com/jobs/919407/information-technology-technician

Government Jobs. (2015c). *Criminal intelligence analyst I.* Retrieved from https://www.governmentjobs.com/jobs/868532/criminal-intelligence-analyst-i

Government Jobs. (2015d). *Parking enforcement officer PT—Police Department.* Retrieved from https://www.governmentjobs.com/jobs/1009616/parking-enforcement-officer-pt-police-department

INTERPOL. (2015). *Criminal intelligence analysis.* Retrieved from http://www.interpol.int/INTERPOL-expertise/Criminal-Intelligence-analysis

Johnston, C. (2016). *Force in law enforcement* (1st ed., Vol. 1, p. 218). San Diego, CA: Cognella Academic Publishing.

LawEnforcementEDU.net. (2015). *Parking enforcement officer careers.* Retrieved from http://www.lawenforcementedu.net/parking-enforcement-officer/

Monster. (2015). *Animal control officer.* Retrieved from http://job-openings.monster.com/monster/8bcb0998-a2f9-44be-a0c4-bae3dbf4ff4f?mescoid=3300592001001#

Morley, E. M., & Jacobsen, M. J. (2007). Building a successful public information program. *Police Chief Magazine, 74*(12). Retrieved from http://www.policechiefmagazine.org/magazine/index.cfm?fuseaction=display_arch&article_id=1345&issue_id=122007

O*NET Online. (2015). *Summary report for: 33-3021.06—intelligence analysts.* Retrieved from http://www.onetonline.org/link/summary/33-3021.06

Pinellas County Sheriff's Office. (2015). *Job descriptions.* Retrieved from http://www.pcsoweb.com/administration/human-resources/job-descriptions

Town of Gilbert, Arizona. (2015). *Career opportunities.* Retrieved from http://www.gilbertaz.gov/departments/human-resources/job-opportunities

U.S. Department of Labor, Bureau of Labor Statistics. (2015). *Occupational employment and wages, May 2014: 33-3041 Parking enforcement workers.* Retrieved from http://www.bls.gov/oes/current/oes333041.htm

7

Jailers, Detention Officers, and Corrections

Many criminals have the opportunity to see the inside of a local jail, but only a small portion ever sits in a prison cell. According to the FBI Unified Crime Report (2013), over 10 million people were arrested for a criminal offense in the United States, which is a consistent statistic every year. Some are released to appear in court at a later time. Others are locked in a jail cell and see a judge (usually within 24 hours) before they can be released. If a suspect is held on bail, he or she is generally transported to a county facility where convicted offenders and suspects can be held for longer periods of time, up to a year.

Throughout the entire criminal justice process from the initial arrest to the conviction and incarceration, one of the largest liability exposures takes place in the local jail facility. Suspects arrested for a crime, whether guilty or not, are usually unhappy with their circumstances. They look for reasons to sue the department. Although most lawsuits against a police department are facetious, the few valid ones can be devastating. In order to avoid losing the inevitable law suites, police departments strive to hire competent personnel that can deal with the limitless rules, procedures, dangers, complaints, health hazards, and pressures that collectively accompany the law enforcement careers.

In this chapter we will explore the careers associated with local jails, county detention, and state correction facilities. We will explore the job descriptions, qualifications, requirements, and salaries. We will look at some of the specific skills needed for this type of work, and some advice on how to become more hirable through college courses, internships, and volunteer programs.

Local Jails

Standard police procedures require that suspects arrested for certain offenses be handcuffed and transported to the police station for booking or further follow-up. Police departments need the ability to temporarily detain those who are arrested during routine police work. At the station, an officer needs to be able to make phone calls; collect records; run computer queries; interview victims, witnesses, and suspects; eat lunch; and use the restroom. Leaving a suspect unsupervised is usually unauthorized and can be unsafe to the prisoner and coworkers. About half of the police departments in the United States employ fewer than 10 sworn personnel, thus making it unlikely that they have full-time jails. Smaller police departments often get by with lockable interview rooms or holding cells. Without an operating jail, officers depend on one another to watch arrestees while they move around the building to accomplish routine tasks. Larger departments that can afford full-time jails are taxed with the expense of a full-time jail staff.

City jailers take on a huge responsibility as they process prisoners, attend to prisoners' needs, and transport them to court or another jail facility. Not everyone is cut out for this type of work. Just like county detention officers and state correction officers (who house some of the most dangerous offenders), jailers are constantly faced with the possibility of assaults from prisoners. City jailers search prisoners (who have already been searched by officers), finding drugs and dangerous weapons hidden under clothing, under the hair, and in body cavities. It is common for prisoners to escape from jailers, usually during court transports. Prisoners in city jails have been killed during fights with one another, during fights with officers, and by suicide. Each time an incident such as this happens, city departments face possible payouts in lawsuit settlements.

As a city jailer in Avondale, Arizona, you would provide care, custody, and control of inmates in city jail; transport inmates (adults and juvenile) and their property to proper locations, ensuring that documentation is completed properly; and administer work furlough and inmate work programs at the discretion of the supervisor. You would complete all bookings and processing for newly arrested subjects on misdemeanor or felony offenses. You would maintain proper accountability and use of supplies for staff and inmate population. You would have full responsibility for a clean, safe environment in the jail. You would conduct numerous counts of the inmate population, conduct fire and safety inspections, and ensure that inmates are released appropriately. Your responsibilities would include supervision of visitations, notification of victims when inmates are released, warrant pickups, and servicing orders of protection and injunctions against harassment.

As an Avondale jailer, you would assist in the functions of patrol units to pick up and transport prisoners when required. You would assist the general public with questions regarding the status of housed inmates, direct callers to appropriate agencies, and provide notary service for patrol when juveniles are referred. Your job duties would include maintaining daily logs of shift activities and creating and maintaining arrest files on all prisoners processed through the police department. Processing prisoners would include paperwork, searching for contraband, fingerprinting, interviewing for any medical conditions, packaging prisoner property, and taking photos. You would need to ensure timely court appearances for all prisoners, escort prisoners to city court for appearances, prepare bond receipts, and collect bonds. There would also be times when you would supervise inmate visitation by contacting visitors, making sure they are allowed to visit, checking visitors for warrants and contraband, supervising actual visits, tracking the number of visitors per inmate, searching inmates upon returning to jail, and performing interviews as required. Jailers also purchase food and prepare meals for inmates, including shopping for and storing food, preparing food, and dispensing meals on weekends and holidays. Jailers handle inmate work details by classifying inmates (often called trustees) who are allowed to work, instructing them in what is expected of them, and transporting inmates to off-site locations. There may also be times when jailers would need to respond to various locations to assist patrol officers or detectives on the scene by taking custody of prisoners. Last, you might find yourself performing warrant pickups or turnovers, picking up wanted persons at other jails, prisons, or outside agencies at various locations.

Qualifications for most jailer positions include the following:

- A high school diploma or GED certificate, no felony convictions, and no dishonorable discharge from the U.S. Armed Forces
- Any equivalent combination of experience, education, or training that provides the required knowledge, skills, and abilities, including course work, experience, or demonstrated work abilities in the areas of criminal justice, customer service, communication, social work, psychology, or sociology
- Terminal operator certification, cardiopulmonary resuscitation certification, first aid certification, and impact weapons and firearms certification
- Passing results on a physical fitness test, a panel interview, an extensive background investigation, a polygraph examination, a psychological evaluation, a medical exam, and a pre-employment drug test
- For candidates with prior experience, a valid diploma from an approved correctional or detention officer academy or proof of comparable tenure and law enforcement experience as a certified peace officer

The physical fitness test for an Avondale jailer position includes a pass/fail 1.5-mile run in 14 minutes 15 seconds, 23 push-ups in 1 minute, and 31 sit-ups in 1 minute. These are the minimum requirements to pass, but the Cooper Age and Gender Base Standards for Law Enforcement are used to determine an overall fitness percentage that will be averaged and combined with the panel interview scoring percentage to proceed to the next phase. The pay for this position is $18.05 to $26.17 hourly (Avondale, Arizona, 2013).

Some smaller agencies combine different positions together in order to accomplish their needs within the scope of the available budget. In Killeen, Texas, the jailer is also a detective and communications specialist. This position is titled police service officer. This person has the following responsibilities (City of Killeen, Texas, 2013):

- Receiving initial reports, via phone or in person, of potential offenses from citizens
- Documenting initial reports using accepted law enforcement report-writing techniques
- Interviewing victims to document initial reports to assist officers in developing leads and tips and interviewing witnesses and taking statements of crimes reported
- Notarizing complaints and statements
- Analyzing and evaluating information reported and determining if reported offenses are violations of civil and/or penal codes
- Summoning ambulances and law enforcement officers as needed
- Investigating and preparing initial reports for minor vehicular damage reported
- Preparing criminal cases for giving testimony and providing testimony in court proceedings
- Carrying out duties in compliance with federal, state, county, and city laws and ordinances
- Providing citizens with assistance with matters such as crime prevention, drug abuse resistance education, and traffic safety
- Maintaining communication and coordination with other law enforcement agencies regarding the location of wanted persons and service of their warrants
- Booking, searching, and releasing prisoners, maintaining security in the jail
- Administering and supervising mealtimes, visitation, counseling, and work assigned to prisoners and monitoring all phone calls and jail access and egress
- Responding to and investigating incidents, crimes, disturbances, disputes, fights, and abuse of drugs among prisoners and taking appropriate action, which includes physical restraint
- Answering questions from bondsmen, lawyers, family members, and courts
- Providing backup in performing responsibilities as a communications officer, including entering data into the computer-aided dispatch system for Bell County Communications Center and operating the National Crime Information Center and Texas Crime Information Center terminals
- Assisting in training new personnel as they are hired

You qualify for this position if you have a high school diploma or GED certificate and are able to complete the 200-hour Public Service Officer Training

Course. You would also need to undergo security clearance, a background check, a psychological test, and a polygraph test and be able to obtain a notary license. Within the first year of employment, you would be required to obtain a Department of Public Safety Texas Law Enforcement Telecommunications System terminal operator certificate and 911 training. You must not have been convicted of or placed on court-ordered community supervision or probation for any offense above a class B misdemeanor or for a class B misdemeanor within the past 10 years. You must not be under any current indictment or have committed any family offense. This position pays $13.57 per hour.

Working as a jailer in a local facility is generally a non-sworn position. Police agencies prefer to hire those with prior law enforcement or detention-related experience but may hire an impressive inexperienced candidate and have the employee attend a detention-related academy. Detention academies are not as intense as the academy that sworn police officers and deputies are required to attend. If you get hired as a detention officer at a local police department, the agency will generally pay your way through the academy while giving you a paycheck throughout the duration.

You can become an attractive candidate without directly related jail experience. It is possible to find internships or other types of training opportunities to help make you more hirable for a full-time jail position. One example is the Summer Basic Jailor Academy offered at Virginia Commonwealth University in the L. Douglas Wilder School of Government and Public Affairs. The 8-week course provides top-flight instruction to rising juniors and seniors while preparing them well for the rigors of detention work. Graduates of the program receive certification as a correctional deputy through the Department of Criminal Justice Services, and become eligible for part-time employment in Henrico's Sheriff's offices. Preference is given to declared criminal justice majors, but any student meeting the requirements for eligibility may apply. Eligible academy recruits must be:

- At least 18 years of age, be a U.S. citizen, and should pass a criminal history records check
- A rising junior or senior undergraduate student or master's student currently enrolled at VCU
- Have a minimum GPA of 2.7 and be in good academic standing
- Have completed CRJS 181, "Introduction to Criminal Justice," and CRJS 253, "Introduction to Corrections" (Virginia Commonwealth University, L. Douglas Wilder School of Government and Public Affairs, 2015)

Several state correctional facilities provide volunteer programs that can expose a person to the various jobs within the prison as well as add a nice entry to a résumé for jailer jobs. One example is the Washington State Department of Corrections, which offers opportunities for volunteers in providing educational tutoring, social services support, religious programming, or reciprocal community stakeholder involvement on boards, steering committees, and advocacy councils. The department also seeks community collaborations such as grant projects, staff and volunteer memberships on boards and councils, proactive partners with law enforcement agencies, members of offender change programs, advisers on management teams, and helpers with transitional programs. The qualifications and requirements include the following:

- Applicants must be 18 years or older.
- Applicants must have photo identification.
- Applicants must provide services DOC needs in accordance with the department's guidelines.
- Applicants must have a valid driver's license if duties include driving while on state business. Volunteers must have permission to use state vehicles.
- Volunteers and interns may not be a member of the immediate family or friend of offenders at the facilities at which they seek to serve.
- Volunteers may not be under the supervision of any local, county, state, or federal corrections agency or under indictment for any felony.
- Criminal History Records checks . . . are required on all volunteer applications. Volunteer positions and duties may be restricted for individuals with a past criminal history. (Washington State Department of Corrections, 2015)

At Washington State Department of Corrections, volunteers are covered under the Department of Labor and Industries Workers Compensation Industrial Insurance while on assignment for the department. Volunteer experience may be counted toward qualification for state employment and actual work experience. Volunteer experience is defined as work experience for which no salary was received, which may be credited toward meeting the minimum qualifications for a classification of state employment. Volunteer experience for which academic credit was granted may be used to satisfy either the educational or the experience requirements of other state employment, but may not be used as both. Volunteer experience of 174.3 hours is equivalent to 1 month of work experience (Washington State Department of Corrections, 2015).

An internship with the Ada County Sheriff's Office in Idaho allows college students the opportunity to get hands-on experience while obtaining credit for school. . . . Internships are unpaid, which allows flexibility for students, as they can volunteer with a variety of divisions throughout the semester. Interns can be placed in positions throughout the Ada County Jail, Work Release Center, Medical Unit, Patrol Division, Detectives, Community Resources Division, Crime Lab, Crime Research Unit, Records Division, Dispatch Center, Human Resources, and the Training Unit. (Ada County Sheriff's Office, 2015)

To become an intern, you must complete the same hiring process as paid employees, which includes the following:

- Criminal Records Check, where we review the applicant's criminal history.
- Polygraph Examination, where applicants are asked to undergo a polygraph examination by a certified polygraph examiner on our staff. After the polygraph session is completed, the examiner writes up a report, which is later reviewed.
- Credit Check Background Investigation, in which a background investigator will do further research and conduct some interviews about the applicant. Once this is completed, the investigator writes up a report, which is later reviewed. (Ada County Sheriff's Office, 2015)

Some of the additional intern/volunteer opportunities at the ADA County Sheriff's Office include:

- *Greenbelt Patrol*—Provide a friendly and reassuring presence on the greenbelt to promote a safe and secure environment for greenbelt users in Eagle and East Ada County.
- *Armory Assistant*—Clean and inspect firearms, and check out ammunition and weapons to deputies at the range.
- *Misdemeanor Probation Assistant*—Answer phones, reschedule appointments, enter data, file, and conduct other office assistant duties as needed.
- *Pre-trial Assistant*—Notify clients of their court dates, track inventory, log drug testing results, install TAD devices, and conduct other case management tasks as needed.
- *Victim Services Support*—Compile information packets for victim services. This task can be done at your home!
- *Marine Patrol*—The marine patrol unit contacts boaters daily to enforce state boating laws and conducts boat inspections. This volunteer would assist the marine deputies with these duties. This position can be done any day of the week and can be done year round. (Ada County Sheriff's Office, 2015)

County Detention Officer

People arrested by county officers and those arrested by state or city departments and not released within 24 hours are normally housed in county jails while awaiting their case resolutions. County jails also hold convicted criminals sentenced to 1 year or less. Usually the most dangerous convicted criminals are sentenced to longer terms, which are completed in state and federal correctional facilities (prisons). But even the worst of the worst are held in county jails while they await trial and sentencing. Similar to a prison environment, detention officers deal with long-term relationships (up to 1 year) with criminals who can be dangerous, manipulative, hostile, seductive, and intelligent. The ideal candidate for a detention officer is ethical, genuine, a good listener, empathetic but not gullible, trustworthy, respectful, patient, and objective.

The hiring process may or may not include a polygraph test. If you are not concerned about passing a polygraph yourself, it might benefit you to join an agency that requires its employees to pass a polygraph. In this type of work, you are constantly in close proximity to criminals, but generally armed with only pepper spray. You need to be able to trust those you work with to not be part of the problem by sneaking in weapons or other contraband for the inmates. Just as in police work, employees can be easily corrupted by the enticing seductive temptations and opportunities that surround them. With that being said, working as a detention officer can be a satisfying career for those who are a good fit.

If you were to work as a detention officer for the Guilford County Sheriff's Department in Greensboro, North Carolina, you would be assigned to one of its three facilities, monitoring inmates to ensure a safe and secure environment for sheriff's office personnel, civilian staff, and those incarcerated. Your pay range would be $33,963 to $45,850, but there are also some incentives that can boost your salary. You would be paid extra for having a bachelor's degree, being fluent in Spanish, having served in the military, and willingness to work rotating shifts. The qualifications to work for Guilford County include the following:

- Citizenship of the United States and age at least 21 years at the time of employment
- Residency in Guilford County or one of the contiguous counties
- Ability to perform all of the essential job functions of an inexperienced officer (unassisted) at a pace and level of performance consistent with the actual job performance requirements
- Possession of a high school diploma or GED certificate
- Weight that is proportionate to height
- Ability to pass a drug test and a complete medical examination by a licensed physician, including psychological testing and evaluation
- Ability to pass a comprehensive background investigation by the sheriff's office, which includes work history, fingerprints, and polygraph test
- Good moral character and have no history of conviction of a felony or a serious misdemeanor by a local, state, federal, or military court
- Good financial status and history (not in bankruptcy, no unpaid past-due accounts or judgments)

The hiring process for the Guilford County Sheriff's Department begins with an application, either online or in writing. The next steps include orientation, a physical fitness test, a written test, an oral interview, a background investigation, a psychological exam, and a medical exam.

Dahmar Wartts-Smiles—Police Officer, Arizona State University Police Department

CJ: What is your current position?

DW: My current position is police officer in the Patrol Division assigned to the downtown Phoenix campus.

CJ: What are your typical job duties?

DW: My typical job duties include the investigation and enforcement of state law and local ordinance on ASU property as well as a large focus on community policing with our students, facility, staff, and visitors.

CJ: How long have you been at your current assignment?

DW: I have been in my current assignment at the downtown campus for approximately 2 months.

CJ: What other positions have you held prior to this one?

DW: In addition to spending a year at the Tempe Campus of ASU on weekend nights, I was a police officer in the Patrol Division at the University City Police Department. I was a police officer there for 2 years and I was a parking enforcement officer for a year at the same department before becoming a police officer.

CJ: What are the requirements/qualifications for your job?

DW: As a fully sworn police officer in the State of Arizona, I am required to comply with the standards of the Arizona Peace Officer Standards and Training Board (AZPOST). This includes graduation from a police academy with a minimum of 585 hours of mandated training. This consists of written tests, defensive tactics, driving proficiency, firearms qualification, and a physical agility test. In addition to those requirements, I must be CPR/AED certified and Mountain Bike Officer certified (IPMBA).

CJ: What steps did you go through during hiring?

DW: First, I applied just like I would any other job online and submitted my résumé. Then, I went on a ride-along with an officer from ASU to ask questions and get a feel of what the environment was like around campus. Next, I had to take a written test specific to ASU and a physical fitness test which included push ups, sit ups, and a 1.5 mile run.

Next, I had to complete an oral board in which a panel of three people asked me questions about my personal and professional experiences.

Next, I had to complete a background check, which included a polygraph and a physiological assessment.

Last, I had to have an interview with the chief of police before being offered a position.

The entire process from start to finish was approximately 6 months.

CJ: What advice can you offer students who might be interested in pursuing a similar career?

DW: The best advice I can offer someone interested in pursing a similar career would be to take advantage of any type of observation or ride-along programs that any local agencies offer. Next would be to talk to any officer you may encounter and ask them any questions you may have. As a police officer, I love talking to people and sharing my experiences with others who like to do the same. Communication is key in this line of work, so don't be afraid to introduce yourself to as many people already in the field as possible and make yourself and your interests known. You never know who you may meet that will make a huge difference in your career and give you a leg up against the competition.

Guilford County Sheriff's Department does not require a polygraph test for its detention officers or deputies. Within the detention division, there are opportunities to move around and work on the Detention Response Team, as a field training officer, on the Gang Intelligence Unit, on the intake crew, or on the K-9 unit (Guilford County Sheriff's Office, 2014).

State Correctional Officer

Corrections is a field in which polygraph tests are not routinely conducted as part of the hiring process. This may be important to some students. Too many students make mistakes early in life that disqualify them from some government jobs because of criminal histories or drug use. Such persons who are seeking careers with the thrill and excitement of law enforcement might find jobs in corrections or private security attainable and satisfying. Although there is less variety in corrections than in police work, and the pay is lower, it is easier to be hired in corrections, and the academy training is shorter as well. Not all applicants for corrections consider it a step on the ladder toward a different goal, such as police work or federal law enforcement. There are correctional officers who complete their whole career in jails or prisons and are quite satisfied.

Some law enforcement officers who chose to start their careers in detention or corrections recount their experience as the best decision they ever made. One of the main reasons is that it taught them (or improved) their "gift of gab," or "verbal judo," as it's known in the police world. They feel the experience made them better interviewers and safer officers.

To survive in the prisons, you either learn how to communicate with criminals or you are dreadfully miserable at work. Convicted criminals will take advantage of a reticent officer. They respond well to firmness as long as it is accompanied with respect. The prison environment introduces employees to a whole new vocabulary. You will learn terms such as *agitator, bean slot, blue bag, clavo, cat head, cho cho, dap,* and *fat back.* If you do use corrections as a ladder rung toward law enforcement, you might be a good candidate for undercover work, buying and selling drugs. Anyone can grow long hair, add a tattoo or two, and not shave or shower. Talking the talk is the difficult part.

After time, many police officers get lackadaisical in their jobs when it comes to officer safety. Those with military or correctional backgrounds are the least likely to experience this injudicious relaxation on the job. Police officers have the privilege of working with law-abiding citizens as well as the criminal element of society, but correctional officers don't enjoy the same variety. They spend their shifts overseeing convicted criminals and those awaiting trial to ensure their safety and overall cooperation. They enforce facility rules and prevent inmate escapes. This requires a good deal of observation and patrolling and a lot of paperwork when security is breached. Correctional officers have the duty of searching convicted criminals at intake and at various other intervals during their sentences. Correctional officers are always at risk for being assaulted, either hand-to-hand or by having items thrown at them, such as food, urine, and feces.

Being a correctional officer for a state prison, or a detention officer for a county or city facility, is a law enforcement–related job with jurisdiction-limited arrest powers and the authority for the use of force. The Arizona Department of Corrections (ADC) employs over 10,000 professionals. To work for ADC, you need to be 21 years old and have a high school diploma or GED certificate. You need to be a U.S. citizen, possess a valid Arizona driver's license, and have no felony convictions. The first step in the hiring process is an entrance exam. You would be assessed through written and oral tests in the areas of general knowledge, human relations, reading comprehension, observation, communication skills, and your ability to follow directions. After passing these introductory tests, you would be given a conditional offer, but you would still have a few remaining hurdles. The first is the background check. As with most law enforcement jobs, you would be required to fill out a background questionnaire that covers your personal, criminal, employment, and driving histories. You would also be asked to submit your proof of age, residency, diploma, and possession of a driver's license. The next step is to pass a medical examination covering hearing, vision, laboratory tests, and medical history. The following step in the process is the physical fitness test, on which you would need to meet the minimum standards of aerobic fitness, muscular strength, endurance, and flexibility. To accomplish this, you might do exercises, such as push-ups, sit-ups, lifts of certain amounts of weight, stretch tests, and stair-step tests. The next test would be a psychological assessment to determine if you fit the profile of a successful correctional officer. A psychologist evaluates the results of these tests, and if there are any discrepancies, the psychologist is empowered to retest you. The final step is drug screening. When taking your first exam, you would be asked to sign a consent form for the screening and would later take that test once you are contacted and asked to appear. You are given 48 hours in which to complete the drug screening test.

Correctional officers attend an academy, which is usually much shorter than police academies. The Arizona Correctional Officer Training Academy (COTA), which is located in the foothills of Tucson, is a 7-week live-in academy with room and board provided for the recruits. While you attend the academy, you receive a salary and benefits. The training curriculum at COTA is divided into nine basic areas: ethics and professionalism, inmate management, legal issues, communications, officer safety, applied skills, security custody and control, conflict and crisis management, and medical and mental health issues. In the academy you are tested weekly through various assessment exercises. A vital component of the training is physical fitness, participation in which is mandatory. There are standards you must meet for aerobic and muscular fitness as well as flexibility. Firearm and self-defense classes are taught at the academy, with the aim of keeping the public, staff, and inmates safe. To graduate, you must demonstrate efficiency in self-defense. As part of firearm education, you would be trained in chemical agents, the use of force, and target identification and discrimination. A key ingredient of the training at COTA is on-the-job experience. Midway through the training, you would be assigned to an institution, in which you are shown a glimpse of the duties and responsibilities of a professional correctional officer (Arizona Department of Corrections, 2015).

Once out of the academy, with a salary between $32,916 and $39,664, you would be assigned to one of the 10 ADC facilities statewide to begin your career. Your job would be to maintain order at an institution crowded with disorderly guests. You would do more than just watch for problems to occur. Inmates are better off being active, so you would be supervising work activities and other organized affairs. You would find yourself settling disputes and enforcing rules while conducting searches and moving prisoners to their destinations, such as visitations, court or parole hearings, and medical appointments.

If you lean toward becoming a correctional officer, you will be more successful if you have the "gift of gab." Just as police officers need to be good actors and deceivers, correctional officers need to be able to work with brilliant deceivers while being genuine, firm, and respectable. Most inmates are willing to conform to the rules and to verbal commands if they feel respected. A correctional officer must display a balance between power and control and must convey respect. If you have any issues with racial bias or a negative attitude toward criminals in general, they will pick up on it.

On a good day at an ADC facility, you might routinely check each cell in your assigned area for contraband or signs of tampering and then log any violations. On a bad day, you might be covered with urine or feces thrown by inmates, verbally attacked, or assaulted with a strike, a kick, or an improvised weapon. Meanwhile, you are armed with little more than a communication device. Like any law enforcement officer, you would be held to a high standard in use-of-force decisions. You would continuously have your patience and temper tested. You would periodically find your name on official documents as the victim of assault. Some inmates have nothing to lose, so an assault charge is hardly a deterrent.

If your long-range goal is law enforcement with a city, county, state, or federal agency, correctional work gives you an opportunity for relevant experience. You will acquire valuable practice in communicating with your superiors, peers, and criminals. You will have a lead on most police academy recruits in the areas of officer safety and use-of-force strategies. However, a word of caution: You will also have the potential for annoying entries in your personnel file. When police agencies do their background checks on lateral applicants, they inquire about the candidates' personnel files. The agencies are interested in favorable entries but also in citizen complaints and internal investigations. Even if complaints or accusations are resolved in favor of an officer, the record remains in the file for a significant length of time, usually 3 to 5 years. The everyday work of a correctional officer can result in two or three file entries a year, even for an exemplary officer. It comes with the job. You may have some explaining to do, but the worst-case scenario is that you may never get the chance if a check of your background results in the removal of your application from the potential list of candidates.

If your initial dream job is police officer, but you have used too many drugs or committed too many crimes to qualify, you may find satisfaction in a correctional job. In police work, you are often (but not always) given a polygraph test, and you are faced with mandatory reporting of every crime you have ever committed. To work for the ADC, you are not required to take a polygraph test, and the criminal history requirement is no felony conviction. The department will do a thorough background check in the hope of weeding out any bad apples, but just like corruption that ultimately surfaces in police departments, there are correctional officers who commit vile acts, such as smuggling in contraband or physically and sexually abusing inmates. Agencies do their best to find model employees. As in the police hiring process, you will be up against some outstanding candidates and, conversely, plenty who are not much of a threat to beat you out of the job.

Within the correctional system, there are some job options that are to some extent less dangerous than being a correctional officer and potentially rewarding, especially for those leaning toward the helping professions. These alternative positions include probation officer, parole officer, corrections advisor, treatment officer, corrections counselor, juvenile review and release specialist, community corrections officer, and warden. A popular position tied to law enforcement and corrections is that of a probation or parole officer. The workload is enormous, and the pay is subpar, but that is quite common in most government work. Probation work is a great ladder rung, offering valuable experience and a challenging career for the right type of person, and is a typical second career for those exiting or retiring from law enforcement.

Juvenile probation work is generally sought after more than adult work, but it really depends on the person seeking the job. If you choose to work with juveniles, hopefully it is because you want to help rehabilitate them. Those who are very good at exhibiting power (such as a drill sergeant or an academy trainer) might be a better fit to work with adults than touchy-feely individuals. The roles of an adult probation officer and a juvenile probation officer are actually quite similar, but the methods used are fundamentally different. Rehabilitation and low recidivism are common goals for adults and juveniles alike, but how the two types of probation officers approach their handiwork is befittingly diverse. This is not to say that adults need a firm hand and juveniles need a soft touch. Like police officers, probation officers see new cases and new faces. They need to have flexibility and a remarkable ability to wear different hats.

Probation officers have immense empowerment in their roles. They act as representatives of law enforcement and as judges. Like police detectives, they are assigned more cases than they can feasibly control, and unless an arrest forces their hand, they work their caseloads at their own pleasure, with a constant fear that their competence may be second-guessed if something goes wrong. If a probationer violates the conditions of probation, a probation officer has the discretionary leeway to either issue a violation charge against the client or to offer a second chance. Just as in police work, there are no specific and concrete words written somewhere explaining what discretionary choices a probation officer is permitted to make or prohibited from making. They learn from their coworkers and supervisors what is acceptable and what is not.

Probation officers constantly face dangers in their everyday contacts with their clients. It is common for probation officers to travel to intimidating neighborhoods to visit probationers at their homes. Many agencies have protocols of working in pairs during home visits, but not all employees like to work with partners or may be hesitant to pull others from their own caseloads to assist as a backup. A growing trend in the last decade has been to arm probation officers. Few probation officers are required to carry weapons, but for many it is offered as a choice to do so. An ongoing controversy with gun-toting probation officers is over its arbitrariness. The qualifications are minimal compared to police officers. A short firearms safety course (usually about 40 hours) is the normal extent of training. Some states, such as New York, require the gun carrying candidates to pass a psychological test in addition to firearms training.

As mentioned earlier, there are internships available to make you more hirable as a local jailer, county detention officer, state corrections officer, or probation/parole officer. If you were interested in working in Arizona, you could access the State of Arizona Human Resources website at http://www .hr.az.gov/index.asp, which shows over 50 internships available for state jobs, which include Department of Corrections, Department of Gaming, Auto Theft Authority, Department of Juvenile Corrections, and the Game and Fish Department. Similar websites can be found from other states by searching for the state's human resources division and navigating the site to internships and volunteer opportunities. It is possible, but unrealistic, to expect to be hired at your dream job right out of college without first entering some type of internship or volunteer job to enhance your résumé. Hiring agencies almost always see your résumé or application before they see you. Make sure your paperwork tells an impressive story about who you are.

Summary

According to the FBI Unified Crime Report (2013), over 10 million people were arrested for a criminal offense in the United States, which is a consistent statistic every year. Some are released to appear in court at a later time. Others are locked in a jail cell and see a judge (usually within 24 hours) before they can be released. If an offender is held on bail, he or she is generally transported to a county facility where offenders and suspects can be held for longer periods of time, up to a year.

Suspects arrested for a crime, whether guilty or not, are usually unhappy with their circumstances. They look for reasons to sue the department. Although most lawsuits against a police department are facetious, the few valid ones can be devastating. In order to avoid losing the inevitable lawsuits, police departments hire competent personnel that can deal with the limitless rules, procedures, dangers, complaints, health hazards, and pressures that are part of law enforcement, in which one of the largest liability exposures takes place in the jail.

About half of the police departments in the United States employ fewer than 10 sworn personnel, thus making it unlikely that they have full-time jails. Smaller police departments often get by with lockable interview rooms or holding cells. Without an operating jail, officers depend on one another to watch arrestees while they move around the building to accomplish routine tasks. Larger departments that can afford full-time jails are taxed with the expense of a full-time jail staff.

City jailers take on a huge responsibility as they process prisoners, attend to prisoners' needs, and transport them to court or another jail facility. Not everyone is cut out for this type of work. Just like county detention officers and state correction officers (who house some of the most dangerous offenders), jailers are constantly faced with the possibility of assaults from prisoners. It is common for prisoners to escape from jailers, usually during court transports. Prisoners in city jails have been killed during fights with one another, during fights with officers, and by suicide. Each time an incident such as this happens, city departments face possible payouts in lawsuit settlements.

Working as a jailer in a local facility is generally a non-sworn position. Police agencies prefer to hire those with prior law enforcement or detention-related experience, but may hire an impressive inexperienced candidate and have the employee attend a detention-related academy. Detention academies are not as intense as the academy that sworn police officers and deputies are required to attend. If you get hired as a detention officer at a local police department, the agency will generally pay your way through the academy while giving you a paycheck throughout the duration.

You can become an attractive candidate without directly related jail experience. It is possible to find internships or other types of training opportunities to help make you more hirable for a full-time jail position. Several state correctional facilities provide volunteer programs that can expose a person to the various jobs within the prison as well as add a nice entry to a résumé for jailer jobs.

People arrested by county officers, and those arrested by state or city departments and not released within 24 hours, are normally housed in county jails while awaiting their case resolutions. County jails also hold convicted criminals sentenced to one year or less. Usually the most dangerous convicted criminals are sentenced to longer terms, which are completed in state and federal correctional facilities (prisons). But even the worst of the worst are held in county jails while they await trial and sentencing. Similar to a prison environment, detention officers deal with long-term relationships (up to 1 year) with criminals who can be dangerous, manipulative, hostile, seductive, and intelligent.

Corrections is a field in which polygraph tests are not routinely conducted as part of the hiring process. This may be important to some students. Too many students make mistakes early in life that disqualify them from some government jobs because of criminal histories or drug use. Such persons who are seeking careers with the thrill and excitement of law enforcement might find jobs in corrections or private security attainable and satisfying. Although there is less variety in corrections than in police work, and the pay is lower, it is easier to be hired in corrections, and the academy training is shorter as well.

To survive in the prisons, you either learn how to communicate with criminals or you are dreadfully miserable at work. Convicted criminals will take advantage of a reticent officer. They respond well to firmness, as long as it is accompanied with respect. After time, many police officers get lackadaisical in their jobs when it comes to officer safety. Those with military or correctional backgrounds are the least likely to experience this injudicious relaxation on the job.

Being a correctional officer for a state prison, or a detention officer for a county or city facility, is a law enforcement–related job with jurisdiction limited arrest powers and the authority for the use of force. If you lean toward becoming a correctional officer, you will be more successful if you have the "gift of gab." Just as police officers need to be good actors and deceivers, correctional officers need to be able to work with brilliant deceivers while being genuine, firm, and respectable. Most inmates are willing to conform to the rules and to verbal commands if they feel respected. A correctional officer must display a balance between power and control and must convey respect. If you have any issues with racial bias or a negative attitude toward criminals in general, they will pick up on it.

If your long-range goal is law enforcement with a city, county, state, or federal agency, correctional work gives you an opportunity for relevant experience. You will acquire valuable practice in communicating with your superiors, peers, and criminals. You will have a lead on most police academy recruits in the areas of officer safety and use-of-force strategies. If your initial dream job is police officer, but you have used too many drugs or committed too many crimes to qualify, you may find satisfaction in a correctional job. In police work, you are often (but not always) given a polygraph test, and you are faced with mandatory reporting of every crime you have ever committed.

Within the correctional system, there are some job options that are to some extent less dangerous than being a correctional officer and potentially rewarding, especially for those leaning toward the helping professions. These alternative positions include probation officer, parole officer, corrections advisor, treatment officer, corrections counselor, juvenile review and release specialist, community corrections officer, and warden. Probation officers have immense empowerment in their roles. They act as representatives of law enforcement and as judges. Like police detectives, they are assigned more cases than they can feasibly control, and unless an arrest forces their hand, they work their caseloads at their own pleasure, with a constant fear that their competence may be second-guessed if something goes wrong.

Probation officers constantly face dangers in their everyday contacts with their clients. It is common for probation officers to travel to intimidating neighborhoods to visit probationers at their homes. Many agencies have protocols of working in pairs during home visits, but not all employees like to work with partners or may be hesitant to pull others from their own caseloads to assist as a backup. A growing trend in the last decade has been to arm probation officers. Few probation officers are required to carry weapons, but for many it is offered as a choice to do so.

There are internships available to make you more hirable as a local jailer, county detention officer, state corrections officer, or probation/parole officer. Internship opportunities can be found in many states by searching for the state's human resources division and navigating the site to internships and volunteer opportunities. It is possible, but unrealistic to expect to be hired at your dream job right out of college without first entering some type of internship or volunteer job to enhance your résumé. Hiring agencies almost always see your résumé or application before they see you. Make sure your paperwork tells an impressive story about who you are.

DISCUSSION QUESTIONS

1. Applicants for county detention and correctional jobs rarely undergo polygraph testing. Do you feel that they should? Why or why not? For what other careers would you recommend that polygraph test results be considered when making hiring decisions?

2. In all law enforcement jobs, including jails, county detention facilities, and state corrections, a personnel file is kept that stores records of internal investigations. A record is saved even if the officer being investigated is found innocent of the allegations. Do you feel this is a necessary procedure? Why or why not?

3. What advantages or disadvantages are there in having women working in local and county jails and in corrections? What about minorities? Does your opinion vary depending on the position within the correctional system?

REFERENCES

ADA County Sheriff's Office. (2015). *Internship opportunities*. Retrieved from https://www.adasheriff.org/internships

Arizona Department of Corrections. (2015). *Employment opportunities with ADC*. Retrieved from http://www.azcorrections.gov/adc/employment/ADCCareers.aspx

Avondale, Arizona. (2013). *Employment opportunities*. Retrieved from http://www.ci.avondale.az.us/index.aspx?NID=13

City of Killeen, Texas. (2013). *Employment with the city of Killeen, Texas*. Retrieved from http://www.killeentexas.gov/index.php?section=87

Federal Bureau of Investigation. (2013). *Crime in the United States 2013*. Retrieved from https://www.fbi.gov/about-us/cjis/ucr/crime-in-the-u.s/2013/crime-in-the-u.s.-2013/persons-arrested/persons-arrested

Guilford County Sheriff's Office. (2014). *Personnel & training*. Retrieved from http://www.gcsonc.com/command/operations-bureau/personnel-training

State of Arizona Human Resources. (2012). *Welcome*. Retrieved from http://www.hr.az.gov/index.asp

Virginia Commonwealth University L. Douglas Wilder School of Government and Public Affairs. (2015). *Summer basic jailor academy*. Retrieved from http://www.wilder.vcu.edu/service/intern/jailoracademy.html

Washington State Department of Corrections. (2015). *Volunteering at the Department of Corrections*. Retrieved from http://www.doc.wa.gov/jobs/volunteer.asp

8

Federal Law Enforcement

Introduction

Federal agencies employ over 103,000 full-time sworn personnel (Reaves, 2007). They rarely participate in the hustle and bustle routinely handled by local and county police. With some exceptions, it is uncommon for federal law enforcement agents to be first responders. As enforcers of laws pertaining to federal crimes, they handle such things as terrorism; illegal immigration; bank robberies; drug enforcement; organized and white-collar crime; crimes involving alcohol, tobacco, firearms, and explosives; and interstate crimes. Most federal law enforcement is similar to detective work in local agencies, in which no uniform is worn and employees specialize in areas of expertise without much variation in their caseloads. The U.S. Border Patrol is the federal agency most similar to local departments. Its agents wear uniforms and proactively seek out offenders. They are first responders to law violators along our nation's borders.

Federal law enforcement is prestigious work, and for the most part, federal crimes are serious issues. Some of the crimes and criminals dealt with in federal law enforcement are high profile, receiving a great deal of publicity. Because of the glamour associated with federal jobs, they are extremely competitive, but there are fewer hiring opportunities available than for local work. There are also opportunities for travel in federal work, including international placement. Consider the analogy of the career ladder when vying for a federal position of great demand, such as with the Federal Bureau of Investigation (FBI), the Drug Enforcement Administration (DEA), Immigration and Customs Enforcement (ICE), and the U.S. Marshals Service (USMS). A step that may need to be included in your ladder is the military or local law enforcement.

In this chapter, we will explore some of the more prominent federal agencies, including job descriptions and hiring information. We will also touch on some of the supportive positions for those who are not interested in carrying a gun and handcuffs. Much of the information about law enforcement personalities, behaviors, and other idiosyncrasies discussed in Chapters 2 and 3 applies to federal law enforcement as well and won't be repeated here in Chapter 8.

FBI

The FBI is one of the most sought after federal agencies by students entering their degree programs in criminal justice. The FBI isn't a national police force, as some might misconstrue. The agency is actually more of a national security organization that partners with countries all over the globe to combat serious security threats. As of September 2012, the FBI had a total of 36,074 employees, including 13,913 special agents and 22,161 support professionals, such as intelligence analysts, language specialists, scientists, information technology specialists, and other miscellaneous professionals. The duties are prioritized as follows:

1. Protecting the United States from terrorist attack

2. Protecting the United States against foreign intelligence operations and espionage

3. Protecting the United States against cyber-based attacks and high-technology crimes

4. Combating public corruption at all levels

5. Protecting civil rights

6. Combating transnational and national criminal organizations and enterprises

7. Combating major white-collar crime

8. Combating significant violent crime

9. Supporting federal, state, local, and international partners

10. Upgrading technology to successfully perform the FBI's mission

Although combating terrorism is the number one priority of the FBI, it isn't necessarily where the most manpower is used. Agents enforce many different federal laws and perform various roles in the bureau. Most of the man-hours are actually spent in the United States, involving U.S. victims and U.S. perpetrators. As mentioned earlier, FBI agents do work that is similar to that of a detective in a police department. An agent in a field office, for example, could be testifying in federal court one day and executing a search warrant and gathering evidence the next. Over the course of a week, an agent might meet with an informant to gather intelligence on illegal activities, arrest a suspect, and then head back to the office to talk with her squad members and catch up on some paperwork. Some agents work in specialized areas across the FBI, such as training, fingerprinting, lab services, and public affairs, while many serve as supervisors or managers.

Special agents are always on call and could be transferred at any time, according to the needs of the FBI. The work is challenging and exciting. Although their workload is heavy, special agents still find opportunities to spend quality time with their families. The FBI has a greater variety of laws to enforce (200 categories of federal laws) than most federal agencies, such as the DEA and the Bureau of Alcohol, Tobacco, Firearms, and Explosives (ATF). The FBI also works task forces with local and state agencies.

As an FBI special agent, you would be responsible for conducting sensitive national security investigations and enforcing federal statutes. You might work on matters including terrorism, foreign counterintelligence, cyber-crime, organized crime, white-collar crime, public corruption, civil rights violations, financial crime, bribery, bank robbery, extortion, kidnapping, air piracy, interstate criminal activity, fugitive and drug-trafficking matters, and other violations within federal statutes.

To be hired as an FBI special agent, you must be a U.S. citizen or a citizen of the Northern Mariana Islands. You must be at least 23 years of age to apply and cannot have reached 37 years of age upon your appointment as a special agent. Age waivers may be granted to preference eligible veterans who are older than 37. You must have a 4-year degree from a college or university accredited by one of the regional or national institutional associations recognized by the U.S. secretary of education. You need at least 3 years of professional work experience. You must have a valid driver's license and be available for assignment anywhere in the FBI's jurisdiction.

All applicants for the position of special agent must qualify through one of five special agent entry programs. These programs include accounting, computer science and information technology, language, the law, and diversified fields. After qualifying for one of the five entry programs, applicants are prioritized in the hiring process on the basis of certain skills for which the FBI is recruiting. Since June 2013, the FBI has been recruiting candidates with one or more of the following critical skills:

- Accounting
- Military experience
- Finance
- Computer science and information technology expertise
- Law experience
- Engineering expertise
- Foreign language proficiency
- Physical sciences (e.g., physics, chemistry, biology) expertise
- Intelligence experience
- Law enforcement and investigative experience
- Diversified experience

Candidates with these skills are essential to address the FBI's complex responsibilities. Those with one or more of these skills are prioritized in the hiring process. A recent trend has been to put a higher priority on applicants with military experience.

Applicants must be in excellent physical condition with no disabilities that would interfere in firearm use, participation in raids, or the use of defensive tactics. All applicants must be able to pass physical tests to gain admittance to the FBI Academy in Quantico, Virginia. The tests consist of four mandatory events, generally handled in the following order:

1. Maximum number of sit-ups in 1 minute

2. Timed 300-meter sprint

3. Maximum number of push-ups (untimed)

4. Timed 1.5-mile run

FBI work is very sensitive in nature; so all positions require top-secret security clearance. Once you have received a conditional offer of employment, the FBI will initiate an intensive background investigation that you must pass before your hiring is official. The investigation includes a polygraph examination to investigate illegal drug use, credit and records checks, and extensive interviews with former and current colleagues, neighbors, friends, professors, and others. Besides the requirements that all candidates must meet, there are also some disqualifiers to be aware of. Some FBI employment disqualifiers include the following:

- Conviction of a felony
- Use of illegal drugs in violation of the FBI Employment Drug Policy
- Default of a student loan (insured by the U.S. government)
- Failure of an FBI-administered urinalysis drug test
- Failure to register with the Selective Service System (for men only)

The entire hiring process for special agent consists of seven steps, which are as follows:

1. **Application:** Done online

2. **Phase I testing:** Written tests and some proficiency tests on the basis of the skills you claim to possess on your application (e.g., Spanish speaking; not everyone gets to enter Phase I testing)

3. **Phase II testing:** Writing test and face-to-face interview with a panel

4. **Conditional letter of appointment:** On the basis of budgetary requirements and the critical skills needed by the FBI, qualified candidates will receive conditional letters of appointment; these letters make conditional job offers to candidates and provide details on the FBI's background investigation and ensuing steps

5. **Physical fitness test:** The four mandatory events listed earlier

6. **FBI background investigation:** Includes a polygraph test; credit and criminal history checks; interviews with associates, personal and business references, past employers, and neighbors; and verification of educational achievements

7. **Medical examination:** Each candidate's situation is reviewed on an individual basis; the medical examination also includes vision and hearing exams

All special agent trainees start their careers at the FBI Academy for 21 weeks of intensive training. During your time at the academy, you would live on campus and participate in a vast range of training activities. Classroom time comprises a wide variety of academic and investigative subjects. The FBI Academy's curriculum includes intensive training in physical fitness, defensive tactics, practical application exercises, and firearms training. Several tests are administered in all of these areas to monitor your progress.

As a trainee at the academy, you would be administered the physical fitness test during the 1st, 7th, and 14th weeks of your training. Those trainees who fail the test during the 1st week would be placed in a remedial program and would be subject to certain restrictions. These restrictions include no overnight leave from the academy until they pass the test. Those who fail the 1st week's physical fitness test and the 7th week's test would be dismissed from training. You must pass all training requirements to graduate and be sworn in as a special agent. Special agent trainees start out with a salary of $51,043 (Federal Bureau of Investigation, 2013).

Because of the scope of the FBI's responsibilities, you could also enter the FBI in other fields, such as intelligence analysis, laboratory sciences, linguistics, security, information technology, human resources, general management, and more. In addition to any current job postings for full-time positions, the FBI also offers a paid honors internship program as well as an unpaid volunteer internship program. Student internship opportunities include the Laboratory Division's Visiting Science Program. Students with backgrounds in science, engineering, or technology disciplines are invited to apply. Watch for career fairs and other recruiting events where you may have a chance to meet an FBI employee and learn more about job opportunities.

DEA

The DEA was created through an executive order in July 1973 to establish a single unified command to combat drugs. At the beginning, the DEA had 1,470 special agents. Today, the agency employs nearly 5,000 special agents. The DEA has 223 domestic offices in 21 divisions throughout the United States and 86 foreign offices in 67 countries. Some of the jobs you could enter with the DEA include special agent, diversion investigator, forensic scientist, intelligence researcher, and professional and administrative positions.

The first step in the application process is to contact your local DEA recruitment office. The DEA encourages applicants to attend a special agent applicant orientation session. These are offered only at four locations. You can find information online at the DEA's website (http://www.justice.gov/dea). The first time you try to reserve a seat for an orientation, it may be full, requiring you to wait for the next session. Casual business attire is the appropriate dress. A valid driver's license or military identification may be required for entry. If you live far from the local recruitment office, the office could opt to conduct a phone screening and orientation in lieu of a face-to-face meeting.

To become a special agent, you must successfully complete all phases of a thorough and in-depth hiring process. This process may take up to a year or longer, and includes the following phases:

- Qualifications review
- Written assessment and panel interview
- Urinalysis drug test
- Medical examination
- Physical task test
- Polygraph examination
- Psychological assessment
- Full-field background investigation
- Final hiring decision

To start the hiring process, you can take an eligibility quiz online (U.S. Drug Enforcement Administration, 2013), consisting of the following items:

1. I have one year of experience in narcotics/drug-related investigations of alleged or suspected violations of the law, participating in surveillance and undercover operations, taking part in apprehending/arresting persons suspected of violations, and assisting in the organization of evidence for presentation to prosecution officials.

2. I have an undergraduate (bachelor's) grade point average (GPA) of 2.95 or higher (based on 4 years of education or in the final 2 years of curriculum).

3. I have completed two (2) full academic years of graduate level education or completed all requirements for a master's or equivalent graduate degree.

4. I have an LL.B. or JD degree.

5. At a three plus rating as established by Foreign Service Institute standards, I am fluent in Spanish, French, Russian, Arabic, Hebrew, dialects of Nigerian languages, Chinese, Mandarin, Japanese, Farsi, Urdu, or any Balkan language, AND I possess a bachelor's degree or

higher (no minimum GPA is required) with coursework in a foreign language, composition, literature, writing, communications, or humanities/cultural studies.

6. I possess a current pilots license and have 3 or more years experience as an airline, military and/or private pilot operating multi-engine, fixed-wing, instrument-rated aircrafts to include utilizing state-of-the art equipment and planning for extensive domestic and international travel, including logistical support, loading characteristics, climatic analysis, and equipment operation limitations, AND I possess a bachelor's degree or higher.

7. I have 3 or more years of experience as a first mate, navigational officer, Maritime Academy graduate and/or ship's captain in the shipping industry utilizing state-of-the-art equipment and planning for extensive domestic and international travel, including logistical support, loading characteristics, climatic analysis, and equipment operation limitations, AND I possess a bachelor's degree or higher.

8. I have 3 or more years of professional accounting or auditing experience (public or private), which includes the audit of company or governmental books and records (manual or automated), AND I possess a bachelor's degree or higher with at least 24 semester hours in accounting or auditing.

9. I have 3 or more years of substantial on-the-job indoctrination and "hands-on" experience in electronic theory and application, with emphasis on communications associated with wireless and cable audio and video systems to include listening devices, video equipment (both visible and invisible spectra), teletype and radioteletype (RTTT), and computers and associated interfacing equipment, AND I possess a bachelor's degree or higher with coursework in information systems/technology, telecommunications, or electrical/mechanical engineering.

10. I have 3 or more years of military experience in leadership, travel, and diverse geographical assignments and familiarity with the control mechanisms necessary to operate in a dangerous environment. My experience may include training and participating in court-martials, conducting investigations on their behalf and administering corresponding disciplinary actions, AND I possess a bachelor's degree or higher with coursework in military or political science, government, management/leadership, and/or communications.

If you meet the minimum qualifications, you will be further evaluated on your relevant training and experience as well as your knowledge, skills, abilities, and competencies in written and oral communication, decision making and judgment, interpersonal skills, honesty, flexibility, problem solving, self-management, teamwork, planning and evaluating, technology application, and law enforcement. Evaluation of the aforementioned competencies would be administered at the time of application.

The DEA has a strict drug use policy. The agency requires that all applicants complete a drug questionnaire as part of the application process. Applicants who are found, through investigation or personal admission, to have experimented with or used narcotics or dangerous drugs, except those medically prescribed, will not be considered for employment with the DEA. Exceptions to this policy may be made for those who admit to limited youthful and experimental use of marijuana. Such applicants may be considered for employment if there is no evidence of regular, confirmed use and the full-field background investigation and results of the other steps in the process are favorable.

In 1999, the DEA Training Academy opened on the Marine Corps base at Quantico. DEA trainees live on site and attend classes at the DEA Training Academy, but the facilities for firearms training, physical fitness and defensive tactics training, defensive driving training, and all practical application exercises are held at the FBI Academy. Approximately 60% of all trainees have prior law enforcement experience, while 30% generally come from military backgrounds. The majority of trainees possess bachelor's degrees, and nearly 20% have some postgraduate educational experience (U.S. Drug Enforcement Administration, 2013).

To graduate from the 18-week academy, students must maintain an academic average of 80% on academic examinations, pass the firearms qualification test, successfully demonstrate leadership and sound decision making in practical scenarios, and pass rigorous physical tests. Upon graduation, students are sworn in as DEA special agents and assigned to DEA field offices located across the United States at a starting salary of about $50,000.

ATF

The ATF was transferred under the Homeland Security Act of 2002 to the U.S. Department of Justice in 2003. The ATF investigates and prosecutes terrorist acts and violent crimes that involve explosives, arson, firearms, repeat and violent offenders, criminal gangs, the illegal use and trafficking of firearms and explosives, and the illegal diversion of alcohol and tobacco products. There are positions for special agents, investigators, and attorneys; professional and technical positions; and internships. Working as an ATF special agent is a unique job and one of the most challenging in federal law enforcement.

The ATF has field offices throughout the United States and its territories. Highly trained special agents are responsible for investigating violations of federal laws relating to firearms, explosives, arson, and alcohol and tobacco diversion. Investigations involve surveillance, interviewing suspects and witnesses, making arrests, obtaining search warrants, searching for physical evidence, preparing concise criminal investigative case reports, testifying for the federal government in court or before grand juries, gathering and analyzing evidence through investigative leads, seizures, arrests, execution of search warrants, and a variety of other tasks.

Special agents must be tough physically and mentally. You would need to handle rigorous training, personal risks, irregular hours, and extensive travel. Special agents are subject to reassignment to any ATF office in the United States, including any U.S. territory or ATF overseas assignment. To be a special agent, you would need to meet the following criteria:

- Be a U.S. citizen
- Possess a current and valid automobile operator's license
- Complete the ATF special agent applicant questionnaire
- Take and pass the ATF special agent exam
- Take and pass the ATF special agent applicant assessment test
- Take and pass the ATF pre-employment physical task test
- Appear for and successfully complete a field panel interview (a writing sample will be required)
- Be in compliance with the ATF's drug policy for special agent applicants
- Take and pass a medical examination by an authorized government physician and meet medical requirements
- Weight must be in proportion to height
- Take and pass a drug test
- Take and successfully complete a polygraph examination
- Successfully complete a background investigation for a top secret security clearance

To be eligible for federal employment, male applicants born after December 31, 1959, must certify at the time of appointment that they have registered with the Selective Service System or are exempt from having to do so under pursuant law. Applicants must be at least 21 years of age and not older than 36 at the time of appointment. In accordance with Public Law No. 100-238, this position is covered under law enforcement retirement provisions; therefore, candidates must be appointed before reaching their 37th birthdays unless they are preference-eligible veterans.

The starting salary for special agents ranges from $34,000 to $43,000. As a special agent, you would receive an additional percentage of your base salary, depending on your location. You would also receive 25% law enforcement availability pay, which is added to locality pay.

Investigators are the backbone of the ATF's regulatory mission. To work as an investigator, you would primarily investigate, routinely have contact with, and interview individuals from all walks of life and all levels of industry and government. To be an investigator, you must meet similar criteria as listed for special agents. The basic training for investigators involves an 8.5-week academy. The salary ranges from $28,000 to $42,000 and also includes locality pay. There is a strict drug use policy, which includes no marijuana use in the past 3 years and never more than experimental use.

The ATF has an internship program, which is designed to provide students enrolled in a wide variety of educational institutions, from high school to graduate school, with opportunities to work in agencies and explore federal careers while still in school and while getting paid for the work they perform. Students who successfully complete the program may be eligible for conversion to permanent jobs in the civil service. Here are some key provisions and features of the internship program:

- The internship program is primarily administered by each hiring agency.
- Agencies may hire interns on a temporary basis for up to 1 year for an initial period, or for an indefinite period, to complete the educational requirement.
- Interns may work either part time or full time.
- Each agency must sign a Participant Agreement with the intern that sets forth the expectations for the internship.
- The intern's job will be related to the intern's academic career goals or field of study.
- Flexible schedule of work assignments.
- Students may be employed year round.
- Open to all students enrolled at least half-time in an educational institution that has been accredited by an accrediting body recognized by the U.S. Department of Education in pursuit of any of the following educational programs:
    o High school diploma or General Educational Development certificate,
    o Vocational or technical certificate,
    o Associate's degree,
    o Bachelor's degree,
    o Graduate degree, and
    o Professional degree.

You are eligible under the Internship Program if you are

- At least 16 years old (required by federal, state, or local laws and standards governing the employment of minors);
- Enrolled or accepted for enrollment as a degree-seeking student (diploma, certificate, etc.);
- In good academic standing and maintain at least a 2.5 overall scholastic average on a 4.0 scale or equivalent, with no grade below a C during the internship;
- Taking at least a half-time academic or vocational and technical course load in an accredited high school, or technical or vocational school, 2-year or 4-year college or university, or graduate or professional school that has been accredited by an accrediting body recognized by the U.S. Department of Education;

- A U.S. citizen or a national (resident of American Samoa or Swains Island); noncitizens may be eligible for employment if
  - Lawfully admitted to the United States as a permanent resident
  - Otherwise authorized to be employed;
- A male applicant who can provide proof of Selective Service registration unless you meet the statutory exemption under Selective Service registration, 5 U.S.C. § 3328. (Bureau of Alcohol, Tobacco, Firearms, and Explosives, 2013)

There is also a student volunteer program, which is

an unpaid program that allows students the opportunity to explore career options and develop personal and professional skills. Student volunteers are exposed to the federal work environment and will learn about the mission and responsibilities of the ATF. Student volunteers may or may not be assigned duties that relate to their courses of study. (Bureau of Alcohol, Tobacco, Firearms, and Explosives, 2013)

Border Patrol

U.S. Customs and Border Protection's (CBP) top priority is keeping terrorists and their weapons from entering the United States. While welcoming legitimate travelers, CBP officers and agents enforce all applicable U.S. laws. CBP prevents narcotics, agricultural pests, and smuggled goods from entering the United States and also arrests those with outstanding criminal warrants. On a typical day, CBP welcomes 1.1 million people into our nation, while approximately 2,800 are apprehended for attempted illegal entry (U.S. Customs and Border Protection, 2013).

The Border Patrol, the largest federal law enforcement agency, is under the arm of the Department of Homeland Security (DHS). Its agents are mobile and uniformed. Spread along the U.S. border in 20 different sectors, the Border Patrol employs 21,394 agents. The Border Patrol has grown quickly since 9/11, when it employed only 9,821 agents. Besides the normal agents, there are also three specialty teams that are trained for activities normally outside the scope of the agency. These specialty units are the Border Patrol Tactical Unit, the Border Patrol Search, Trauma, and Rescue Unit, and the Border Patrol Special Response Team.

When most law enforcement agencies slowed or stopped hiring in 2007, the Border Patrol remained consistent in its hiring and still recruits aggressively. Here are some key requirements for border patrol agents:

- U.S. citizenship
- Referral for employment before a candidate's 40th birthday
- Passing a polygraph test

- Passing a background security investigation
- Residency in the United States for the past 3 years
- No convictions for misdemeanor crimes of domestic violence
- Carrying a firearm

If the Border Patrol hires you, you will be selected for the southwestern border of the United States and must be willing to accept placement anywhere along that border. You can identify one regional preference for placement (South Texas, West Texas and New Mexico, Arizona, or California), but this does not guarantee placement in that region. Your primary responsibilities would be the detection, prevention, and apprehension of undocumented aliens and smugglers of aliens at or near the borders by maintaining surveillance from covert positions; following up leads; responding to electronic sensor alarms and infrared scopes during night operations; monitoring low-light-level television systems; checking aircraft sightings; and interpreting and following tracks, marks, and other physical evidence. You would also perform farm and ranch checks; traffic checks; traffic observation; city patrol; transportation checks; and administrative, intelligence, and anti-smuggling activities.

To work as a Border Patrol agent, you would need to meet some experience requirements, educational requirements, or a combination of both. You can get detailed information about these requirements at USA Jobs (http://www.usajobs.gov). The application process includes an entrance examination. This examination consists of general abilities, logical reasoning, and language ability testing. To be a Border Patrol agent, you must speak and read Spanish. You would be required to take either an artificial language test or a Spanish proficiency test designed to test your Spanish language ability.

To be eligible for the position of Border Patrol agent, you must have a score of at least 70 (excluding veterans' preference points) on the written examination. If you take and fail the written examination, you will not be allowed to retake it for 1 year. If you meet the minimum qualifications, you will be placed in one of the following categories:

- Best qualified: Applicants possessing the type and quality of experience that substantially exceeds the minimum qualifications of the position
- Very highly qualified: Applicants possessing the type and quality of experience that exceeds, to a very considerable extent, the minimum qualifications of the position
- Highly qualified: Applicants possessing the type and quality of experience that exceeds, to a considerable extent, the minimum qualifications of the position
- Well qualified: Applicants possessing the type and quality of experience that marginally exceeds the minimum qualifications of the position and who demonstrate average proficiency in most of the critical competencies of the position
- Qualified: Applicants possessing the type and quality of experience that meets the minimum qualifications of the position

You apply for the Border Patrol online, accessible at USA Jobs. You will be directed to a pretest for the Border Patrol agent position. The pretest provides insight into how well you might do on the entrance examination. There is a link to a study guide at USA Jobs and also at the website of CBP (http://www.cbp.gov). After the pretest, you may be selected for the written test portion at a later time, and you will also have a chance to fill out a more complete application. As with other law enforcement jobs, the hiring process for Border Patrol agents includes a polygraph test, background check, medical exam, and physical exam. There will also be an oral board interview.

There is a mandatory basic training program for Border Patrol agents. Soon after entering duty, you would be sent to the U.S. Border Patrol Academy in Artesia, New Mexico, for approximately 11 weeks of intensive instruction in immigration and nationality laws, law enforcement and Border Patrol–specific operations, driving, physical techniques, firearms, and other courses. All trainees are tested in their language abilities. Those who score below an established benchmark are assigned to an additional 8-week Spanish class at the Border Patrol academy, which will extend their stay to 19 weeks. Upon successful completion of the academy training, all Border Patrol agents begin the Field Training Program and the Post Academy Training Program at their stations and sectors. The Field Training Program will consist of on-the-job, hands-on training with an experienced agent. The Post Academy Training Program is a combination of web-based training and instructor-led training and will require an agent to successfully pass 7 unit exams and 10 web-based scenario exams. The salary range for Border Patrol agents is $38,619 to $63,259.

ICE

ICE is the principal investigative arm of the DHS and the second-largest investigative agency in the federal government. ICE has more than 20,000 employees in offices in all 50 states and 47 foreign countries. Jobs within ICE include deportation officer (DO), detention and deportation officer (DDO), special agent, immigration enforcement agent (IEA), intelligence positions, and investigative support positions.

DOs conduct legal research to support decisions on deportation and exclusion cases and assist attorneys in representing the government in court actions. DOs work with other federal law enforcement officials to identify, locate, and arrest aliens and are responsible for ensuring the physical removal of aliens from the United States. DOs also prepare, present, and defend deportation or exclusion proceedings.

As a DO, you would be working with both criminal and noncriminal aliens at various stages of their deportation and exclusion proceedings. Additional responsibilities include conducting complex investigations, conducting surveillance work, preparing investigative reports, and assisting in seizures.

DDOs are responsible for directing, coordinating, and executing detention and removal activities. DDOs recommend administrative procedures and policies; participate in long-range planning; and provide guidance on detention and removal operations, policies, and requirements. Additional responsibilities may include developing budget estimates and justifications, analyzing programs to recommend improvements, and assisting in investigations.

IEAs are the uniformed presence of immigration enforcement within the U.S. interior. IEAs perform enforcement functions related to the investigation, identification, arrest, prosecution, detention, and deportation of aliens and the apprehension of absconders from removal proceedings. IEAs assist in the processing and removal of aliens to their countries of citizenship.

Criminal investigators, also referred to as special agents, conduct criminal and civil investigations involving national security threats, terrorism, drug smuggling, child exploitation, human trafficking, illegal arms export, financial crimes, identity fraud, benefit fraud, commercial fraud, and more.

[Intelligence officers'] responsibilities include analyzing and evaluating information and preparing intelligence products, along with interfacing with other ICE components and the larger intelligence community, providing on-site intelligence input to field offices involved in major criminal investigations, and coordinating and monitoring ICE intelligence operations.

[Intelligence research assistants'] responsibilities include technical and administrative support and assistance for intelligence operations through a wide range of procedural work and data gathering. [Intelligence research specialists'] responsibilities include analyzing and evaluating information and coordinating and preparing intelligence products.

[Management and program analysts' and mission support specialists'] responsibilities include administrative and management services essential to the operations of the office, including management and information systems, telecommunications, budget, finance, procurement, human resources, training, logistics, property, space, records and files, printing and graphics, mail, travel, and office equipment. (Immigration and Customs Enforcement, 2013)

If you worked as an auditor, you would

plan, perform, and advise on a variety of external audit assignments in connection with financial and work site enforcement audits of suspected criminal organizations and businesses. You [would] provide technical assistance and analysis to criminal investigators and others as required in the course of investigations, including participating in on-site reviews of financial documents and employment documents. You [would] support the other offices by working directly with criminal investigators and other auditors in financial investigations and identifying unauthorized workers in both critical and noncritical sectors during administrative and criminal work site investigations. You [would] be responsible for conducting highly complex financial audits of criminal organizations and business entities. You [would] use a variety of audit procedures, statistical techniques, and data analyses to assemble and develop findings. (Immigration and Customs Enforcement, 2013)

As a criminal research specialist, you would perform

a wide range of duties on criminal, civil, and administrative investigations relating to financial, smuggling, public safety, critical infrastructure, national security, arms and strategic technology, and human smuggling. You [would] provide briefings, advice, and assistance to management on government-wide intelligence operations for the promotion and implementation of a criminal analysis program. Based on reports, assessments, and statistical summaries, you [would] be responsible for planning, conducting, and coordinating complex, multifaceted analytical assignments and research projects in support of diverse investigations on matters involving Homeland Security Investigations (HSI). (Immigration and Customs Enforcement, 2013)

If you were hired as an investigative assistant, you would

provide a wide range of technical, administrative, and clerical support to the investigations program. This includes gathering data and conducting limited inquiries regarding individual case assignments; assisting in and accomplishing case research and trial preparation; and researching, assembling, compiling, and tabulating information and figures for agents' use in investigations, seizures, and evidence in various cases. During mobile investigative activity, you [would] monitor the base station's radio; coordinate and relay information among agents when radio transmissions are hampered; respond to requests by agents for investigative information, which may be of an urgent nature; and use personally developed contacts from other law enforcement agencies [and] state government agencies . . . to obtain the required information. In addition, you [would] compile reports on the progress of various cases, seizures, and arrests and perform a variety of clerical duties for the office and the agents, including typing, receiving and screening mail, and acting as the office timekeeper.

[Mission support specialists] coordinate and perform a wide variety of administrative and management services essential to the operations of the office (including, but not limited to, management and information systems, telecommunications, budget, finance, procurement, human resources, training, logistics, property, space, records and files, printing and graphics, mail, travel, and office equipment) and serve as an advisor to management on assigned administrative matters. In addition, you [would] conduct or participate in the evaluation of administrative programs, systems, and methods and identify ways to improve the efficiency and effectiveness of these services at the local level. You [would] also represent the office in dealings with vendors and organizations within the agency that have primary responsibility for these services. (Immigration and Customs Enforcement, 2013)

As a technical enforcement officer, you would

participate with criminal investigators and other law enforcement officers in active criminal investigations and apply advanced investigative techniques to gather evidence and intelligence that facilitates the prosecution of violations of criminal laws of the United States. You [would] have an extensive working knowledge in the use, instruction, installation, maintenance, troubleshooting, and integration of the full range of electronic surveillance devices, including telephone, video, audio, tracking, radiofrequency technologies, and associated unique surveillance systems. You [would] provide extensive expertise in the planning and execution of the electronic surveillance phases of major investigative and enforcement operations. You [would] serve on high-risk special operations teams. You [would] make covert court-ordered entry into the property of targets of criminal investigations to install equipment for collecting evidence. You [would] also serve as a technical authority and provide training and guidance to journey-level technical enforcement officers, HSI special agents, and other law enforcement officers engaged in electronic surveillance and investigative work, ensuring that mission requirements are fulfilled. (Immigration and Customs Enforcement, 2013)

For all positions, except special agent, you would use an automated, online application system. You can search USA Jobs for openings. Some positions are open to the general public, and others are open only to current government employees. Applications for special agent positions are accepted during an open vacancy announcement. During an open announcement period, applicants will be required to submit résumés with their original applications. Applicants must be at least 21 years of age. The day immediately preceding an individual's 37th birthday would be the last day to be referred for selection consideration. You cannot have a domestic violence or a felony conviction.

Once officially selected as a special agent, you would be required to attend 22 weeks of paid training at the Federal Law Enforcement Training Center (FLETC) in Brunswick, Georgia. The training program is a formalized course of required basic technical instructions that must be successfully completed according to the standards of ICE. Failure to successfully complete the

Jeremiah Deegan: Special Agent – Homeland Security

CJ: Can you give some information about yourself and your job?

JD: My name is Jeremiah Deegan and I have spent the majority of my adult life serving the United States of America. I have served 14 years in the military, serving in both the United States Army—within the United States Army Special Operations Command—and the Air National Guard as a commissioned officer. I have further served in a law enforcement capacity for approximately 8 years now in both munici-pal and jurisdictions. I graduated from the American Military University in 2011 with a bachelor's degree in criminal justice. I am currently a special agent with Homeland Security Investigations (HSI). A special agent with HSI serves as a criminal investi-gator and is responsible for investigating complex transnational crimes including, but not limited to, drug smuggling/trafficking, alien smuggling/human trafficking, firearms trafficking, finan-cial crimes, organized crime, intellectual property rights violations, counterproliferation, national security, and cyber-crimes. The typical duties of my position consist of surveillance, execution of search warrants, execution of arrest warrants, conducting interviews/interrogations, drafting affidavits, report writing, and much more. Special agents work together with the United States Attorney's Office and the local county attorney's offices to ensure that the prosecutors have the facts and evidence required to obtain criminal convictions. Special agents also serve as liaisons with other state and local law enforcement entities in order to exploit all possible investigative methods when conducting a criminal investigation.

CJ: What is your current assignment?

JD: My current assignment involves investigating the illegal transportation of illicit drugs into the United States and the illegal transportation of firearms and currency out of the United States. I have been working in my current assignment for approximately 5 years now and I absolutely love what I do! No two days are ever the same. One day you may be stuck at your desk all day, the next day you could be executing a search warrant and seizing large amounts of drugs and money. However, if somebody is looking for a typical nine to five, Monday through Friday career, this may not the right job for them. This particular position can be very demanding at times. Although there are times where I may not be home for dinner or may get called in to work on a weekend, in my opinion it is well worth it to see some of our nation's worst criminals lose their ill-gotten gains and freedom.

CJ: What are the requirements to be an HSI special agent?

JD: The requirements for an HSI special agent position vary depending on the pay grade the applicant is applying for and may change slightly from vacancy announcement to vacancy announcement. However, a few require-ments always remain the same. First, the applicant must be a United States citizen. The applicant must also be able to legally possess a firearm. This means the applicant cannot have been convicted of a felony or misde-meanor of domestic violence. Aside from the above, the applicant cannot further be a prohibited possessor as per federal statutes. The applicant must also be able to enter on duty with the agency prior to their 37th birthday. The applicant must also be physically able to perform the duties of a criminal investigator and must be able to obtain a top secret security clearance. Although a college degree is preferred, a combination of education and experience may make you a qualified candidate. During the hiring process applicants will go through a series of steps as part of the hiring process. These steps include, but are not limited to, initial application, written exami-nation, interview panel, individual interview, drug screening, medical evaluation, physical fitness test, and back-ground investigation. Once an applicant is contacted and offered a position within the agency, they select their location and await an academy date. Applicants are required to attend two paid academies in Glynco, Georgia, totaling 6 months, which must be completed to continue on as a special agent.

CJ: What advice can you offer students who are interested in pursuing a career with Homeland Security?

JD: If I could offer students pursuing a similar career any advice, it would be to keep yourself out of trouble when you are younger. Social media has become a huge part of our everyday society and adverse information about an applicant on social media could be the deciding factor when it comes to hiring you or the next applicant.

My second piece of advice would be get your foot in the door somewhere within the federal government if you are ultimately aspiring to become a special agent. Once you are in, lateral movement between agencies may be easier than being hired directly off the street. Again, this is an exciting and rewarding career and I hope this gives some insight into the world as a special agent with HSI.

Disclaimer: I am writing this interview on my own behalf and neither ICE/HSI nor DHS are endorsing Arizona State University, the author of this publication, its class, textbook, or program.

training would be grounds for mandatory removal from the position. Failure would result in reassignment to a different position, demotion, or separation by appropriate procedures. ICE agents' salaries vary widely depending on their areas of assignment. An ICE agent in Phoenix could earn $53,000, while an agent in Washington, D.C., might make $75,000 (Immigration and Customs Enforcement, 2013).

U.S. Secret Service

The U.S. Secret Service was created on July 5, 1865, in Washington, D.C., to suppress the creation and circulation of counterfeit currency. The Secret Service's responsibilities were broadened to include the detection of persons perpetrating frauds against the government. This resulted in investigations into the activities of the Ku Klux Klan, nonconforming distilling, smuggling, mail theft, land fraud, and a number of other infractions against federal laws. As the years passed, the Secret Service increased its responsibilities to include protecting the president, president-elect, and former presidents and their spouses and family members, as well as investigating espionage, crimes against federally insured financial institutions, identity theft, telemarketing fraud, computer crimes, and counterfeiting.

In 2008, the Secret Service marked 5 years under the DHS. Since 2003, the Secret Service has made nearly 29,000 criminal arrests for counterfeiting, cybercrimes, and other financial crimes (98% of which resulted in convictions) and seized more than $295 million in counterfeit currency. The Secret Service investigated and closed financial crimes cases in which actual losses amounted to $3.7 billion and prevented a potential loss of more than $12 billion.

Positions with the Secret Service include special agent, uniformed division officer, special officer, administrative personnel, and technical and administrative and clerical support. There are opportunities for veterans, students, those with disabilities, and women. To be considered for a special agent position, you must be a U.S. citizen and meet the following additional criteria:

- Be at least 21 years of age and younger than 37 at the time of receipt of a conditional offer of employment to continue in the application process; applicants with veterans' preference must be at least 21 years of age and younger than 40 at the time of receipt of a conditional offer of employment to continue in the application process

- Have (a) a bachelor's degree from an accredited college or university, (b) 3 years of work experience in the criminal investigative or law enforcement fields that require knowledge and application of laws relating to criminal violations, or (c) an equivalent combination of education and related experience
- Have uncorrected vision no worse than 20/60 binocular, correctable to 20/20 in each eye
- Be in excellent health and physical condition
- Pass a written examination
- Qualify for top secret clearance and undergo a complete background investigation, including in-depth interviews, drug screening, and medical and polygraph examinations
- Certify that you have registered with the Selective Service System or are exempt from having to do so if you are a male applicant born after December 31, 1959

The Secret Service prohibits employees from having visible body markings (including tattoos, body art, and branding) on the head, face, neck, or any area below the wrist bone. If you have visible body markings, you will be required to medically remove such visible body markings at your own expense prior to entering duty with the Secret Service.

Special agent trainees and new uniformed division officer trainees undergo months of intensive training through established programs at the FLETC. For officers, this is followed by a 14-week specialized training program at the Secret Service's training facilities outside Washington, D.C. Training includes coursework in police procedures, firearms, physical fitness, psychology, police-community relations, criminal law, first aid, laws of arrest, search and seizure, physical defense techniques, diplomatic immunity, and international treaties and protocol. On-the-job training and advanced in-service training programs complement the classroom studies.

Upon successful completion of the Criminal Investigator Training Program at FLETC, special agents continue with the 18-week Special Agent Training Course at the Secret Service's training academy. This course focuses on specific Secret Service policies and procedures associated with the dual responsibilities of investigations and protection. Trainees are provided with basic knowledge and advanced application training in counterfeiting, device fraud, and other financial criminal activity; protective intelligence investigations; physical protection techniques; protective advances; and emergency medicine. The core curriculum is augmented with extensive training in marksmanship, control tactics, water survival skills, and physical fitness.

Secret Service agents and officers receive continuous advanced training throughout their careers. In part, this training consists of regular firearms requalification and emergency medicine refresher courses. Agents with protective assignments also participate in unique crisis training simulations that present agents with a variety of real world emergency situations. Agents assigned to offices in the field have the opportunity to acquire advanced training in the area of criminal investigations and are also encouraged to attend training sessions sponsored by other law enforcement agencies. As with other federal law enforcement jobs, the pay scale varies with experience and location. The starting salary for a low-ranking agent is about $44,000 per year. The average Secret Service agent makes closer to $74,000 per year. Top pay for Secret Service agents can be as much as $89,000 per year (U.S. Secret Service, 2013).

U.S. Marshals

The offices of U.S. marshals and deputy marshals were created by the first Congress in the Judiciary Act of 1789. The USMS is the nation's oldest and most versatile federal law enforcement agency, occupying a uniquely central position in the federal justice system.

The USMS is the enforcement arm of the federal courts, involved in virtually every federal law enforcement initiative. Presidentially appointed, U.S. marshals direct the activities of 94 districts, one for each federal judicial district. Approximately 3,925 deputy U.S. marshals and criminal investigators form the backbone of the agency. Among their many duties, they apprehend more than half of all federal fugitives, protect the federal judiciary, operate the Witness Security Program, transport federal prisoners, conduct body searches, enforce court orders and orders of attorneys general involving civil disturbances and acts of terrorism, execute civil and criminal processes, and seize property acquired by criminals through illegal activities (U.S. Marshals Service, 2013).

Career opportunities with the USMS include deputy positions, administrative positions, and detention and aviation enforcement positions. Experienced former law enforcement officers, having served in various capacities and specialties throughout their careers, comprise the agency's court security officer (CSO) program. These contracted CSOs receive limited deputations as special deputy marshals and play a vital role in courthouse security. Using security-screening systems, CSOs detect and intercept weapons and other prohibited items that individuals attempt to bring into federal courthouses. Senior inspectors, deputy marshals, and CSOs provide security at facilities that house court operations. The agency also oversees each aspect of courthouse construction projects, from design through completion, to ensure the safety of federal judges, court personnel, and the public.

In 1995, the USMS and ICE merged air fleets to create the Justice Prisoner and Alien Transportation System (JPATS). The merger created an efficient and effective system for transporting prisoners and criminal aliens. Managed by the USMS, JPATS is one of the largest transporters of prisoners in the world, handling more than 950 requests every day to move prisoners between judicial districts, correctional institutions, and foreign countries. JPATS completes more than 350,000 prisoner and alien movements annually via coordinated air and ground systems.

The USMS currently leads 75 district fugitive task forces and 7 regional fugitive task forces dedicated to locating and apprehending wanted criminals. The USMS has developed close working relationships with other law enforcement agencies on fugitive matters and provides assistance, expertise, and training to agencies on the federal, state, local, and international levels. The USMS is the premier agency to apprehend foreign fugitives believed to be in the United States, and it is the agency responsible for locating and extraditing American fugitives who flee to foreign countries. In fiscal year 2010, the USMS coordinated 805 extraditions and deportations involving 67 countries.

The USMS houses over 63,000 detainees in federal, state, local, and private jails throughout the nation. To house these presentenced prisoners, the USMS contracts with approximately 1,800 state and local governments to rent jail space. Seventy-five percent of the prisoners in USMS custody are detained in state, local, and private facilities. The remainder are housed in Federal Bureau of Prisons facilities.

Each year, the USMS carries out hundreds of special missions related to its broad law enforcement authority and judicial security responsibilities. It also responds to homeland security crises and national emergencies. The USMS Special Operations Group is a specially trained tactical unit composed of deputy marshals who can respond immediately to incidents anywhere in the United States or its territories.

The USMS is responsible for managing and disposing of seized and forfeited properties acquired by criminals through illegal activities. Under the auspices of the U.S. Department of Justice's Asset Forfeiture Program, the USMS manages nearly $3.9 billion worth of property and promptly disposes of assets forfeited by all Department of Justice agencies. The program's goal is to use the net return from forfeited property for law enforcement purposes.

U.S. marshals ensure the safety of witnesses who risk their lives testifying for the government in cases involving organized crime and other significant criminal activities. Since 1971, the USMS has protected, relocated, and given new identities to more than 8,300 witnesses and more than 9,800 of their family members. The successful operation of the Witness Security Program has been recognized as providing a unique and valuable tool in the government's battle against major criminal enterprises and international terrorism. Witness Security Program personnel are the world's leading authorities and foremost experts on witness security matters, providing guidance and training to numerous government officials throughout the world.

To work for the USMS you must be a U.S. citizen and meet the following additional criteria:

- Age 21 to 36 years (must be appointed before 37th birthday)
- Possession of a bachelor's degree, completion of 3 years of qualifying work experience, or a combination of education and experience equivalent to the GL-07 level
- Successful completion of a structured interview, background investigation, and other assessments
- Medical qualifications and excellent physical condition
- Passing a rigorous 17.5-week basic training program at the USMS Basic Training Academy in Glynco, Georgia

The hiring process for the USMS may take from 9 to 12 months depending on the various assessment phases. If you are hired, you may be placed within any of the 94 districts throughout the continental United States. Deputies are assigned to their first duty stations at the need of the USMS. All candidates are required to remain at their initial duty stations for a minimum of 3 years. A mobility agreement and memorandum of understanding must be signed prior to employment. The pay scale is similar to other federal jobs. You would start at between $38,511 and $48,708.

TSA

Resulting from the terrorist attacks on September 11, 2001, the Aviation and Transportation Security Act established TSA and required the completion of more than 30 mandates by the end of 2002. In the largest civilian undertaking in the history of the United States, TSA met each one of these initial requirements including:

- Assuming responsibility for all civil aviation security functions from the Federal Aviation Administration
- Hiring, training, and deploying security officers for over 400 commercial airports from Guam to Alaska in 12 months
- Providing 100 percent screening of all checked baggage for explosives by December 31, 2002

In March 2003, TSA transferred from the Department of Transportation to the Department of Homeland Security (U.S. Department of Homeland Security, Transportation Security Administration, 2015). Programs within TSA include:

- Federal Air Marshals
- Visible Intermodal Prevention and Response
- Federal Flight Deck Officer
- Armed Security Officer
- Crew Member Self Defense
- LEO Travel
- LEO Reimbursement

Federal air marshals (FAMs) are deployed to detect, deter, and defeat hostile acts targeting U.S. air carriers, airports, passengers, and crews. They operate independently without backup and rank among those federal law enforcement officers that hold the highest standard for handgun accuracy. They blend in with passengers and rely on their training, including investigative techniques, criminal terrorist behavior recognition, firearms proficiency, aircraft specific tactics, and close quarters self-defense measures to protect the flying public. They work closely with other law enforcement agencies to accomplish their mission, and staff several positions at different organizations such as the National Counterterrorism Center, the National Targeting Center, and on the FBI's Joint Terrorism Task Forces (U.S. Department of Homeland Security, Transportation Security Administration, 2015).

After the Madrid train bombing in 2004, TSA developed the Visible Intermodal Prevention and Response (VIPR) program to allow TSA security and law enforcement assets to enhance federal, state, and local law enforcement and security agencies in the transportation domain. TSA's VIPR teams provide a full range of law enforcement and security capability; the exact makeup of VIPR teams is determined jointly with local authorities and can include federal air marshals, transportation security officers (TSOs), behavior detection officers (BDOs), TSA certified explosive detection canine teams, transportation security inspectors (TSIs), transportation security specialists–explosives (TSSEs), explosives operational support, security and explosive screening technology, radiological/nuclear detection, and local law enforcement officers (U.S. Department of Homeland Security, Transportation Security Administration, 2015).

Adding to improved security at airport checkpoints, the use of federal air marshals, and the hardening of cockpit doors, the Transportation Security Administration developed the Federal Flight Deck Officer program as an additional layer of security. Under this program, eligible flight crewmembers are authorized by the Transportation Security Administration to use firearms to defend against criminal violence or any attempts to gain control of an aircraft. A flight crewmember may be a flight engineer, pilot, or navigator assigned to the flight (U.S. Department of Homeland Security, Transportation Security Administration, 2015).

The Crew Member Self Defense Training (CMSDT) program is available to all actively employed or temporarily furloughed U.S. passenger and cargo crewmembers. The program is available at 22 sites nationwide. Crewmembers are encouraged to register to attend this 4-hour hands-on training developed by the Office of Law Enforcement/Federal Air Marshal Service to help prepare them to face potential threat situations—both on and off the aircraft. CMSDT is provided at no cost to crewmembers. They are welcome to attend the training as often as desired (U.S. Department of Homeland Security, Transportation Security Administration, 2015).

Armed security officers (ASOs) are specially trained law enforcement officers who are authorized by the TSA to fly on each general aviation aircraft operating into or out of Ronald Reagan Washington National Airport (DCA). In order to serve as an ASO, you must be nominated by a DCA Access Standard Security Program approved (or pending) company, meet certain eligibility criteria, and complete an application process that includes background, criminal history, and employment verification checks. Applicants meeting the established criteria must then successfully complete two days of training with the Federal Air Marshal Service, at which time they will be credentialed and authorized by the TSA to serve on general aviation flights into DCA (U.S. Department of Homeland Security, Transportation Security Administration, 2015).

The Office of Law Enforcement/Federal Air Marshal Service oversees the Law Enforcement Officers Flying Armed program. To qualify to fly armed, federal regulations require that an officer meets the following basic requirements:

- Be a federal law enforcement officer (LEO) or a full-time municipal, county, or state LEO who is a direct employee of a government agency
- Be sworn and commissioned to enforce criminal statutes or immigration statutes
- Be authorized by the employing agency to have the weapon in connection with assigned duties
- Have completed the training program "Law Enforcement Officers Flying Armed"

In addition to the above requirements, the officer must need the weapon to be accessible from the time he or she checks the weapon until being claimed after deplaning. The need to have the weapon accessible must be based on one of the following:

- The provision of protective duty, for instance, assigned to a principal or advance team, or on travel required to be prepared to engage in a protective function
- The conduct of a hazardous surveillance operation
- On official travel required for reporting to another location, armed and prepared for duty
- Employed as a federal LEO, whether or not on official travel, and armed in accordance with an agency-wide policy governing that type of travel established by the employing agency by directive or policy statement
- Control of a prisoner, or an armed LEO on a round trip ticket returning to or from escorting a prisoner

The LEO Reimbursement Program (LEO RP) was established to provide reimbursement to airport operators in the wake of the new LEO require-ments mandated by the Aviation Transportation Security Act (ATSA). The LEO RP continues maximizing the mutual benefits of the program through consolidated efforts with our airport stakeholders, industry partners, and TSA stakeholders to fulfill their common goal of ensuring traveler safety (U.S. Department of Homeland Security, Transportation Security Administration, 2015).

To apply for a position with TSA, you need to first find the job that is the best fit for you. Learn about the TSA and decide what part of their agency interests you. Next, find an opportunity near you by viewing announcements on their website: https://www.tsa.gov. The job announcement will provide important information about job qualifications, duties, salary, location, benefits, and security requirements. You will be able to determine if your interests, education, and professional background make you a good candidate. All TSA jobs require U.S. citizenship and successful completion of a full background investigation. In addition, all candidates interested in security officer positions must pass a medical examination, be able to read, speak, and write English, and pass a physical ability test, a drug and alcohol screening, and an aptitude test. Many careers have different application instructions, so you need to carefully follow instructions posted for each job. The instructions guide you through the application process, providing detailed information on the questions, forms, and format that must be addressed and used to capture your qualifications for the job. Make sure to submit all required documents and pay close attention to the application due date and application procedures, which vary for different jobs. The names of best-qualified candidates will be forwarded to a hiring official. If you are one of the best qualified candidates, the supervisor or hiring official may interview you in person or by telephone, or in rare cases may hire you based solely on your application materials. Once an offer is extended, you receive further instructions.

Non-Sworn Positions

Just as with local and state police, all federal law enforcement agencies are composed of sworn and non-sworn employees. With rare exceptions, if sworn employees take polygraph tests, civilians, interns, and volunteers will also be required to take them. Some non-sworn positions are paid as well as or better than the sworn assignments. Some positions can offer challenges and excitement without the person ever carrying a gun. The application process differs somewhat for each type of job. At a minimum, most non-sworn hiring processes involve a résumé review, an interview, a background check, and a polygraph test. Non-sworn positions are just as hard earned as sworn jobs, but you may find a better fit for your interests and skills outside of enforcement responsibilities. It is easier to move around in federal jobs once inside than it is to enter a federal job initially.

Diversity in Federal Law Enforcement

Just like local police agencies, federal law enforcement agencies need representation from all cultures, races, and genders. According to the Bureau of Justice Statistics (Reaves, 2012),

Women accounted for 15.5% of federal officers with arrest and firearm authority in 2008. This was a slightly lower percentage than in 2004 (16.1%) but higher than in 1996 (14.0%). About a third (34.3%)

of federal officers were members of racial or ethnic minorities in 2008. This was only a slight increase compared with 2004 (33.2%) but more substantial compared with 1996 (28.0%). The increase in minority representation from 1996 to 2008 is primarily attributable to an increase in the percentage of Hispanic or Latino officers, from 13.1% to 19.8%. The percentage of African American or black officers in 2008 (10.4%) was lower than in 2004 (11.4%) or 1996 (11.5%).

Women and minorities currently hold leadership positions as well. The DEA is currently under the direction of administrator Michele Leonhart, the first female career law enforcement officer to lead a federal law enforcement organization. Janet Napolitano is the first woman to serve as the U.S. secretary of Homeland Security, the third largest cabinet department. And of course, the current president of the United States, Barack Obama, is the first African American to hold that office. Don't let the fear of discrimination hold you back from your dream job! Great things are happening in our country in the area of diversity; come be part of it!

Experience

Common requirements among federal law enforcement jobs are a college degree and experience. Most students obtain the degree without difficulty, but getting the required experience is a tougher hurdle. When trying out for a federal position, you will be going up against those who have experience, so why would a federal agency choose you if you are fresh out of college and have no background in a related field? If you focus more on getting the experience during and after college instead of the long-range goal of a federal job, the climb will be much smoother. Consider either military or local police experience as part of your ladder. If the public sector is closed down at the time you graduate, consider working in the private sector in loss prevention, risk management, or corporate security. Settle for earning your way to the top and not counting on a boost. Get the experience! If you resolve to climb each rung of the career ladder, you are likelier to make the right decisions at the right time.

Summary

Federal law enforcement is prestigious work and therefore very competitive. Most federal law enforcement is similar to detective work in local agencies in which no uniform is worn and employees specialize in areas of expertise without much variation in their fields of work. As enforcers of federal crimes, they handle such things as terrorism; illegal immigration; bank robberies; drug enforcement; organized and white-collar crime; crimes involving alcohol, tobacco, firearms, and explosives; and interstate crimes.

The FBI is basically a national security organization that partners with countries all over the globe to combat serious security threats. The FBI has a total of 36,074 employees, including 13,913 special agents and 22,161 support professionals, such as intelligence analysts, language specialists, scientists, information technology specialists, and other miscellaneous professionals. All applicants for the FBI special agent position must qualify through one of five special agent entry programs. These programs include accounting, computer science and information technology, language, the law, and diversified fields.

The DEA was created through an executive order in July 1973 to establish a single unified command to combat drugs. Today the DEA employs nearly 5,000 special agents. Some of the positions you could obtain with the DEA include special agent, diversion investigator, forensic scientist, intelligence researcher, and professional and administrative positions.

The ATF was transferred under the Homeland Security Act to the Department of Justice in 2003. The ATF investigates and prosecutes terrorist acts and violent crimes that involve explosives, arson and firearms, repeat and violent offenders, criminal gangs, the illegal use and trafficking of firearms and explosives, and the illegal diversion of alcohol and tobacco products. There are positions for special agents, investigators, and attorneys, as well as professional and technical positions and internships.

The Border Patrol, the largest federal law enforcement agency, is under the aegis of the DHS. Its agents are mobile and uniformed. Spread along the U.S. border in 20 different sectors, the Border Patrol employs 21,394 agents. Besides the normal agents, there are also three specialty teams that are trained for activities normally outside the scope of the agents. These specialty units are the Border Patrol Tactical Unit, the Border Patrol Search, Trauma, and Rescue Unit, and the Border Patrol Special Response Team. The Border Patrol still recruits aggressively.

ICE is the principal investigative arm of the DHS and the second-largest investigative agency in the federal government. ICE has more than 20,000 employees in offices in all 50 states and 47 foreign countries. Jobs within ICE include DO, DDO, homeland security special agent, and IEA, as well as intelligence positions and investigative support positions.

The Secret Service was created on July 5, 1865, in Washington, D.C. The Secret Service's responsibilities include protecting the president, president-elect, former presidents, and their spouses and family members, as well as investigating land fraud, espionage, crimes against federally insured financial institutions, some telemarketing frauds, some identity thefts, computer crimes, and counterfeiting. Careers with the Secret Service include special agent, uniformed division officer, special officer, administrative personnel, and technical and administrative and clerical support. There are opportunities for veterans, students, those with disabilities, and women.

The USMS was created by the first Congress in the Judiciary Act of 1789. It is the nation's oldest and most versatile federal law enforcement agency. The USMS occupies a uniquely central position in the federal justice system. It is the enforcement arm of the federal courts, involved in virtually every federal law enforcement initiative. Among their many duties, U.S. marshals apprehend more than half of all federal fugitives, protect the federal judiciary, operate the Witness Security Program, transport federal prisoners, conduct body searches, enforce court orders and orders of attorneys general involving civil disturbances and acts of terrorism, execute civil and criminal processes, and seize property acquired by criminals through illegal activities. Career opportunities with the USMS include deputy positions, administrative positions, and detention and aviation enforcement positions.

Resulting from the terrorist attacks on September 11, 2001, the Aviation and Transportation Security Act established TSA and required the completion of more than 30 mandates by the end of 2002. Programs within TSA include Federal Air Marshals, Visible Intermodal Prevention and Response, Federal Flight Deck Officer, Armed Security Officer, Crew Member Self Defense, LEO Travel, and LEO Reimbursement. To apply for a position with TSA you need to first find the job that is the best fit for you. Next, find an opportunity near you by viewing announcements on their website: https://www.tsa.gov. You need to carefully follow instructions posted for each job. Make sure to submit all required documents and pay close attention to the application due date and application procedures, which vary for different the jobs. The names of best-qualified candidates will be forwarded to a hiring official.

There are sworn and non-sworn positions at all law enforcement agencies. Some non-sworn positions are just as challenging and pay as well as (or better than) sworn law enforcement positions. Women and minorities are well represented in federal jobs and are continuously being recruited. Students who want to work for the federal government should gain experience first to increase their chances of being hired.

DISCUSSION QUESTIONS

1. Should all federal law enforcement agencies standardize and use the same requirements for all positions? Why or why not?

2. Should state and local police be held to the same standards for hiring as federal law enforcement (education, experience, drug use, etc.)? Why or why not?

3. Do federal law enforcement (sworn) employees have more authority than state and local police? Explain.

4. Do any of the requirements for federal law enforcement seem unnecessary or too strict? Explain.

5. Which federal agency interests you the most? Why?

REFERENCES

Bureau of Alcohol, Tobacco, Firearms, and Explosives. (2013). *Internships*. Retrieved from https://www.atf.gov/careers/internships

Federal Bureau of Investigation. (2013). *Careers*. Retrieved from https://www.fbijobs.gov/?

Immigration and Customs Enforcement. (2013). *Occupations*. Retrieved from http://www.ice.gov/careers/occupations

Reaves, B. A. (2007, June). Census of state and local law enforcement agencies, 2004 (NCJ 212749). *Bureau of Justice Statistics bulletin*. Retrieved June 3, 2013, from http://bjs.ojp.usdoj.gov/content/pub/pdf/csllea04.pdf

Reaves, B. A. (2012, June). Federal law enforcement officers, 2008 (NCJ 238250). *Bureau of Justice Statistics bulletin*. Retrieved June 7, 2013, from http://www.bjs.gov/content/pub/pdf/fleo08.pdf

U.S. Customs and Border Protection. (2013). *Careers*. Retrieved from http://www.cbp.gov/careers

U.S. Department of Homeland Security, Transportation Security Administration. (2015). *Transportation Security Administration*. Retrieved from https://www.tsa.gov

U.S. Drug Enforcement Administration. (2013). *Careers: Occupations*. Retrieved from http://www.justice.gov/dea/careers/occupations.shtml

U.S. Marshals Service. (2013). *Career opportunities*. Retrieved from http://www.usmarshals.gov/careers/

U.S. Secret Service. (2013). *Special agent*. Retrieved from http://www.secretservice.gov/join/careers/agents/

9

Private Security and Investigations

Introduction

The terrorist attacks of September 11, 2001, initiated drastic changes in the United States, including enhanced security along our borders and within our cities, counties, and states. The private security business boomed and was at long last recognized as an important appendage to law enforcement. Why weren't private security personnel used to a greater degree prior to 9/11? Why did private security rapidly expand faster than law enforcement (other than border patrol, of course)?

Security officers have been employed for a very long time at hospitals, shopping malls, apartment complexes, and individual businesses after hours; for transporting money and guarding buildings during remodeling or new construction; at the entrances to big events or important government buildings; and during temporary hoarding, such as in Black Friday or Christmas sales at retail stores. Sometimes the presence of security is essential for insurance purposes, and sometimes businesses hire security officers just because the benefits outweigh the costs.

Sometimes businesses choose to hire off-duty police officers as security personnel even though the cost is greater. They may feel that the advantage of having a sworn peace officer on the premises offsets the additional cost. What are the advantages? It depends on the purpose of the security. When a business is concerned mainly with deterring crime, a security officer's visibility will likely do the job just fine. If a business or government agency foresees a likelihood of arrests and physical confrontations, using a trained, certified, gun-toting peace officer may be the most prudent choice.

There has traditionally been some tension between private security and the public police. Although there have been substantial improvements, many police officers have long looked at security officers as inferior and thus have not displayed adequate respect. Security officers who might already feel inferior to sworn law enforcement personnel don't appreciate being made to feel that way by the police. Why the lack of respect? Well, it is no secret that being hired as a police officer is difficult, the training is intensive, and the authority and empowerment are inimitable and comprehensive. Being hired at a private security firm sometimes entails mediocre standards (with no polygraph testing) followed by minimal training and resulting in slightly higher than minimum wages in exchange for undesirable hours. This is not to say that security officers are any less qualified than police officers, but likely those who crave law enforcement careers, and could qualify, would choose to do so over working in private security. Also, those who desire police work but don't feel that they can qualify, or those who leave or retire from police work, can find great satisfaction in security work. One can also find positions in the security arena that are practical careers with good pay, reasonable benefits, and enough challenge and excitement to impel someone out of bed each day for work.

A new trend during the community era, and particularly following 9/11, has been for law enforcement to work closer with the community, especially all the personnel who may find themselves as first responders to terrorist activities or other catastrophic events. There has been an increase in training for schools, hospitals, and security firms in the area of incident command. Some police agencies have invited security officers to join them in certain training activities. Many police personnel, who have historically had the "us versus them" attitude, have reconsidered the way they view civilians, including security officers, and respect them as important parts of a larger team. Police officers, as well as the community as a whole, realize the benefits of having full-time, visible, security at places such as water treatment plants, power plants, dams, financial centers, oil refineries, and railroad lines. Why did it take a catastrophic event such as 9/11 to connect law enforcement to all these available sources? Why didn't law enforcement involve its community partners more efficiently in crime prevention strategies decades ago? This can be answered with this parable, which has been used throughout the world, called "The Flying Turkeys":

> There once was a group of turkeys. They spent their days doing turkey stuff—gobbling, hanging out, dreading Thanksgiving, and not flying.
>
> Then one day, one of the turkeys announced that they were all invited to a seminar where they would be trained by a flying turkey. They were so stoked, because this flying turkey was going to teach them how to fly! They couldn't believe it. They got their group together and walked to the seminar.
>
> They stood around in their group waiting.
>
> Then all of a sudden, one of the turkeys noticed something in the sky coming toward them. As it got closer, they saw that it was a flying turkey!
>
> He swooped down and landed in the middle of the group. It was incredible!
>
> For the next few hours, the flying turkey taught them all about flying. He showed them how to use their wings and the wind to fly.

Later that day, he brought them to a cliff, and one by one, each turkey jumped off and flew. It was amazing. The turkeys couldn't believe it. They soared through the air. They went above the clouds. They did flips and dive bombs. They did things they never could have imagined.

It was the greatest experience of their lives. They now knew how to fly. They were so excited. They would never have to touch the ground again! They felt amazing. This was so much better and quicker than walking. Why didn't they learn this before?

The seminar ended and they all landed back at the main seminar area. The turkeys waved goodbye as their flying instructor took off and flew to another turkey seminar.

The group of turkeys then talked all about their great day as they walked home.

It is a normal tendency for all of us to be somewhat slow to change. We tend to enjoy our comfort zones. For years, police officers would have briefings, drive to and around their beats looking for bad guys and answering calls, and then return to the station to let someone else have a turn. The crime rate continued to rise, more officers were hired to drive around, and the crime rate continued to rise. Then someone came up with the idea of crime analysis, and someone else suggested a repeat-offender program, and yet another innovator realized the value of involving the community in crime prevention and problem solving. Yet even today, not every agency has adopted these programs and strategies to their fullest potential. Although using resources such as private security in conjunction with police isn't necessarily a cutting-edge vision, it's exciting to see these two powerhouses start to come together toward a common goal.

Some of the prominent jobs related to private security include security officer, private investigator, loss prevention officer, and armed security guard. These jobs carry a level of danger, but most do not involve carrying a firearm. Many security jobs are also done independently, without backup close by. In some positions, such as loss prevention, you are rarely empowered to make arrests even if the law allows you to. When you are in uniform, the public associates you with peace officers and therefore has high expectations of your assistance, regardless of your limited authority and responsibility. Nonetheless, private security work is a necessary entity in our nation and a continuously growing industry. Some positions in the private sector are actually very similar to law enforcement work. An important difference for students is the age requirement. Most security agencies hire applicants at 18 years old. This could be a great way to get work experience on your résumé and make some decent money while going to school. Let's explore some of the possible careers.

Security Officer

AlliedBarton Security Services provides trained security personnel to many industries, including commercial real estate, higher education, health care, residential communities, chemical and petrochemical, government, manufacturing and distribution, financial institutions, and shopping centers. Their more than 55,000 employees and 120 offices across the country service a client base of several thousand, which includes approximately 200 Fortune 500 companies nationwide. AlliedBarton is headquartered in Conshohocken, Pennsylvania, and has been American owned and managed since 1957. AlliedBarton was the first security service company selected as one of *Training Magazine*'s Top 125. They offer on-the-job, web-based, and ongoing training programs for all personnel, from security officers through executive-level managers. Their training includes industry-specific programs that are customized for the security challenges in several of the markets they serve. By using employee retention programs and promotions from within, AlliedBarton is able to foster a culture of quality security officers and customer satisfaction. AlliedBarton's security officers are proactive, responsive, and ever ready to meet clients' needs. A security officer position with AlliedBarton in Scottsdale, Arizona, would include patrolling facilities or manning a post as instructed and serving as a general security presence and visible deterrent to crime and client rule infractions. You would detect suspicious activities and watch for criminal acts or client rule infractions at or near an assigned post, which may be a threat to the property, client, or employees at the site. You would report all incidents, accidents, and medical emergencies and respond to emergencies, such as medical and bomb threats, and to alarms, such as fire and intrusion, by following emergency response procedures. AlliedBarton requires its security officers to be at least 18 years of age, to have a high school diploma or General Educational Development (GED) certificate, to have at least 10 years of verifiable employment history, to have at least one verifiable employer, to have no criminal convictions as specified under AlliedBarton's guidelines, to have the ability to communicate effectively both orally and in writing in the English language, to be authorized to work in the United States, and to have the ability to perform the essential functions of the position with or without reasonable accommodation. To work for AlliedBarton, you would need to pass a pre-employment drug screening, to successfully complete AlliedBarton's security officer basic course exam, the ability to maintain satisfactory attendance and punctuality standard, a neat and professional appearance, a friendly and professional demeanor, the ability to provide quality customer service, and the ability to handle typical and crisis situations efficiently and effectively at client sites. AlliedBarton also prefers that you have customer service experience, above-average computer skills, and report-writing experience.

AlliedBarton is the largest American-owned security company in the United States. Hiring military veterans and reserves is an important part of AlliedBarton's recruiting strategy. The company values the dedication, leadership skills, and commitment to excellence that the nation's military personnel bring to the organization. The position in Scottsdale pays $11.28 per hour (AlliedBarton Security Services, 2013).

Some colleges employ security officers to supplement their campus police forces. One such institution is the University of Arkansas at Little Rock, which has a position for a security officer who also doubles as a dispatcher. The basic duties include the following:

- Operating computer consoles, video monitoring equipment, and other communication devices in the public safety department to receive requests for assistance, identify the nature of a situation, and dispatch public safety officers or other personnel as required
- Performing security checks of campus buildings for unauthorized persons, illegal entry, and damaged or missing property
- Monitoring fire, security, and environmental alarm systems and notifying the proper authorities
- Maintaining accurate records of calls and other communications using the methods prescribed by the public safety department
- Acting as a link for coordinating the activities of police officers, security guards, and emergency responders from outside agencies
- Preparing required reports, including incident reports, lost and found, and any reports requested by public safety officers
- Operating the Arkansas Crime Information Center terminal in accordance with state law, Arkansas Crime Information Center rules, and university public safety procedures
- Notifying the public safety supervisor of any observed safety concerns on the campus
- Directing traffic and assisting with crowd control and emergency situations as directed by public safety officers
- Providing routine information to visitors and directing them to campus departments and services

The education requirement for this position is the formal equivalent of a high school diploma plus 1 year of specialized training in communications or a related field, plus 1 year of experience in the public safety environment. For this position, you would also need the following skills and knowledge base:

- Knowledge of communication equipment and the procedures and federal rules and regulations concerning dispatch equipment
- Knowledge of emergency response procedures and practices
- Ability to direct traffic for an orderly flow
- Ability to prepare reports of incidents and accidents

For this job, activities occur inside and outside in extreme cold temperatures (below 32°F) for periods of more than 1 hour and in extreme heat (above 100°F) for periods of more than 1 hour. You might be in situations of extreme noise requiring you to shout in order to be heard. There are hazards with a job such as this that can cause bodily injury, such as proximity to moving mechanical parts and electrical currents, directing traffic, and, of course, dealing with disruptive individuals.

This position is subject to a pre-employment criminal background check, sex offender registry check, and drug screening. A criminal conviction or an arrest pending adjudication alone will not disqualify an applicant in the absence of a relationship to the requirements of the position. The background check information is used in a confidential, nondiscriminatory manner consistent with state and federal law. The salary for this job is $18,885 (University of Arkansas at Little Rock, 2013).

Surely you have noticed security personnel at the airport. They are the men and women who examine your license and boarding pass, check them again at another point, and stand at the scanners looking over your shoes, purse, computer, and carry-on bags. You could be one of them! As a transportation security officer at Klamath Falls Airport in Oregon, you could earn anywhere from $29,131 to $43,697 per year, depending on your value, which is based on experience and expertise.

As a transportation security officer in Klamath Falls, you would provide security and protection for air travelers, airports, and aircraft. This includes the following:

- Operating screening equipment to identify dangerous objects in baggage, cargo, and on passengers and preventing those objects from being transported onto aircraft
- Performing searches, both hand-wand and pat-down
- Controlling terminal entry and exit points
- Staying focused amid crowd distractions, time pressure, and disruptive and angry passengers
- Identifying and locating potentially life-threatening or mass-destructive devices
- Making effective decisions in both crisis and routine situations

For a position such as this, you would need to be a U.S. citizen or U.S. national at the time of your application submission; to be at least 18 years of age; to be proficient in English (i.e., able to read, write, speak, and listen); and to have a high school diploma or GED certificate or at least 1 year of full-time work experience in the security industry, aviation screening, or as an x-ray technician.

If you were to meet the minimum qualifications, you would be invited to take a computer-based test to confirm English-language proficiency and evaluate your X-ray interpretation aptitude. Upon passing this test, you would be eligible to be scheduled for additional assessments, which include a color vision test; a structured interview to determine, among other qualities, your decision-making skills and your ability to work with teams and the general public; a drug screening; and a job-related medical evaluation that includes a vision exam, hearing exam, and adequate joint mobility exam. Upon passing these assessments, you would be subject to a prehiring background investigation. After passing this background investigation and undergoing a qualitative evaluation of the criteria above, you would be placed in one of the following categories:

- Best qualified: Applicants demonstrating a superior level of all evaluation criteria
- Highly qualified: Applicants demonstrating a more-than-satisfactory level of the evaluation criteria
- Qualified: Applicants demonstrating minimal or basic satisfactory qualifications, with general knowledge, skills, and abilities

The Transportation Security Administration provides employment preference to eligible veterans as defined in the Aviation and Transportation Security Act and to those eligible under the provisions of Title 5 of the U.S. Code, Section 2108 (Transportation Security Administration, 2013).

Private Investigator

An enjoyable position for some may be as a private investigator. Investigators are often hired by large businesses, attorneys' offices, and insurance companies. An example of an investigator position exists in the California Department of Insurance. In this position, you would conduct felony criminal investigations of insurance fraud and related penal statutes, both state and federal. You would make arrests, interrogate suspects, interview witnesses, work with informants, prepare comprehensive written reports, and use sophisticated surveillance and electronic evidence-gathering equipment. Investigators are expected to work undercover and to testify as expert witnesses for prosecutors in state and federal courts. Investigators must work unusual hours on short notice and also travel throughout the state. As an investigator, you would have to carry a weapon and successfully qualify at quarterly weapon qualifications and meet all California Commission on Peace Officer Standards and Training requirements. In this position, you would perform a full range of peace officer duties and responsibilities in the accomplishment of your assignments. Because this position is designated as a peace officer, a background check, fingerprinting, and a psychological screening and medical examination are required. Applicants with prior fraud investigation experience are preferred.

To be eligible for a position such as this, you would need to possess a degree from a 4-year college with a major in criminal justice, law enforcement, criminology, administration of justice, or police science or a minor in

Tim Newton: Patrol Sergeant Private Security

CJ: What is your current position?

TN: I am currently a patrol sergeant for a proprietary security company (Cojak Properties, LLC) in Phoenix, Arizona.

CJ: What are your typical job duties?

TN: I supervise deployment of armed security officers to two large apartment complexes. We deal with a variety of scenarios, including criminal trespass, possession of illegal drugs, graffiti/vandalism, burglary, and domestic violence. We perform foot patrol of the properties and watch for signs of criminal activity. We do have arrest powers on the properties that we patrol, but we must witness a crime take place in order to make an arrest.

CJ: How long have you been at your current assignment?

TN: I have been in my current position since January 2012.

CJ: What other positions have you held prior to this one?

TN: I have over 8 years of experience in the security field, including both armed and unarmed. I was employed as a mall security officer at Fiesta Mall in Mesa, Arizona, in 2008 and was promoted to day shift supervisor in January of 2009. I have also been employed as a security officer at a homeless shelter in Phoenix, Arizona, and at a gated community. I enjoy my current position as a patrol sergeant with Cojak Properties, LLC, the best. I feel that we are helping to provide a safer environment for the families who live in the apartment complexes, while at the same time assisting Phoenix Police with getting some truly bad people off of the streets.

CJ: What are the requirements/qualifications for your job?

TN: A common prerequisite for promotion into management in the private security field is a minimum educational level of an associate's degree in criminal justice or criminal investigations. Good, concise report writing skills are also a must, as are good communication skills in general.

CJ: What steps did you go through during hiring?

TN: I submitted my résumé and went through the interview process, where I was questioned regarding how I would react to certain incidents and scenarios that may arise during the performance of my duties, as well as questions related to my education and work experience.

CJ: What advice can you offer students who might be interested in pursuing a similar career?

TN: Private policing/security can be very challenging, particularly in urban housing projects and apartment complexes. This is not a career for everybody, but it can be very rewarding knowing that you are helping to provide a safer place for people to live. Many tenants regularly express their thanks and appreciation for performing our duties. I would advise college students who would consider this career path to focus on report writing, criminal justice management, and policing. Be prepared to be occasionally subpoenaed to testify in court. Listen to your instructors, in particular if they are retired or former police officers. These folks have so much knowledge and experience to draw from and give very useful advice.

law enforcement, criminology, administration of justice, or police science, with evidence that the following courses or their equivalents have been completed:

- Introduction to criminal justice
- Introduction to criminal law
- Basic investigation
- Evidence
- Criminal procedure
- Philosophy of law

The California Department of Insurance also accepts a minimum of 2 years of peace officer experience in a criminal investigative assignment at a government agency and 2 years of college or recent experience in state service as a peace officer investigating automobile, workers' compensation, or property and casualty insurance fraud. The department also desires that an investigator have the ability to liaise with other law enforcement and prosecuting agencies in the region, be a graduate of the Regular Basic Course or the Specialized Investigators Basic Course, and have verbal and written fluency in Spanish, Vietnamese, Tagalog, Russian, Korean, Chinese, or another foreign language. The salary for this position ranges from $46,824 to $74,328 (California State Personnel Board, 2013).

Another example of an investigator position is Medicare fraud investigator in Hingham, Connecticut. The mission is to detect and deter fraud and abuse in Medicare. This position requires the use of a variety of tools to initiate referrals, identify subjects, develop investigations for law enforcement, and assist in education and overpayment recovery. The investigator works with internal resources and external agencies to develop investigations and take corrective actions as well as respond to requests for data and support.

The essential functions for this job include performing research and drawing conclusions; presenting issues of concern; citing regulatory violations; alleging schemes or scams to defraud the government; organizing case files accurately and thoroughly documenting all steps taken; communicating effectively and professionally, internally and externally; composing correspondence, reports, and referral summary letters; educating providers, provider associations, law enforcement, and other contractors and beneficiary advocacy groups on program safeguard matters; interpreting laws and regulations; handling confidential information; reporting work activities on a timely basis; working independently and as a member of a team to deliver high-quality work; and attending meetings, training sessions, and conferences.

The prerequisites for this position are a bachelor's degree, 3 to 5 years of Medicare experience, and a law enforcement background. It is necessary to have strong investigative skills, strong communication and organization skills, and experience in reviewing claims for technical requirements, analyzing data, and developing fraud investigations. Investigator positions can pay very well depending on experience and expertise.

Innovative Systems Group (ISG), in Chicago, employs a private investigator part time (paid per diem). ISG is a national investigative and medical management services firm specializing in cost containment and antifraud services. This position involves surveillance and field investigative work. The ideal investigator has a strong work ethic, is self-motivated, has good problem-solving skills, and is team oriented. If you had this position you would need to be able to work independently, have strong time management skills, have the flexibility to travel, and have strong communication skills. You would need to be willing to work flexible hours, including weekday, weekend, and evening hours.

It is preferred that a private investigator at ISG have a criminal justice degree, but it is required that the candidate for this position have a permanent employee registration card, experience in workers' compensation surveillance, a reliable vehicle, a cell phone, a hard-drive camera and Pinnacle software with the ability to upload video with a time stamp to the server, proficiency using Microsoft Word, and the ability to write detailed reports (Innovative Systems Group, 2013).

You could join a special investigations unit (SIU) such as the one in Portland, Oregon, with GlobalOptions, an international investigative firm servicing the insurance, government, and legal communities. They perform surveillance, activity checks, and background investigations on workers' compensation, auto liability, general liability, and long- and short-term disability claims. An SIU investigator conducts red-flag file reviews, claim file evaluations, and field investigations to investigate and document suspected fraudulent activity related to insurance claims.

If you worked with the SIU as an investigator, you would prepare evaluation reports, updates, state-mandated reporting forms, and documented fraud referrals. You would obtain, document, and organize evidence that is suitable for presentation in a court of law to establish the presence of material misrepresentations. You would educate claims staff regarding insurance fraud, red flags, and the SIU process. You would need to be familiar with the claims processes for multiple lines of the insurance business, including workers' compensation, general liability, automotive, and property claims. Three to 5 years' experience investigating insurance claims is a must. In this job, you would make recommendations to claims staff to ensure that insurance fraud is properly identified and to promote claims savings through the application of investigative best practices. You would provide in-service training, including annual antifraud training, to the claims staff. As an SIU investigator, you would be required to work a varying schedule, including nights, weekends, and holidays. GlobalOptions prefers applicants with bachelor's degrees in criminal justice, business, or related fields from 4-year colleges; at least 3 years of experience conducting client-facing activities; and 3 years of experience as a full-time investigator assigned to a carrier or contract SIU. As an SIU investigator, your essential functions would be as follows:

- Educating claims staff regarding red flags and the identification of insurance fraud as it relates to their line of business, workers' compensation, general liability, automotive, and property
- Conducting verbal consultations with adjusters to discuss suspected fraudulent claims activity and assisting in the identification of industry-accepted red flags
- Completing red-flag file reviews, claims file evaluations, investigative updates, state-mandated reporting forms, and documented fraud referrals
- Making sound investigative recommendations to claims staff that will assist in the identification and investigation of insurance fraud and promote claims savings
- Coordinating investigations of suspected fraudulent activity with GlobalOptions investigators, case managers, third-party vendors, and prosecuting authorities
- Obtaining, documenting, and reporting statistical information related to suspected fraudulent activity, red flags, state-mandated reporting, arrests, convictions, sentencing, restitution, and claims savings
- Establishing appointments to conduct field investigations within established time frames
- Conducting interviews and obtaining recorded statements from a wide variety of individuals in varying environments
- Obtaining supporting documentation, including claim documents, releases, and other records
- Documenting all investigative efforts and case-related communication in GlobalTrak case notes
- Completing expense reports on a biweekly or monthly basis

To perform the SIU investigator job successfully, an individual must be able to perform each essential duty satisfactorily. The following requirements are representative of the knowledge, skills, and abilities required to do this job (GlobalOptions, 2013):

- Ability to operate a motor vehicle in a safe manner
- Ability to operate a digital audio recorder in a manner that produces evidence that can be presented in a court of law
- Ability to operate a computer and related software to complete daily reports, evidence transfers, time sheets, and expenses
- Ability to read claim file documents, including but not limited to medical reports, investigative reports, deposition transcripts, correspondence, and claim payment histories
- Ability to write investigative reports in a clear and concise manner using proper grammar and spelling

Loss Prevention

Large retail chains hire security personnel to control shoplifting and internal thefts. Positions in loss prevention can be hazardous enough for thrill seekers, a ladder rung for college students pursuing law enforcement, and an alternative to law enforcement for those who fear the dreaded polygraph test. The position of loss prevention officer doesn't usually pay well enough to support a prosperous family life, but it is ideal for part-time work, and it can also be a gateway to innumerable administrative and supervisory positions in the security and investigative arena, with career potential.

An example of a loss prevention job is store detective for the TJX Companies, Inc., at HomeGoods in Utah. HomeGoods is a store that offers a selection of home merchandise, including giftware, home basics, accent furniture, lamps, rugs, accessories, and seasonal merchandise. TJX is one of the largest off-price apparel and home fashion retailers in the Unites States and worldwide. TJX is composed of four major divisions: Marmaxx (T.J. Maxx and Marshalls) and HomeGoods in the United States, TJX Canada (Winners, HomeSense, and Marshalls), and TJX Europe (T.K. Maxx and HomeSense).

Store detectives take an active role in identifying all forms of loss within retail outlets. In this position, you would be responsible for heightening loss prevention awareness, conducting physical security checks, making recommendations for ways to prevent loss, conducting safety inspections and communicating hazards to store management, participating in the orientation and training of new hires, and conducting surveillance to detect and apprehend shoplifters.

The basic requirements for a store detective are a strong desire for a career in retail loss prevention, the ability to work independently, excellent written and verbal communication skills, experience in retail loss prevention and store operations, or a criminal justice background. This job, like most loss prevention jobs, pays by the hour. As with many hiring processes, TJX prefers a résumé as opposed to an application (The TJX Companies, Inc., 2013).

In Grand Island, Nebraska, the JCPenney store in the Conestoga Mall employs a loss prevention specialist whose role is to keep the store safe and profitable at all times by investigating any suspicious customer activities or behavior in the store, taking action when needed, and executing company programs. This includes conducting surveillance, for which you would need to blend in well with other shoppers. You would observe customers and contractors in the store and look for any activities or behaviors that may be associated with theft, fraud, or impending violence. Some loss prevention specialists who monitor shoplifters with camera equipment associate this type of job with the omnipresence of God. They watch everyone in the store, without anyone knowing that they are being observed. These employees describe the experience as very exciting. They also make contacts with police officers during shoplifting investigations.

As a loss prevention specialist, you could find yourself interviewing suspects and writing reports. To accomplish this, it would help if you are skilled at using words in lieu of force when it comes to difficult situations. It would require you to listen effectively and probe for further details when conducting interviews with shoplifters. You would need to be an accurate and descriptive writer who can communicate exactly what happened during a situation to any audience. You would be expected to support shrinkage and safety awareness programs. Letting team members know what's going on and what they need to do to create the right store experience would facilitate this. Your job would also include maintaining records. You would be in charge of a great deal of detail. The company and law enforcement agencies would be depending on you to have complete and accurate reports to assist any investigation that may need to occur in the store.

In addition to the above jobs, you would participate in court hearings. You would need to become an expert when it comes to the witness stand. You would need to know the facts and deliver them like a seasoned pro. Your job would also include supporting workplace safety by walking the floor to identify and address potential hazards to customers and the staff. You would sometimes be called upon to support internal investigations. As the talent who handles loss prevention issues, there may be times when your assistance will be needed to investigate your peers, who may be acting inappropriately within the store. Your observation skills, loss prevention knowledge, and ability to remain objective with your teammates will greatly assist you with this sensitive undertaking.

JCPenney hires those who have a passion for loss prevention. They want someone who is a sponge for learning new loss prevention techniques and is driven to stop crime. They hire those who have a balanced temperament with "a level head," who can handle difficult situations with discretion. They favor detail-oriented personnel who never leave their *T*s uncrossed or their *I*s undotted, individuals who check and double-check to ensure that the final product is right. JCPenney likes a person of influence: not a pushy person, but someone who knows how to maneuver in a conversation to get someone to act differently. They want decisive employees who can make good decisions quickly, even when they may not have all the information available. Last, they look for accountability: very responsible employees who can take ownership of their mistakes as well as their triumphs (JCPenney, 2013).

You could be a regional loss prevention manager (LPM) such as the one with Energi Inc. in Mississippi. Working for Energi as an LPM would give you the opportunity to work with the regional operation of a dynamic growing company in various segments of the United States. You would complete compliance audits, deliver safety trainings, and determine if risks meet best-practice guidelines. You would provide detailed reviews of risks, hands-on safety training, and program development. The goal would be to identify and assess risks and effectively implement safety programs to reduce losses on prospective and existing risks. In addition, open and clear communication would need to be maintained with underwriting, claims, broker services, and agents. You would conduct field investigations and site reviews for initial claim assessments and oversee extended environmental cleanups with the ability to manage remediation vendors, contractors, and other vendors. Some additional responsibilities for LPMs include the following:

- Following up on recommendations with risks
- Ensuring that all work flows, procedures, departmental manuals, and standards are being adhered to
- Acting as a resource for all departments with regard to loss prevention and risk management, providing support to regional sales managers
- Constantly communicating with interrelated departments and agents to ensure open communication and cohesiveness
- Timely and accurate development of all management and productivity reports

To fit the requirements for the LPM position, you would need to be detailed oriented and have good analytical skills and decision-making initiative. You would need excellent oral and written communication skills; in-depth understanding of National Fire Protection Association, National Propane Gas Association, U.S. Department of Transportation, and Occupational Safety and Health Administration regulations; and proficiency with computers and Microsoft software. Prior experience in fuel distribution, oil and gas exploration, fleet operations, and agricultural risk is preferred. A bachelor's degree and loss prevention, risk management, or claim designations are also preferred (Energi Inc., 2013).

Armed Security Guard

Some security positions require you to carry a firearm. An example of a position such as this is in Sacramento, California, for Construction Protective Services, Inc. (CPS). An armed security officer is responsible for a safe and secure environment for CPS's clients. To work as an armed guard, you would need to know and understand post orders and assigned posts, be alert and observant, communicate unusual activity, and observe, deter, and report theft, vandalism, and illegal entry at client sites.

Headquartered in California, CPS has over 2,500 employees working in more than 18 offices across the United States, including Arizona, Arkansas, California, Florida, Georgia, Louisiana, Nevada, North Carolina, and Texas. CPS provides security, remote management solutions, video management systems, and high-tech staffing. To work for CPS, you would need to have the following qualifications:

- Be at least 18 years of age
- Have at least one verifiable employer
- Have no criminal convictions
- Have a state guard card and guard license
- Have your own authorized gun and equipment

- Have the ability to communicate effectively both orally and in writing in English for the purposes of public interaction and report writing
- Be authorized to work in the United States
- Have the ability to perform the essential functions of the position without reasonable accommodation
- Have the ability to pass pre-employment screening, which includes drug testing, a background check, and a Social Security check
- Have a neat and professional appearance at all times
- Have the ability to handle crisis situations efficiently and effectively at client sites

The pay for the armed guard position is $14 per hour (Construction Protective Services, Inc., 2013).

Another example of an armed guard position is with G4S in Towson, Maryland. G4S is a world-leading private security organization, providing security for the U.S. government, Fortune 500 companies, nuclear power plants, oil and gas companies, airports, seaports, banks, hospitals, factories, warehouses, commercial facilities, residential communities, and much more. An armed guard with G4S has the following responsibilities:

- Performing security patrols of designated areas on foot or in a vehicle
- Watching for irregular or unusual conditions that may create security concerns or safety hazards
- Sounding alarms or calling the police or fire department in case of fire or the presence of unauthorized persons
- Warning violators of rule infractions, such as loitering, smoking, or carrying forbidden articles
- Permitting authorized persons to enter property and monitoring entrances and exits
- Observing departing personnel to protect against theft of company property and ensuring that authorized removal of property is conducted within the appropriate client requirements
- Investigating and preparing reports on accidents, incidents, and suspicious activities
- Providing assistance to customers, employees, and visitors in a courteous and professional manner

The ideal candidate would possess a high school diploma or equivalent, be able to pass any state-required training or other qualifications for licensing, be able to pass a state licensing test, possess a valid and current Maryland State Police handgun permit and security guard certification, and have at least one of the following:

- Law enforcement experience
- Service in the elite military forces, military police, or combat arms
- Graduation from a police or corrections academy

- A criminal justice degree (associate's or higher)
- Career military experience

An armed guard with G4S would need the ability to operate radio and telephone equipment and console monitors, the ability to interact cordially with the public with effective oral and written communication skills and active listening skills, the ability to assess and evaluate situations effectively, the ability to identify critical issues quickly and accurately, and a natural attention to detail.

To work for G4S as an armed guard, you would need to be at least 21 years old, have access to reliable transportation, and not use illegal drugs. You would be required to pass a drug test and an extensive background check, including criminal history, personal references, employment and education verification, and Motor Vehicle Administration and credit checks. If you are accepted as an employee, you would need to pass the Minnesota Multiphasic Personality Inventory and a physical exam (G4S, 2013).

Diversity Issues in Private Security

Minorities, women, and physically challenged individuals have become valuable resources for organizations in need of security specialists. Today's security professionals are part of a multicultural workforce representing a variety of racial, ethnic, religious, and gender backgrounds. Despite the workplace diversity in the security sector, men still represent the majority of employees. More and more women are entering the field because of the wide range of opportunities that are available.

Summary

Since the terrorist attacks of September 11, 2001, the security industry has grown enormously. Working in private security or investigations doesn't always pay well, but it can represent a step on the ladder toward police work, or it can be a gateway job for a career in an advanced or supervisory position. This type of work is also popular for retired law enforcement personnel.

Police have historically looked at private security as inferior. Since 9/11, police agencies around the United States have made great steps in including private security in trainings to enhance defenses against catastrophic events, including terrorism.

Some of the prominent jobs in private security include security officer, private investigator, loss prevention officer, and armed security guard. There are various levels of danger in these positions but often less authority than police officers have, and very few security jobs involve backup or carrying a weapon. Some jobs can be exciting and rewarding.

Most jobs in private security and investigations require applicants to be at least 18 years of age and prefer degrees and/or related work experience. Rarely does a job in the private sector require a prospective employee to undergo a polygraph test, but all hiring processes include background checks. Women, minorities, and those with physical handicaps are continuously entering the private security sector.

DISCUSSION QUESTIONS

1. What might be some reasons a person would enter security work as opposed to law enforcement?

2. Should security officers all undergo polygraph tests, be trained equally as thoroughly as police, and receive better pay? Explain.

3. How can law enforcement work with private security in crime prevention and responding to threats or incidents of terrorism?

REFERENCES

AlliedBarton Security Services. (2013). *Jobs at AlliedBarton*. Retrieved from http://www.jobs.alliedbarton.com

California State Personal Board. (2013). *Careers in California government*. Retrieved from http://jobs.ca.gov

Construction Protective Services, Inc. (2013). *Careers*. Retrieved from http://www.cpssecurity.com/careers/

Energi Inc. (2013). *Home page*. Retrieved from http://www.energi.com

G4S. (2013). *Security and facilities management jobs and careers with G4S*. Retrieved from http://careers.g4s.com

GlobalOptions. (2013). *Jobs*. Retrieved from http://www.globaloptions.com/careers

Innovative Systems Group. (2013). *Innovative systems group candidate options*. Retrieved from http://www.innovativesys.com/index.php?option=com_wrapper&view=wrapper&Itemid=72

JCPenney. (2013). *Jobs*. Retrieved from http://jobs.jcp.com

The TJX Companies, Inc. (2013). *Careers*. Retrieved from http://www.tjx.com/careers.asp#&panel1-1

Transportation Security Administration. (2013). *Careers*. Retrieved from http://www.tsa.gov/careers/

University of Arkansas at Little Rock. (2013). *Applicant portal*. Retrieved from https://ualr.peopleadmin.com

SECTION 3

Preparing

10 Getting a Foot in the Door

Introduction

The goal is the job, the objective is the interview, the catalyst is an impressive résumé, and the means is a comprehensive portfolio. If you don't get called in for an interview, you weren't impressive enough on paper. In this chapter, we will look at effective preparation for the application, the interview, and the job itself. Review this chapter, and start doing all the preparation pragmatic to your present circumstances. You can be sure your competitors are!

Portfolios

A fairly recent trend in job applications is the electronic submission. This method has numerous advantages. All of your documents can be scanned and compiled into one file, ready for posting. You can easily add to your portfolio and update the files periodically. You can have it ready for those tight deadlines when you happen across job postings. It can be at an employer's computer in minutes if need be. What types of items are appropriate for your portfolio?

Your portfolio contains all the useful documents you can collect, including your résumé and curriculum vitae (CV). Potential items include recommendation letters, certificates, thank-you letters, school transcripts, sample reports or school research papers, and anything else possible. You will scan everything electronically, but you will also keep everything together as hard copies, ready to take with you to interviews. Keep your portfolio organized, and update it electronically after every semester. You should at least have a recommendation letter from your professor and a list of completed classes to add.

Letters of Recommendation

Applications routinely require letters of recommendation. These can take considerable time to collect. Once you determine the best people to ask, you need to genteelly relay the information you want covered, request that the letters be provided quickly, and meet with the letter writers to pick up their recommendations. A practical option is to collect generic letters early on each time you encounter a person who would be favorable for your background check. These can be nonspecific and all-inclusive letters that recommend you for employment, graduate school, internships, and volunteer programs. You can scan the letters into your computer and include them in your portfolio. If your source keeps your recommendation letter saved on his or her computer, you could easily go back and ask for an updated version with the current date and a more specific objective. An adjusted letter would take little effort once the original letter has been created. You may need four or five modified letters before you finally land a job. If your contact is willing to send you letters electronically, you can simply e-mail your request for any changes, and a new letter could be on your computer relatively quickly. Consider obtaining letters right away from friends, family, and acquaintances in respectable positions in the community, such as clergy members, lawyers, police officers, council members, and prominent business owners. These are important because some applications stipulate that your references have known you personally for a particular period of time. Often the duration of acquaintance is merely requested information, with no other specified criteria.

Some professors are willing to write letters for students provided they get to know the students well enough. Approach your professor at the beginning of the semester and find out if he or she would be willing to write you a letter if you prove worthy of it. Bringing attention to yourself early on is key. Some professors can have a student pool of 400 to 500 per semester. Participate often in class, sit near the front, talk to the professor periodically, have great attendance and punctuality, get at least an A–, and then ask for a letter near the end of the semester. Consider college as assertiveness practice and job preparation, not just an annoying stumbling block of life.

The types of compliments you want to see included in your letters involve attendance, punctuality, communication skills (both oral and written), critical thinking skills, interaction skills with individuals and groups, integrity, work ethic, organization, stress and anxiety control, work quality, and overall attitude and demeanor. These are some common traits that are explored during background checks. Professors may not be able to witness all of these, but make sure they witness as many as possible.

Certificates

Certificates are impressive and can nudge you ahead of others who haven't collected any. Certificates demonstrate recognition for accomplishments. They generally accompany awards and trainings. People start receiving certificates early on in life for things such as Eagle Scout, honor roll, student of the month, student council service, spelling bees, and so on. You might take these certificates for granted when you are younger, but they are still pieces of your life story. Each time you find an opportunity to obtain a certificate for an accomplishment, put a priority on it. If there is a free seminar offered at school or anywhere else, ask if certificates or training records will be provided. Scan certificates and add the files to your electronic portfolio.

Were you aware there are some online certificates you can earn for free? A good resource for a quantity of certificates with a variety of choices is the Federal Emergency Management Agency (FEMA) at http://training.fema.gov/nims. At this website, you will find several trainings for the National Incident Management System (NIMS). NIMS (also known as the Incident Command System) is a standardized approach to the preparation for, response to, and management of catastrophic events. NIMS was developed in 2004 by the U.S. Department of Homeland Security. It establishes a standard set of procedures used by emergency responders at all levels of government to conduct large-scale response operations. NIMS enables responders at all levels to work together more efficiently to handle domestic incidents, no matter the cause, size, or complexity, including catastrophic acts of terrorism and disasters. NIMS is also functional for small-scale and routine incidences, such as traffic accidents, fires, and even parades. FEMA desires that everyone learn the NIMS and thus furnishes this comprehensive website as a resource for training. After completing the interactive training, you should be knowledgeable enough to pass the quiz. After passing the quiz, you will be asked for your identification, including your Social Security number. The link for the certificate is then e-mailed to you, usually within 24 hours. Figure 10.1 displays a sample certificate.

It doesn't matter if incident management training is related to the job you are seeking. All certificates add pizzazz to your portfolio and show accomplishments. An employer may not even examine what certificates are awarded for, but 5 to 10 certificates mentioned on your résumé will surely be noticed.

You can also obtain online training from the National Institute of Justice, at http://www.nij.gov/training/welcome.aspx. After completing an easy registration, you can select online courses in different areas of criminal justice for free. A certificate can be printed out immediately. This site has an assortment of courses ranging from forensics and criminal investigations to corrections and courts.

Another option is to create your own certificates. As specialized training comes along in which you can obtain some level of expertise, ask the providers if you can create your own certificate for them to sign. Some trainers will be happy to accommodate you. You can purchase certificate-making software for a reasonable price or use the templates included in Microsoft Word and start creating your own. An example might be a club or volunteer program you participate in at school, in church, or in the community. Not all agencies take the time to hand out some form of acknowledgment. Sometimes you will get a thank-you letter, which is also valuable for your portfolio, but why not ask for a signed certificate as well? You can design it yourself and, although unnecessary, you can ask for logos electronically to really spice up the aesthetics of your masterpiece.

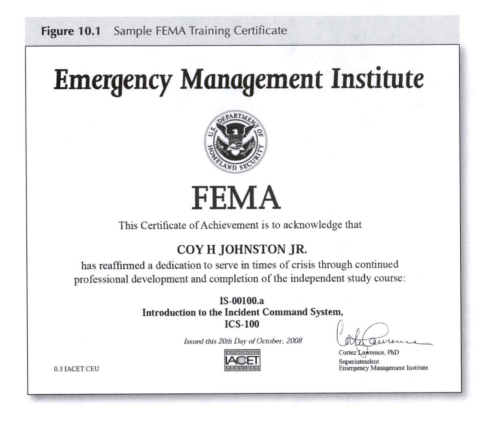

Figure 10.1   Sample FEMA Training Certificate

Volunteer Service

Now is a good time to start looking for volunteer opportunities and internships to collect kudos for your résumé. Volunteer for as much as you can, even if it doesn't appear relevant to your career choice. Many employers are impressed with the quantity of life experiences you obtain as much as their relevance. If you want to be an attorney and your certificates are for volunteering with the optimist club and the governor's grant-reviewing committee, you still reveal significant attributes about yourself. Selfless service is an indicator that you are an individual who will likely endure hard work and extra hours without complaining. Presenting evidence that you are an unselfish person might jump you ahead of other applicants who have too much white space on their résumés. Records of volunteer work can corroborate your words when you declare in an interview that you care about others. Many candidates will say it; you can back it up!

There is an advantage in having a supervisor of an internship or volunteer program who can be contacted for a background check. Experience is a key factor in an employer's decision. You might be the best candidate in person, but without the right attractions on paper, those who can demonstrate stronger employment or volunteer experience may pass you over for an interview.

Education Documentation

Although you are rarely asked to submit your transcripts initially with your résumé, it does sometimes happen. Eventually you will have to provide your transcripts to your employer, so why not get those ready to go? If you have an associate's or a bachelor's degree, get four or five sealed and certified transcripts added to your hard-copy portfolio packet. If you have not yet completed your degree, you can obtain transcripts early on that verify what credits you have already earned. If you are just a semester or two away from a minimum educational requirement, you may receive an exception and get an interview. If an employer is looking for a woman with a bachelor's degree who speaks Spanish, she might choose to hire a fluent Spanish-speaking female student close to finishing her degree over another candidate with a completed degree who speaks only basic Spanish.

Curriculum Vitae and Résumé

A curriculum vitae (CV) is less than a portfolio but more than a résumé. In terms of length, a résumé is best kept to a one-page, one-sided document listing your skills, relevant experiences, education, and awards. A CV is a longer, more detailed synopsis than a résumé and could be anywhere from two to five pages in length. A CV is more commonly used for academic jobs, but it could be beneficial to have one prepared and ready to use if an opportunity arises allowing you to submit more than what is on your résumé. Your CV provides an overview of your accomplishments throughout your life. There is no standard format, but you should always make sure the most relevant information comes first. Your goal should be to keep it short but inclusive of everything remarkable. One helpful trick is the use of incomplete sentences. Instead of saying "I received 40 hours of grant-writing training," you could shorten it to "40 hours' grant training." You will use bullet points more on a résumé than on a CV. When it is appropriate to add bullet points to your CV, use them modestly.

The résumé will be the document most frequently attached to your job applications. For some jobs, your résumé is the application, but for some criminal justice jobs, you could find yourself filling out 25- to 30-page applications. For most volunteer opportunities, internships, and employment (other than positions requiring polygraph testing), the résumé and letters of recommendation will be significant in the decision of whether you are called for an interview. Here are some typical components (the order can be changed) of a résumé:

Name: Should stand out at the top of the résumé

Contact information: Include address, phone number, and e-mail address

Objective: What job are you seeking?

Education:	This area can include trainings
Experience:	Any job or volunteer experience is important, but especially that which is relevant to the job you are seeking
Skills:	This is where you include everything else, such as typing, Spanish speaking, grant writing, and so on
Awards/Activities:	Mention certificates, memberships, and volunteer programs such as scout leadership, church choir, campaign volunteer, dean's list, honors, etc.

In deciding how much information to include on your résumé, look at the aesthetics from the critical viewpoint of the employer. A résumé needs a balance of white space and a blend of bullet points, boldface, italics, and underlining. If your résumé has too much white space, go ahead and include a few of the things you left off for the more important items. If it appears too full, work with the formatting or remove some less relevant minutiae, but keep it at a 12-point font. It is best to single-space your résumé, with spaces between different sections. Make sure to include a heading for each section. Remember the rule "KISS": keep it simple, stupid.

Should a résumé be colorful? Great question! You want readability, which is why you spread out the white space and include a variety of bullet points, boldface, italics, and underlining. Another supportive feature for a readable document is contrast. Not knowing how your electronic document will look after an employer prints it out, you are always safer with black ink on white background, like most résumés. If you will be submitting your résumé as a hard copy, you may choose to risk adding some boldface, strong colors, such as red or blue, on some expensive paper, but be aware that yours would stand out. That may be good, but maybe not. Figure 10.2 displays a sample résumé.

A key phrase to have on your résumé is "grant writing." Government agencies and supportive agencies have had to depend on grants for some of their key programs to exist. By hiring grant writers, an agency increases its potential to secure available government money and improve the likelihood of retaining current grants. Grant-writing training is offered all over the country, with costs ranging from $100 to $200. Training is available online or in person and can be done in as short as 2 days or spread out in weekly classes for a longer period. At the conclusion of the training, you receive documentation of your certification. This could be the best $100 you spend for job preparation.

Another eye-catcher to have on a résumé is "Spanish speaking." Even if your level of expertise is only basic or conversational, the opportunity to list it among your skills can push you ahead of monolingual candidates. Taking Spanish classes at college is sufficient and can be credited toward your bachelor's degree. The more proficient you become in Spanish, the more value you will have in the job force. Even if you could list on a

---

Figure 10.2 Sample Résumé

Juan Díaz **July 21, 2013**

2620 N. Circle West • Beverly Hills, CA 90210 • (310) 555-9880 • jdiaz1@aol.com

---

Objective: Fish and Game Ranger

Profile: *Motivated and assertive 22-year-old male with a mild-mannered personality, accustomed to multitasking and being diplomatic and tactful with professionals and nonprofessionals at all levels*

Relevant Skills

- Report writing
- Grants
- Computer savvy
- Emergency procedures
- Project management
- Spanish speaking
- Organization and scheduling
- Communications

Relevant Experience

- Preparation of police reports as a police explorer with Beverly Hills PD (2007–2009)
- Grant writing certified (2013)
- Volunteer with California Fish and Game as a ranger aide (2012 to present)
- Participated in 22 police or ranger ride-alongs (2007–2013)
- Organized two statewide explorer conferences (2008–2009)

Employment History

- Night manager at Wal-Mart, Beverly Hills, CA (2012–2013)
- Criminal justice tutor, Beverly Hills Community College (2011–2013)
- Manager at In-N-Out Burger, Beverly Hills, CA (2006–2007)

Educational History

- Bachelor's degree in criminal justice, UCLA (2013)

Relevant Awards

- Distinguished Service Award, Explorer Division, Beverly Hills PD (2008)
- Five certificates from FEMA for emergency procedure training (2013)
- Dean's list at UCLA for 4 straight years (2009–2013)

---

résumé that you are currently enrolled in a Spanish class and a grant-writing class, it could effectively push you ahead of others who haven't matched your efforts.

Naturally, your educational level will be influential on job applications, even if a degree is not required. The word *degree* is another strategic one to use. If you have just started your degree program, list on your résumé that you are currently enrolled in a particular degree as opposed to just attending college. If you are attending a community college, you might not currently be enrolled in an actual bachelor's degree program, but you can mention "associate's degree" with an added note of your intention to transfer to a bachelor's degree program. If you haven't actually completed any degree, being enrolled in college (with a plan for a degree) will be better than not listing the key words at all.

Interview Preparation _____

What have you done to prepare yourself for this job? Plan on encountering a question such as this in the interview. Better yet, hope for such a question. You will want the opportunity to sell yourself. Too many applicants take the hiring process for granted or don't really want the job badly enough. They don't commit themselves adequately to the preparation phase and lose the job to someone not so indolent. A new trend in hiring interviews is to let the candidate do all the talking. More and more agencies are handing out the questions prior to the interview (usually just three or four) and then giving the candidate 20 to 25 minutes to narrate the answers. Some candidates waste the opportunity and finish their narration in 5 to 10 minutes. Maybe they didn't have many skills and didn't do much preparation. Do you have enough material to sustain a 20-minute speech about your skills, strengths, experiences, and preparation? There are some activities you can participate in that will exhibit your seriousness about the job and will help prepare you for this type of an interview.

Police Ride-Along

Many agencies allow citizens to participate in citizen ride-along programs. A ride-along can be anything from a 4-hour stint to the full 10-hour shift. Some agencies require that you live in their cities in order to ride with their officers. Exceptions to this rule might be for school projects or to investigate an agency for possible employment. Most students have at least four different agencies they qualify to ride with, including campus police, city police, county sheriffs, and their state police agencies. Agencies that don't regularly allow citizens to ride along will usually permit their officers to provide such opportunities for family members or friends.

The protocol for a ride-along ordinarily involves a short request form to be filled out to allow a background check to be done. You will also be asked to select what days and times you are available for the ride-along. The agency will call you back within 2 to 7 days with your scheduled time. You will be asked to be at the police station at a certain time, where the officer will meet you. Some students are able to attend the briefing at the start of the shift, which can be very enlightening. In the briefing, you get to meet the other officers you will be seeing again and again at the various calls for service throughout your ride-along. You start picking up bits and pieces of clearer understanding right from the start as the officers train, share information, and get mentally ready for their tour of duty.

A ride-along is an opportunity for a potential police applicant to see and feel things that could not be experienced any other way than being right there in the action. It is easier to answer scenario-based interview questions when you have been in the unique situations officers encounter. One-on-one time with an officer is a great time to ask questions. Ask her why she touched the trunk of the car as she approached the driver. Ask why she called in a traffic stop before she turned on her overhead lights. Ask why she made a particular driver get out of his car, but not other drivers. Ask for some advice on the oral board questions. Obtain her e-mail address so that you can ask more questions in the future.

Most agencies won't allow more than one ride-along within 6 months. However, it would be beneficial to ride with a variety of agencies and officers, so sign up for more than one department at a time. Try not to key only on the organization you hope to work for. If you hit it off with the officer, he or she can get approval to let you ride again without going through the paperwork and without waiting for 6 months. Most officers have permission to invite friends and family on ride-alongs with just their sergeant's approval.

Dress like a detective! Your opportunity for exposure to the most exciting parts of police work correlates with your appearance. If you look like a student riding along, you will be treated like one and will likely spend a lot of time in the car. If you look professional and could pass for a detective, the officer can reasonably allow you to be closer to more scenes without distracting the citizens he or she is gleaning information from. Although it would be beneficial to be in jeans and tennis shoes in anticipation of a foot chase, your potential for a better experience is increased in slacks and a buttoned shirt for males, with professional shoes. Polo shirts are also acceptable, but a buttoned shirt is even more prudent. Women should apply the same strategy. Female detectives generally wear nice slacks, a buttoned top, and classy shoes, with their hair back. Dressing the way you would for an interview would be impressive and could get you more exposure to the routine calls and possibly to some daunting crime scenes.

Court and Attorney Observations

Most students have not been in a courtroom other than for a traffic ticket or a minor criminal offense. Court expertise in police work is as important as any other faction of the job. If asked what you have done to prepare yourself for a job, internship, or a volunteer position at a criminal justice–related agency, what do you have on your list so far? How would it sound if you were able to say, "I have attended various court proceedings, including misdemeanor and felony trials, in both state and federal court. I have also shadowed two different attorneys for a day, in which I accompanied them to court and assisted in their everyday workloads, including court preparation and follow-up"?

Just like police, many attorneys will allow students to meet with them and follow them around for a day. Often a student can participate in some of the work, including case preparation, court note taking, and client follow-up. What you actually learn from the experience is secondary to the value of demonstrating your assertiveness and motivation to prepare for the hiring process and for your career. If you don't find an opportunity to shadow an attorney, you should at least visit some courtrooms and observe the proceedings. Other than some civil and family cases, all criminal trials are open to the public. You can walk into any courtroom at the city, county, or federal level and observe the hearings that are taking place at that time, as long as seats are available. No appointment is necessary, but you could call and find out if anything interesting is happening, when the proceedings will occur, and in what courtroom they will be held. Most court personnel are familiar with student projects and are happy to assist you with advice. Once you are in the court building, you will walk through the security scanners at the entrance, which are usually much less intrusive than those at airports. If you prefer help, you can contact the information desk for advice on what types of cases are in the works. You could also just walk around the court and read the dockets, which are usually posted outside each courtroom, to see if anything sounds interesting.

A variety of hearings take place at the courthouse. Observing 1 day of a 2-week felony murder trial would certainly be interesting, but even the misdemeanor courts have some eye-opening and rewarding activities to witness. If you are pursuing a law enforcement career, it is advantageous to witness what goes on during the initial appearances. It will give you a genuine understanding of the types of information the judge and attorneys use in the process. Spending 2 hours watching initial appearances will leave no doubt in your mind that our court system has all the work it can possibly manage. You may be able to handle it better emotionally, later on in your police career, when you watch numerous criminals get released on their own recognizance on a second, third, or even a fourth violation.

Firearms

Firearms are another aspect of police work, like driving, report writing, handcuffing, and fighting, in which you will need to become proficient. You will have the opportunity to learn and/or improve on all these skills in the academy. Often, range masters need to help recruits change their bad habits from years of shooting the wrong way. For this reason, shooting experience isn't always a positive thing, but firearms training (with instruction) can be. You are not likely to be asked in an interview if you are a good shooter, and you should likewise avoid sounding as though you put too much importance on your shooting ability. However, adding this to the list of what you have done to prepare for police work could be beneficial if it comes across properly: just one small part of a larger picture. If the topic doesn't come up in the interview and is thus of no avail to your hiring, prior firearms training will still pay off during the academy, especially for women. In general, women struggle more than men with firearms proficiency in the academy.

Chances are there is a firearms range within an hour of where you live. Our nation is heavily dotted with gun ranges of all types. Look for an indoor range in your area with trainers on site. Most ranges rent guns, eye protection, and ear protection and allow you to buy ammunition if you are at least 21 years of age. If you are under 21, you will need to bring someone with you who is of age. Trainers are usually on duty and normally do not cost you any extra. They will teach you the proper stance, proper gun handling, proper target acquisition, tactical loading, and jam-clearing techniques.

The price can range anywhere from $40 to $75 for a 50-round session. You normally don't need an appointment, but all ranges differ in their every-day operations. Again, this type of experience and training is relevant to police work but is rarely usable in an interview. If you are male and choose to refer to your firearms experience in an interview, it should be downplayed as just one of many things you have done to prepare yourself. Women, how-ever, can get away with giving firearms training more emphasis. If a female job applicant were to say that she went on her own to learn firearms skills because she knew that women struggle with firearms proficiency in the academy, it would come across as a positive.

Physical Fitness

For law enforcement and detention-related jobs, physical fitness plays an important role. Even if you aren't the biggest and the strongest, you need to be able to chase, fight, and overpower people for the safety of yourself and others. The hiring process doesn't normally involve any fighting or arrest tactics, but assessing basic physical fitness is almost always a part of the procedure. The physical fitness test differs among agencies but can include things such as an obstacle course; a distance run; some push-ups; some sit-ups; jumping; stretching; a wall climb; and a body drag using a heavy, full-size dummy. Getting physically fit will not only help you ace the physical fitness test but also help you look better in the interview that follows. If you are overweight, make sure you are a member of a gym and have an exercise plan in place when you walk into your interview. You could resolve concerns an employer might have cultivated from the first impression. If you have already dropped some significant weight, let interviewers know so that they won't assume you are sedentary.

Some women seeking law enforcement jobs need to practice climbing a 6-foot block wall. This requires upper body strength as well as some tech-nique. The 6-foot wall is often part of an obstacle course, so climbing the wall quickly is important. There are several sources online including YouTube videos that you can view before you actually attempt this task. Some women may have problems with push-ups if they are not properly prepared. Even if a woman outruns every applicant and doubles everyone in sit-ups, she will be disqualified if she fails even one part of the test.

A battle for men is the stretch and reach component. You may be asked to perform a stretch test in which you sit with your legs straight in front of you and reach forward as far as you can. This is usually a pass-fail test with a standard number of inches you have to reach from a certain designated point.

Lori Ohrt: Property and Evidence Supervisor – Goodyear Police Department

CJ: What is your current position?

LO: Property and evidence supervisor.

CJ: What are your typical job duties?

LO: I supervise and manage the appropriate storing of criminal evidence, found property, impounded vehicles, and other property. I manage and supervise the identification and collection of evidence from crime scenes. I plan, organize, supervise, and evaluate the functions and the staff within the property and evidence section of the police department. I safeguard and maintain the integrity of all police evidence/property in accordance with state laws, city ordinances, and departmental policies and procedures. I prepare and implement the budget for the property and evidence section. I forecast the need for additional staffing, equipment, and materials. I monitor and control expenditures, develop and evaluate recommendations for changes in policies, procedures, and practices through proposal and/or reports. I plan, coordinate, assign, and supervise the work of subordinate personnel, and prepare and review performance evaluations.

CJ: How long have you been at your current assignment?

LO: Ten years with the department and 3 years in a supervisory role.

CJ: What other positions have you held prior to this one?

LO: Business owner, surveillance officer, and forensic specialist.

CJ: What are the requirements/qualifications for your job?

LO: My work requires knowledge of a specific vocational, administrative, or technical nature, which may be obtained with a 2-year associate's degree, diploma, or equivalent from a college, technical, business, vocational, or correspondence school. Appropriate certification may be awarded upon satisfactory completion of advanced study or training. This job requires a minimum of 3 years' experience in a related field and a valid driver's license. It requires the ability to read reports, correspondence, software manuals, management books, trade journals, and policies at a college level. It requires the ability to perform general and advanced math calculations, including calculating distances and creating charts at a college level. It requires the ability to write memos, letters, reports, e-mail, correspondence with customers, policies, and bulletins at a college level. It requires supervising and monitoring performance of a regular group of employees including providing input on hiring/disciplinary actions and work objectives/effectiveness, performance evaluations, and realigning work as needed. It requires a comprehensive, practical knowledge of a technical field with use of analytical judgment and decision-making abilities.

CJ: What steps did you go through during hiring?

LO: My position was reclassified at that time.

CJ: What advice can you offer students who might be interested in pursuing a similar career?

LO: Twenty credit hours of chemistry; volunteer, volunteer, volunteer; internships. Full time students . . . join the International Association for Identification (www.theiai.org). Take photography courses (in addition to what is required).

Athletic women can sometimes touch their noses to their knees, so the stretch test isn't as much of an issue for them. Male applicants often struggle with this.

Most agencies will alter the requirements for different ages, such as a longer time allowance for the 1.5-mile run for those over 30 years old. However, it is rare for an agency to make any exceptions for gender. Not only would it be unfair to men if women had a shorter fence to climb, but it would also be insulting to capable women who want to earn the job on their own merits.

Volunteering vs. Internships

Volunteer work is great for the résumé and doesn't have to be job related. Because of unexpected hiccups in the economy and subsequent budget cuts, many agencies have made available more opportunities for volunteer positions. The word *volunteer* implies that you donate some time for the benefit of others with no expectation of payment or reward. Although this is true, you can still reap huge benefits by including the word *volunteer* on your résumé, revealing your aggressiveness in your approach to job preparation.

Popular volunteer or intern positions in law enforcement involve victim services, crime scene work, police aide, detective aides, pawn detail, evidence managing, auto theft and impound lot assistance, and data entry for records. There are also volunteer and intern positions at courts and law firms. Most agencies will post volunteer openings on their websites. Volunteer work is normally not too taxing on your time. A typical program might require 8 to 12 hours a month. Your supervisor will usually agree to write a letter of recommendation or provide some type of certificate of appreciation.

Internships differ from volunteer jobs because you expect something in return. It is more of a work contract. Internships are harder to find than volunteer positions because they involve more responsibility from a supervisor. Supervisors generally feel an obligation to create useful experiences for you, whereas in a volunteer position, you are there for the company and will do whatever they need you to do. If you volunteer for a law firm, you may spend much of your time filing papers. If you intern for a law firm, you may find yourself in the courtroom taking notes for an attorney and, after court, making follow-up phone calls to clients. Some internships are paid positions, but this is rare and should not be too high of a priority. Don't pass up great opportunities being penny-wise and pound-foolish.

Whether you apply for a volunteer position or for an internship, if it is for a law enforcement agency, you will generally undergo a grilling testing process, which includes a background check and polygraph test. The testing experience will be valuable. If you intern at an agency you hope to work for someday, your foot is far in the door. Most agencies won't pick up interns they wouldn't consider hiring.

Education and Grades

Put importance on your grades and on being liked by your professors. To improve on your grades, research the professors and choose those who will award an A+. Look at what others are saying about the professors on Rate-MyProfessors.com. Try to find professors who would be a good fit for your learning style. If possible, find out what professors have reputations for writing recommendation letters. Stay in contact with the professor. Professors rarely get to know the outstanding students as well as the needy students. Make sure the professor can remember you when he or she gets a call for your background check.

Not all jobs require a bachelor's degree. It is common, though, for the requirement of a bachelor's degree for law school and federal law enforcement. It might surprise you to see what types of degrees are relevant. You might think the best degree for any law enforcement job would be in criminal justice. That is a good degree to have, but if you are interested in working for the Federal Bureau of Investigation (FBI), they also look strongly at accounting, psychology, biology, and chemistry. The FBI generally requires either law enforcement or military experience as well. You are generally better off working for a municipal agency for 4 or 5 years before applying to the FBI. Municipal agencies often offer tuition reimbursement as well. You can finish your degree after graduating from the police academy.

The Application

There is so much competition for positions that some applicants are weeded out before they get an opportunity to participate in any part of the testing process. It isn't always because of a drug history or a criminal record; sometimes, it is for very minor mistakes on the application or seemingly incomplete information. An application for a law enforcement job can be 25 pages or more in length. You may start doubting how much you want the job by the time you complete the application. Most applications ask for similar information, so each time you fill one out, it should get easier, especially if you prepare a good portfolio to work from.

You want to stay consistent on all of your applications, so make a copy of your first one and use it as a reference for subsequent agencies. If you declare that you used marijuana 15 times on one application, stay with that number on all applications. Also, stay consistent with dates for your jobs and degrees. You can use the same references, so keep their addresses and phone numbers together. Keeping everything together will minimize the tediousness of filling out additional applications, preventing you from giving up too easily.

Written Tests

Law enforcement (and sometimes corrections) hiring includes a written test. The written test isn't something you can prepare for, but here are some samples of what you can expect to come across:

Read the notes from this call for police service. Pick the answer that most completely and correctly represents the information.

1. Responded to domestic at 100 Main Street. Spoke with victim Jane Jones. Observed visible injury laceration on Jane Jones' right forearm. Jones refused to cooperate.

   a. I responded to a domestic. Upon my arrival, I spoke with the victim, Jane Jones.

   b. I observed a visible injury laceration on her right forearm. Ms. Jones refused to cooperate with my investigation.

   c. I responded to 100 Main Street in reference to a domestic. Upon my arrival, I spoke with the victim, Jane Jones. I observed a visible injury laceration on her right forearm. Ms. Jones refused to cooperate with my investigation.

   d. I spoke with the victim, Jane Jones. I observed a visible injury laceration on her right forearm. Ms. Jones refused to cooperate with my investigation.

   e. I responded to a domestic. Upon my arrival, I spoke with the victim, Jane Jones. I observed a visible injury laceration on her right forearm.

   Answer: C

2. Officer Harper responded to a residential burglary. The victim stated that while he was on vacation between 7/2/08 at 4:00 pm and 7/8/08 at 11:00 am, a person or persons unknown did unlawfully enter his residence and take his property.

   When did the victim discover the burglary to his residence?

   a. 7/2/08 at 4:00 pm

   b. 7/2/08 at 11:00 am

   c. 7/8/08 at 4:00 pm

   d. 7/8/08 at 11:00 am

   Answer: D

3. Deputy Williams responded to an armed robbery in progress. Upon his arrival, he was advised that the suspect fled in a late model blue Honda Accord sedan.

   The vehicle was described as a:

   a. 2008 blue Honda Accord

   b. late model dark blue Honda Accord

c. late model blue Honda Accord sedan

d. late model blue Honda Accord

Answer: C

4. Referring to the last scenario, Deputy Williams responded to:

a. A robbery in progress

b. An armed robbery in progress

c. A burglary in progress

d. An armed robbery that happened in the past

Answer: B

5. Gang Unit Investigator Smith fills out a field interview (FI) card on a suspected gang member. The gang member's street name is "Killer G" and he is a documented member of the Eastside Boys. "Killer G" has numerous tattoos that help to verify his gang status including a tear tattoo on his face, an "EB" tattoo on his left chest over his heart, and a tattoo of a compass with a large "E" on his right forearm.

"Killer G" has how many tattoos?

a. 1

b. 2

c. 3

d. 4

Answer: C

6. "Killer G" had an "EB" tattoo on his

a. right forearm

b. right chest

c. face

d. left chest

Answer: D

7. Departmental policy requires that all officers that use force must complete a written use of force report. The report must include the circumstances leading up to the officer's decision to use force, the level of force used, the justification for the force used, and the outcome of the officer's use of force.

The departmental policy requires:

a. That officers explain to suspects why they are using force before such force is utilized.

b. That officers explain verbally the circumstances leading up to the decision to use force, the level of force used, the justification for the force used, and the outcome of the use of force.

c. That officers explain in a use of force report the circumstances leading up the officer's decision to use force, the level of force used, the justification for the force used, and the outcome of the officer's use of force.

d. That no use of force report be filled out if no injury resulted from said use of force.

Answer: C

8. You are a city police officer on patrol and observe a car driving left of center and not stopping for a stop sign. You stop the car and, upon speaking with the driver, you believe that the driver is DUI. You also note that the driver is a member of your employing municipality's city council. You should:

a. Give the city council member a ride home.

b. Allow the city council member to go on his way in his car.

c. Continue as you would normally with your investigation and notify your supervisor.

d. Write a citation for the two traffic violations and release the driver.

Answer: C

9. You are on patrol with your Field Training Officer (FTO) and respond to a commercial burglar alarm at a grocery store. Upon responding, you and your FTO find an open door with no sign of forced entry. After successfully clearing the store, your FTO grabs a case of water and says no one will miss it. You should:

a. Ask for your share of the water

b. Tell him to put the water back

c. Ignore the situation since you are new to the department

d. Report the situation to your FTO's supervisor.

Answer: D

10. Your department has a written policy that forbids officers from taking any bribes, gratuities, or gifts. You stop at a local diner and find that the waitress wants to give you, the police officer, a 50% discount. Of these four options, you should:

a. Leave money on the table equal to the full amount of the menu price and normal tip you would have left, avoiding a scene.

b. Argue with the waitress and manager, insisting on paying the full bill.

c. Walk out not paying anything.

d. Pay the bill as indicated with the 50% discount.

Answer: A (Even if you might narrate a different answer in an interview, you would need to select the best choice from what you are offered. The key word is *argue*. If the wording were different and instead said, "Politely discuss," B would be a valid choice. An argument could create more of a problem than giving the impression that you accepted a gratuity.)

11. *Miranda v. Arizona* was a very important U.S. Supreme Court case from 1966 that affected law enforcement officers. Among other things, the rape case involving migrant farm worker Ernesto Miranda dictated that a warning must be given to suspects who are not free to leave if they are questioned as to specifics of the case. What this says is:

   a. Miranda warnings must be given anytime a suspect is placed in handcuffs

   b. Miranda warnings must be given if the suspect is questioned as to the specifics of the crime and he or she is not free to leave.

   c. Miranda warnings must be given in rape cases.

   d. Miranda warnings must be given to all people interviewed by law enforcement officers.

   Answer: B

12. *Carroll v. United States* was a 1925 U.S. Supreme Court case that clarified a law enforcement exception to the search warrant requirement of the Fourth Amendment. Under the Carroll Doctrine, as it is now known, law enforcement officers may search automobiles without a search warrant as long as they have probable cause to do so and the automobile is movable. In other words:

   a. Officers may only search an automobile with the written voluntary consent of the driver.

   b. Officers may search an automobile since the car is movable.

   c. Officers may search an automobile without a search warrant as long as they have probable cause to do so and the automobile is movable.

   d. Officers may not search an automobile.

   Answer: C

13. *New York v. Belton*, a 1981 U.S. Supreme Court case, clarified that law enforcement officers, upon making an arrest, may search any the immediate "lunge area" within the reach of the arrestee including any open or closed containers. Such a search may be conducted at the same time as the arrest. Therefore:

   a. Officers may search the vicinity of the arrestee including any open or closed containers.

   b. Officers must have consent to search the area around the arrestee.

   c. Officers may search beyond the reach or "lunge area" of the arrestee.

   d. Officers may not search any further than the person they have arrested.

   Answer: A

14. Which sentence below is grammatically correct?

   a. I am an educated person who wants to be a police officer.

   b. I am an educated person whom wants to be a police officer.

   c. I am an educated people who wanted to be a police officer.

   d. I was an educated person who wants to be police officers.

   Answer: A

15. While conducting traffic enforcement in an area with a posted speed limit of 45, the reading on your radar for a passing car is 73. How many miles over the speed limit is the vehicle driving?

   a. 23

   b. 26

   c. 28

   d. 32

   Answer: C

Some agencies will use pictures as part of their written exams. You are asked to view a picture for a couple of minutes, and then, when the picture is taken away, you answer some questions based on what you can remember. The hiring written test is usually pass-fail, requiring a score of at least a 70%. Although it is a pass-fail test, scores are sometimes used to help recruiters with hiring decisions at the completion of all assessments.

Often, a written exercise accompanies the test. It is usually just a one-page essay on a topic that is not too difficult to write about, such as a personal experience. The papers would be collected and graded by an English expert of the department's choice. These are usually pass-fail, so you should brush up on your grammar and punctuation.

Although the written test isn't something you can study for, you can certainly perform better by getting plenty of sleep the night before. You can also try to take care of the little things that are on your mind so that you can concentrate on the test. Additionally, you can take care of yourself through good nutrition and exercise in order to be alert and prepared on test day.

Psychological Tests

Another step in the process for law enforcement hiring is a psychological test. This is generally a 2- to 4-hour exam consisting of anywhere from 200 to 400 questions. The test is normally multiple choice, which facilitates quick grading. The choices aren't for the right or wrong answer; instead they are "agree" or "disagree," or something similar. The questions often seem alike, even though they are slightly different. The mistake some people make is to answer the questions the way they think they are supposed to instead of just being truthful. If the question changes, it is okay for the answer to change.

It is best to not overthink it and to answer all of the questions fairly quickly. An example of similar but different questions might be the following:

I like socializing in big groups.	Agree	Disagree
I enjoy large groups more than small groups.	Agree	Disagree
Being in groups makes me uncomfortable.	Agree	Disagree
I prefer settings with just a few friends.	Agree	Disagree
I prefer large groups over being by myself.	Agree	Disagree
Large groups cause me to have some anxiety.	Agree	Disagree

You would likely answer these scenarios differently, because they are asked differently. You don't want to go back and worry that you are being inconsistent. Just answer each question according to how you interpret it. If you like socializing in big groups, it doesn't mean you prefer large groups over small groups. You also use your own frame of reference. If you interpret "large group" as referring to the audience at a concert or a professional sporting event, you might answer differently than if you were visualizing a family reunion. Just stay consistent with your interpretations, and you should be fine.

Summary

Having a wide-ranging portfolio is the means to an exceptional résumé, which is key to getting the opportunity for an interview. Building your portfolio and preparing for the testing starts now. Your portfolio is a packet containing all the documents you have collected throughout your life, including awards, certificates, recommendation letters, transcripts, and thank-you letters. You can double or triple the material in your portfolio by collecting letters from your professors and by completing some online training that provides certificates. Some helpful key phrases for your résumé are "Spanish speaking" and "grant writing."

Your one-page résumé is sometimes all you are asked to submit as a job application. Therefore, it is important to build a dazzling one. A CV is two or more pages long, containing much more information than a résumé. It is more common for academic jobs, but if you are allowed to submit more data, it would be best to have a CV ready to go. Applications for law enforcement are lengthy and can disqualify an applicant if not filled out completely. Once you fill out your first application, copy it and use it to fill out other applications. This will save you time and help keep all applications consistent.

To prepare for tests and interviews, go on a police ride-along, visit court proceedings, get some firearms training, get physically fit, volunteer wherever feasible, and apply for internships. Although written tests for law enforcement aren't something you can study for, you can prepare more effectively by getting plenty of sleep and by taking care of any responsibilities that might be on your mind and taking away your full focus. Psychological tests are the norm for law enforcement and can be long and tedious. The key is to stay consistent and answer quickly without overthinking. Search out professors at RateMyProfessors.com and find those who are a good fit for you. Find a professor who will award an A+ and will also write a recommendation letter.

DISCUSSION QUESTIONS

1. What types of items are appropriate for your portfolio?

2. What traits are common for an employer to check into during a background check?

3. What are some sources for certificates?

4. What are some typical components of a résumé?

5. What can you do to prepare for the written test?

11

The Interview

Not many jobs require written tests in the hiring process. Rarely does the process include a physical test or a polygraph exam. But almost every job in the United States involves some type of hiring interview in the selection process. Would you do the same thing if you owned your own business? What would you hope to accomplish in your interviews with applicants? What would you be looking for? Is it safe to say that you would want to know as much as possible about the applicants so that you could choose the best one possible for your open position? What types of things can you reasonably expect to learn about a person in a 20- to 30-minute interview?

In the case of police officers, the various types of written tests and psychological tests can weed out those who don't have the necessary intelligence. The background investigation and polygraph test can weed out those who are an integrity risk. Anything else that is important must be determined in the short dialogue of the interview. Therefore, the interview can (and does) weed out applicants for a variety of reasons. It also serves as the best opportunity to move ahead of other candidates who may be less prepared or just aren't right for a position.

In a perfect world, the most qualified person would be hired for an open position, but the truth is it's the best interviewees who are getting the callbacks. You may be the ideal person for the position you seek, but it is unlikely that you could just walk into an interview, tell that to the interviewer, and ask when you start. Part of being that ideal person is to know how to perform well in an interview. Knowing the answers to interview questions is significant, but there are additional factors to consider if you want to have the edge over other candidates. In this chapter, we will explore some generic and specific interview hints, followed by common questions and appropriate answers. Some of the upcoming information is relevant solely to police or detention jobs. As in many areas in life, there are a good, a better, and a best. Let's go for the latter!

Punctuality

Your goal should be to show up at the office lobby about 10 minutes early. It is a good idea to be even earlier to the building and use the extra time to get focused, pray or meditate, and review this chapter and any other helpful items you brought with you. About 20 to 30 minutes of reflection and review could be beneficial after your drive. If you are driving from a long distance, you should factor in some of the predictable holdups, such as rush-hour traffic, accidents, or a long line at your habitual coffee stop. If you haven't already seen the building you are driving to, you should plan some time to find the location and a parking spot. You also should plan a restroom break. These are just the things you can plan for. Now add another 10 minutes as a cushion for unpredictable obstacles. It is best to spend your drive focused on your interview rather than on the long lights, heavy traffic, and those drivers who do not belong in the fast lane. You will likely feel some anxiety about the interview, so why add to it by having to rush past bad drivers to get there? It could be difficult to calm down after feeling so much anger toward those who choose to drive the speed limit for whatever reason. If nothing goes wrong, you may have 45 to 60 minutes to sit in your car and prepare. Is that so bad?

Appearance

As mentioned earlier, there are a good, a better, and a best for almost everything. This is true with the routes we choose to take, the products we buy, the careers we choose, how we cut our hair, and the clothes we wear. One thing you can't avoid is making a first impression. You are stuck with that! This is especially critical for interviews. Why not shoot for the best you can?

Men need a suit in a dark color. Black, dark blue, and dark gray are power colors. These colors are always best if you want to influence others. A white shirt with a tie is best. Wear a conservative tie of either a plain color or a symmetrical design, such as stripes. The color of the tie can make a difference in how you are perceived. Consider a blue, burgundy, green, or yellow tie. You can also get away with wearing a red tie, but it can come across as too emotionally strong. As far as hair, wear it short. If it is extremely long and you are interviewing for a job in which long hair is okay, wear it back in a ponytail. It is best to be clean shaven, but you might be able to get away with neatly trimmed facial hair for some jobs. Cover as many of your tattoos as possible. Remove your earrings, nose rings, lip rings, tongue studs, and any other face metal.

Women need a dark-colored dress, a dark skirt, or dark pants. It is best to wear a white top and possibly a dark, matching jacket over the top. The dress or skirt should be no shorter than just above the knee. In general, your apparel should not be overly revealing; at the same time, you shouldn't come across as too conservative. It is best to wear black, closed-toe heels that are no higher than 2 inches; you might be able to get away with stylish, open-toe shoes. When it comes to makeup, keep yourself looking as natural as possible. Avoid anything that would bring too much attention and cause distractions. The eyes are the most important, because that is where you want the interviewer to be focused the most. Wearing your hair up or back is the safest approach. It needs to look as if you put a lot of time into it, even if you didn't. Having your hair up or back will look professional and keep you from absently playing with it, revealing nervousness, during the interview. Wear nice earrings or studs, but nothing that catches the attention of the interviewer too much.

Attractiveness is one of the most important factors in influencing others. Attractiveness goes beyond your facial features. Attractiveness includes the totality of your look and your aura. You want to exude confidence. That is easier done if you know that you look good. It also helps to know some tricks of body language.

Body Language

Imagine a boss who tells her recruiters something like this: "We are looking for people who think they are all that, and then some. Try to find us someone who has the 'I'm too cool' look on her face. We want someone who doesn't smile, someone who acts like he has nothing left to learn. We're looking for someone blasé, with a negative point of view, and an uncaring demeanor."

Is there any job out there for which you would prefer someone who is unfriendly or unapproachable? If you are thinking of correctional officers or probation officers, you are misinformed. In these jobs, you want your employees to be firm and careful of the boundaries they set, but you also want someone who is part of the solution, not the problem.

If you don't naturally smile, start practicing. It needs to be part of the new you. Smile at every person you pass. Smiling makes you likable. When you are being interviewed, your body language needs to coincide with your assertions. Smiling is the easiest and most effective body language you can use. If you are a friendly person, show it. If you are not, maybe you could be a custodian or a warehouse worker, with minimal interaction with others.

The first impression you make includes the person working the front desk. Sometimes the person who greets you and asks you to have a seat will make comments to the interviewer before or after your interview. It may be something sarcastic before the interview, such as "You guys are going to love this one." It could also be something after the interview, such as "Did that blonde girl with the nice dress suit do well? I really liked her!" If the receptionist doesn't like you, he or she is not going to push for you if the opportunity arises. You should smile at everyone, but especially the receptionist.

Make eye contact with everyone involved in the interview as evenly as possible. Be careful not to stare too deeply or too long. Keep the eye contact to short intervals so that the other person doesn't feel uncomfortable or get distracted. If someone gets left out of your conversation, he won't feel enough connection to you. Looking at people will make them feel that you respect them individually.

Introductions

Let the interviewers dictate your behavior. In most cases, someone will come to get you and walk you to the interview room. When that person approaches you, stand and listen carefully to everything said. In almost any other circumstance, it would be an appropriate gesture to offer a handshake. For job interviews, it is usually best not to offer your hand unless an interviewer offers hers first. People have different comfort spaces. The safest way to learn another's comfort space is by letting him dictate how close you get. Sometimes handshakes are not practical because of a room's layout.

The eye-contact rule is especially important in the introduction phase. Look at each individual as you are introduced, and at least nod your head in acknowledgment. Let the interviewers dictate your behaviors. If they haven't yet asked you to sit, remain standing during the introductions. Again, do not walk around the table and reach your hand out to shake hands unless the interviewers invite it. Hugs are out! Just a smile, a nod of your head, and a response to whatever they say. If they say something such as "Thanks for coming," just respond succinctly with something such as "Thanks for this opportunity." If they say something along the lines of "Nice to meet you," it is best to either say "Likewise" or "Nice to meet you, too." Your eye contact lets them know you are acknowledging them individually. Clichés are fine. It's best not to try to say something clever or witty at this time. The interviewers' job is to study you and learn as much as they can about you. Let them ease into it at their pace. You will have 20 to 30 minutes to present your personality.

When you are seated at the table and ready to go, what do you do with your hands? If you naturally use your hands to articulate, set them on the table and clasp your hands so that you don't fidget. After each answer, clasp them back in place. If you don't need them to articulate, set them in your lap. That way you can fidget with them out of sight if need be to hide your nervousness. Women also need to moderate jewelry on their wrists and fingers, making sure any bracelets and rings are not distracting. Sit as calmly and comfortably as possible. The interviewers will be looking at you and will notice nervous movements. You want them to be paying attention to what you are saying.

Although it is important to be comfortable, you will want to sit up and lean in slightly toward the interviewers. This body language makes you appear interested. Folding your arms or sitting back could make you look uninterested, defensive, and/or less welcoming. Look at the person talking, and try to stay focused on the entire question. While answering, share eye contact with everyone.

A more advanced body language trick (used with one-on-one interviews) is called mirroring. The idea is to subtly behave or speak in the same way as the person you are visiting with. Subconsciously, this sends a message to the person that you are on the same level. This can help build rapport faster. However, mirroring is not something you want to do in an interview until you get good at it. When you are in a conversation with someone with whom you want to connect, try practicing this technique. If the other person crosses his legs, wait just a moment and then cross your legs. If the other person leans on the palm of her hand, do the same thing a moment or two later. If the other person talks quietly, keep your own voice at a lower level. Skilled law enforcement interviewers use this technique on suspects and victims to break through defenses and build a rapport as quickly as possible. As a side note for you future interviewers, mirroring works well when interviewing children.

In a hiring interview, it is best to use the words *sir* and *ma'am* sparingly. Do use them, because it is an easy way to say "I respect you," but overdoing it can have an adverse affect. These words are often used too much in response to closed-ended, yes-or-no questions. It is perfectly fine to just say "yes" or "no."

Sample Questions

Can you answer these three questions with unmistakable articulation?

- What word describes the asexual reproduction of a genetic carbon copy of a plant or an animal?
- Which Kurdish chemical element has the shortest name?
- What three impugnations in the 18th century best refute Einstein's theory of relativity?

If you're not prepared for your hiring interview, it will feel as if you're answering questions such as these. Reading through this chapter will be valuable before an interview, but also consider visiting with at least one person in the agency you are applying to or at least someone in the same field of work. Ask every question you can think of, and take notes. Do this type of preparation within a couple of days of the interview, each time you interview.

Interviews for law enforcement jobs generally consist of two types of questions. You will normally start out with generic questions about yourself and about your goals or intentions. The interviewer will then transition into scenario-based questions to assess your knowledge and thinking process. Scenario-based questions generally cover topics of ethics, teamwork, and the use of force. In this section, we will look at questions that have actually been used or are similar to questions actually used in oral board interviews. You are also provided here with comments and reasonable answers that might be helpful.

1. What have you done to prepare yourself for this position, and what goals have you established for your professional life?

Hopefully you have a list of examples to offer for the first part of this question, such as college classes, ride-alongs, interviews with others in the field, tours of relevant facilities, court observations, volunteer or internship opportunities, and any extra trainings or studies. Each of these should already be listed in your portfolio for easy review. Some agencies will ask for a portfolio or curriculum vitae prior to or during your interview, but even if they don't, it is best to bring it, review it in the car, and then carry it into the interview.

You can be somewhat relaxed with questions about your goals or what you want to accomplish. Answers to these types of questions aren't meant to make or break you. It is fine to be predictable and ordinary. Interviewers hear the same things over and over. It is better to stay on the safe side and not try to be too creative. Let them hear the same things again. There really isn't a lot of variety you can add to your answers to questions such as these. One piece of advice for this question, and throughout the entire interview, is to focus on what sounds good for the agency and not too much on what is best for you. Obviously, you should avoid answers such as "I plan to be your boss someday" or "I hope to ride motorcycles." Use this opportunity to articulate well, because this is a predictable question to which you should have a well-rehearsed answer. Consider an answer such as this:

> My goals are to become a well-rounded and well-trained police officer. I've reviewed the department's mission and vision statements, and I understand that the chief expects her officers to be well rounded, dividing their time between responding to calls for service, investigating crimes, conducting high-visibility patrols in residential, commercial, and retail areas, making positive contacts with citizens, using person and vehicle stops to detect and deter criminal activity, addressing neighborhood traffic concerns, and making crime prevention contacts with citizens and business owners. My goal is to become proficient in as many facets as possible to best represent my department.

This answer can be modified to fit other criminal justice jobs. Impress interviewers by letting them know that you did your homework.

2. What attributes do you feel are important for a law enforcement officer to possess, and how would you apply these attributes to your performance as a police officer?

Just as with the first question, there are generic answers to this question, and it is best to not go off on tangents. Include things such as honor, integrity, courage, and professionalism, but avoid attributes such as being a good shooter, a good pursuit driver, proficient in martial arts, or physically strong. With good articulation in the early, predictable questions, interviewers will be hopeful for you before you even get to the scenarios. For a question such as this, it would be best to name just the main attributes and then spend a little time relating each one to your performance. Spending too much time coming up with attributes will only make the second part of the question more difficult. Stick with three or four, and give an example of each one in order. Use acronyms or phonetics to help you remember what you plan to say and to help you remember the order. For example, the attributes listed above could be remembered using the word *hiccup*, for HICP. Then, when you start to give examples of how you would apply these attributes, you would be well organized. An example could be something like this:

> I know that as a police officer, I represent the city, the chief, and all other brothers and sisters in blue. I would conduct myself ethically at all times in a way that would bring honor to my profession. I would use the empowerment and trust given me with honesty and integrity by adhering to all federal, state, city, and department guidelines. I know that part of my job is to protect citizens and their property. I would face those who challenge the safety of our citizens with courage and steadfastness. I would perform professionally in all my encounters with citizens, attorneys, judges, supervisors, and fellow officers. I would keep myself physically fit and neatly groomed, and wear the uniform with pride.

Questions such as this might be used in interviews for courts and corrections as well. If you have a planned answer, it can be easily adjusted to fit the way the question is asked. Again, why not prepare for these predictable questions? Write down answers for questions you expect, and then go over these answers in your mind while you drive, between classes, in the shower, and on the treadmill.

3. What can you tell us about our agency, and what factors influenced you to apply here?

The U.S. Marshals Service is one agency that puts a lot of weight on how well an applicant researched the organization. Many other agencies use this type of question as well. Try to memorize some important facts about the department or firm, including size, leadership, mission statement, and job description. The more the better! This is a make-or-break question. Always, always research the agency, and be prepared for a question of this nature.

When asked why you chose a particular agency, honesty is really the best way to go. The criminal justice field is very competitive, and students are always advised to apply for all openings that come along. If you apply only at the agency you prefer, you may miss several other opportunities and never get the job you are waiting for. The truth is, you want to be in law enforcement or law or corrections. Where you do the job is secondary. You might prefer another agency just because it is a shorter drive, but be honest with the interviewer. The person doing the interview already knows the truth and will be more impressed if you tell it like it is. After listing several facts about the agency, you could answer the second part of the question like this:

> I have set my goal to become a police officer. I have enjoyed ride-alongs at four different police departments, and although they are different geographically, the work is similar. I know this field is very competitive and that I am competing with hundreds of other candidates. I also realize that departments are not always hiring. I have prepared myself the best I can and hope that I am hired here and can start my career. However, if I am not hired here, I plan to continue applying to other agencies until I succeed. I am prepared to move to another city or state if necessary to work in law enforcement. I am loyal, and whoever hires me will get my best effort. If I am not hired here, I will follow up by asking what I need to improve on, and I will use that information to continue my self-improvement. I have a lot to offer the agency that gives me the chance, and I hope it is this one.

4. Being a police officer can be a stressful job. Please identify some of the aspects of this job you believe would be stressful, and explain how you would cope with the stress of the job.

This kind of question is relevant for any type of work. There has been more emphasis on stress in recent decades. Officers have high suicide and divorce rates. Stress affects health both physically and mentally. Attorneys and correctional officers face similar stresses, with internal politics, heavy workloads, and deadlines. Law enforcement personnel, court personnel, and correctional officers are constantly performing their duties in situations that trigger anxiety. Mandatory stress management trainings have been instituted at many agencies. You answer could be similar to this:

> Putting aside personal feelings and dealing with criminals and their victims can be challenging. Many police officers see examples of human indecency and pain on a day-to-day basis. Seeing people, particularly the elderly and children, who are the victims of murder, beatings, robberies, rapes, and other violent acts can be causes of stress. Police officers also work different shifts. Having to appear in court may interfere with an officer's sleep, personal time, and current work assignments. Changes in work hours can cause the body stress. In addition to working with the public, a lot goes on inside a police department. Dealing with administrative issues, paperwork, and internal investigations can all cause stress.
>
> Police work is also a dangerous job. Officers never know when they show up for work if they'll return home that evening. An officer's day may fluctuate from slow boredom to a sudden dangerous

situation. Dangerous encounters can trigger the fight-or-flight response when presented with a threat. It is important to recognize this condition and to know how to respond to it. The fight-or-flight response has a lot to do with perception. Regular training can help officers manage perceived threats. I deal with stress in a variety of ways.

Exercise has been proven to have a beneficial effect on a person's mental and physical states. For me, exercise is an extremely effective stress buster.

I eat plenty of fruit and vegetables, and I make sure I have a healthy and balanced diet.

I make sure to set aside some time each day just for me. I use that time to organize my life, relax, and pursue my own interests.

An effective breathing technique slows down my system and helps me relax.

I talk to my family, friends, and work colleagues. I try to always express my thoughts and concerns.

There are other stress management tricks you can use that might be substituted or added. Writing your to-do list before retiring to bed can help you sleep better at night. Curbing your caffeine intake can help with sleep. Procrastination can be a stress enhancer. Getting assignments done early and leaving early for appointments can help relieve stress. Doing service for others can help get your mind off your own problems. You can keep a better perspective by having enjoyable events to look forward to, such as vacations or special date nights. Getting sunshine can increase serotonin and improve mood. Self-talk can be helpful. Counselors use this technique as an intervention to help people change self-destructive thought processes.

5. Officers must complete accurate and detailed reports yet still be available to respond to calls for service or perform proactive patrol activities such as monitoring the flow of traffic. Please provide a specific example that demonstrates your ability to multitask.

Questions in which you are asked to give examples are difficult. You will start to think back and try to come up with the best example possible, and you will feel rushed. You know you have several, but your interview is short, and the interviewer is waiting to hear your answer. Similar questions in which you might be asked for examples include the following:

- Tell us about a time when you had difficulty with a coworker or group member and how you handled it.
- Tell us about a time when you had to perform under pressure and how you handled it.
- Tell us about a time when you had to work with a partner or a team and what you did to help the project succeed.

- Tell us about a time when you had to be in charge of a project and what you did to make sure you experienced success.
- Tell us about a time when something went wrong on a project you were involved with and how you handled the turn of events.

These types of questions can be somewhat predictable if you understand how interview questions are created. First, the interview team is presented with the goals of the interview. In other words, it is determined first what an interview is intended to reveal about an applicant. Someone or some group decides what they want to find out, and then they create the questions accordingly. If you look at the examples above, these are all important aspects to explore. If you think as they do, you will be able to have tentative answers prepared. A possible answer could be something like this:

I have had many opportunities to demonstrate my ability to multi-task. I can honestly say that I am good at it and have provided you with three recommendation letters from professionals who have witnessed me handling multiple tasks and mastering my responsibilities. My approach to handling several responsibilities is to write everything down. I prioritize the tasks right away and make a time map of any important time-sensitive details. Writing everything down has improved my quality and timing. Once it is on my to-do list, I know I will be able to stay on task when something new or unexpected comes up. I have also been on three ride-alongs and observed how officers handle all their multitasking. One example that comes to mind is . . .

Make sure to have an example for each of the sample questions above. When you are faced with adversity, handle it well, and then use it to your advantage in future interviews. If you currently do not get along with a coworker, make the steps to correct the problem and use the experience as an example in your interview. If you are in a group in a college course, and one of the members is the worst person ever to walk on our planet, change your purpose, and it will change the outcome. Look at it as an opportunity instead of your awful luck of the draw.

6. Dealing with difficult and noncompliant people is an inherent part of an officer's job. Police officers must deal with people during emotional events and must take people into custody who verbally and physically resist arrest. Describe what actions you will take to deal with these types of situations.

This is the area that can make or break you. Learn the general use-of-force guidelines of the agency you are applying for. Justifications for the use of force are generally just a couple of clicks away on your computer. You can look up your state's statutes and find the section on justifications for

Steve Cervantes: Recruit Training Officer – Mesa Police Department

CJ: What is your current position?

SC: Recruit training officer (RTO) at the Mesa Police Academy.

CJ: What are your typical job duties?

SC: Act as a first line supervisor for police recruits, assist recruits with various problems or concerns. Instruct, educate, evaluate, and mentor recruits on basic police work and physical fitness principles.

CJ: How long have you been at your current assignment?

SC: One year.

CJ: What positions have you held prior to this one?

SC: Patrol officer for 7 years with 3 years as a field training officer.

CJ: What are the requirements/qualifications for your job?

SC: High school diploma for police officer and AZPOST General Instructor Certificate to be an RTO.

CJ: What steps did you go through during hiring?

SC: A written test with a passing score of 70% or better, an oral board interview, and a physical fitness test. All three of those tests are sometimes held on the same day. When I tested for Mesa PD in 2007, the physical fitness test was held on a separate day. The physical fitness test is the Cooper Test. I was tested on the Institute Assessment, which consists of a mile and a half run completed under 15:20, 29 or more push-ups in a minute, and 31 sit-ups or more in a minute.

Once I passed the three requirements, a background investigation was conducted; then a polygraph test was administered. When I was notified that I passed the polygraph test, I was instructed to get a medical physical and a psychological exam done. A short time later, I was sent an offer letter to attend the police academy. The whole process took about 3 months. It takes some applicants over a year to go through the hiring process.

CJ: What advice can you offer students who might be interested in pursuing a similar career?

SC: The hiring process can take a very long time and I suggest testing for multiple agencies. Volunteer or go through a citizen's police academy to get familiar with basic police work and to get your name known. Have some sort of general idea of what police officers do and their responsibilities. Police officers do more than just issue traffic citations. Integrity and having self-confidence is everything in this position. Know-it-all personalities, and the people who aren't willing to adapt to change or learn something new, usually don't do well in this field.

---

force. You need to know what you have the authority to do. If you also understand the atmosphere of the discretionary powers at the agency, the scenarios will be easier to answer. The nice thing about this question is that you are not asked to determine if you would make an arrest or not. Instead, you are being assessed for your thought process on problem-solving skills, human relational skills, safety concerns, mental control, and several other possible traits. The best advice is to answer the way the chief would want to hear it. Remember that the purpose of all questions is to assess certain traits about you, so you can usually hear a question and figure out what they want to assess. These types of questions weed out the candidates who didn't go on ride-alongs or at least get prepped by an officer or a professor. Scenario-based questions are also used in correctional job interviews. You can prepare for scenario questions by practicing with the officer you do your ride-along with. Have the officer ask you questions and critique your responses.

In Chapter 3, you were provided with a brief lesson on the use of force. It is important to understand the use-of-force continuum and the Fourth Amendment connection to this topic. One side of the continuum consists of a scale of different levels of force an officer can use to accomplish the necessary enforcement. The other side of the continuum is different behaviors of the perpetrator that justify an officer's equal or slightly higher level of force. An example would be a suspect who has no weapons and sits on the ground, telling an officer that he is not going to jail. The officer has the authority to use verbal judo or certain pain compliance holds to encourage the suspect's cooperation, but pointing a gun would be unreasonable in this situation. The Fourth Amendment guarantees citizens that they will be treated reasonably. It also restricts the government from going beyond what is necessary. These are good key words for your answers: *continuum*, *reasonable*, and *necessary*.

Going back to Question 6, you can see that it is somewhat vague. The question leaves a lot to a person's interpretation. The question allows for a variety of possible answers. It uses words and phrases such as *people* (children, adults, gang members, known criminals), *emotional events* (car accidents, shootings, stabbings, sexual assaults), and *physically resist arrest* (guns, knives, broken bottles, fists). The best way to answer a question such as this is to cover as many possibilities as you can. It will show that you aren't closed minded and can see that there are many optional routes. It will also let you show off how much you know. You may not get another chance to demonstrate your knowledge of the use of force. One possible answer could be as follows:

> The level of force is dictated by the situation. Officers should use verbal commands in combination with command presence. Whether you instruct a person to "Stop!" "Don't move!" "Be quiet!" "Listen to me!" "Let me see your ID!" or "You're under arrest!" voice commands in conjunction with your mere presence can prevent many situations from escalating. The right combination of words and command presence can deescalate tense situations and prevent the need for a physical altercation. When someone is noncompliant or resisting arrest, soft, empty-hand techniques might be necessary, involving the use of bare hands to guide, hold, and restrain; applying pressure points; and take-down techniques that have a minimal chance of injury. When a suspect is actively resisting, less physical measures

might be insufficient. Pepper spray or a Taser might be a better option, depending on department policy guidelines. Less lethal weapons can be used in accordance with policy when other alternatives are impractical and when lethal force is not justified. Hard, empty-hand techniques, such as kicks, punches, or other striking techniques, such as the use of a baton, could be justified if a suspect is actively attacking an officer. Of course, deadly force should be used only when a peace officer has probable cause to believe that a suspect poses a significant threat of death or serious bodily injury to the officer or others. The main thing is to understand department policy and procedure in terms of use-of-force guidelines and to maintain proficiency with training.

My personal philosophy will always be to only use the amount of force that is necessary and reasonable. I believe I have the ability to communicate with hostile or difficult citizens because of my 2 years of experience working as an intern for the U.S. Marshals Service and 1 year working in corrections as a detention officer. I assisted in over 50 verbal confrontations with hostile suspects or prisoners, which resulted in only one physical fight. I was exonerated for that fight and given a commendation for my self-restraint and overall behavior. My portfolio contains three letters of recommendation from my past supervisors, which all mention my ability to communicate well with combative subjects.

7. You are driving in your marked police car along a canal bank at midnight, and on the other side of the canal, in an open field, you see a man holding an axe standing over another man on the ground. The man with the axe has lifted it over his head, ready to swing down and hit the other man, who is not resisting in any way. What course of action would you take?

Scenario-based questions pertaining to the use of force often deal with lethal force. Interviewers may want to know if you are willing to take a life. They also want to know if you recognize the reality of the situation. You would not want to try to swim across the canal to save the man. The axe is ready to come down. You would not drive around the canal to the other side; you would be too late. You would not drive your car toward the canal and attempt to jump over, because you don't have time and it might not work anyway. You do not want to try to shoot the axe out of the hands of the assailant. You might miss such a small target. The victim might be killed, and the stray bullet might hit someone else on the other side of the field. The sad truth is that a police officer may have to shoot someone during his or her career. You never shoot to kill; you shoot to stop. Your target is the center of mass. The biggest area of mass is the torso. The center of mass is in the area of the lungs and heart, which officers call the 10 ring because in firearms training, 10 points are awarded for hitting the small circular target over the chest area. Although a shot to this area could be fatal, an officer's job is to stop the threat, not to kill the assailant. Hitting the area of the vital organs will stop an axe-wielding killer quicker than a leg shot. Officers don't shoot to wound, and they don't fire warning shots. The only shot allowed at a human is to stop a threat. A possible answer might come across like this:

> I know that taking someone's life is one of the hardest things I might have to do as part of my job. Deadly force should only be used when necessary to protect myself or a third party against serious physical harm or death. In this scenario, I realize that every second counts. I will be yelling commands to the assailant from the moment I step out of my car and also pulling my weapon out as quickly as possible. I will point my weapon at the person wielding the axe and aim at the center of mass. If he does not discontinue immediately, I will fire on the suspect until he is no longer a threat. I realize that I could miss my target, or that he could be under the influence of a drug such as PCP and not be affected immediately by my first shot. I will shoot as many times as necessary to stop the threat. I will be cognizant the entire time of the background so that I can best position myself in a way that avoids hurting anyone who might be in the line of fire.

The interviewers may have follow-up prompts for a question such as this. You may be asked if you would hesitate. You will need to be careful not to ruin the great answer you already gave. The good thing is that interviewers are generally held to strict standards of fairness. So whatever they ask you, they have already asked it of everyone else before you. Make sure to confirm what you have already said, unless the scenario is changed in any way. Come back with the surety that you would shoot the suspect as quickly and as often as necessary to stop the threat.

8. You pull a driver over for speeding and find that it is your mother, who borrowed a friend's car. What is your course of action?

Do not write your mother a ticket! Knowing when to exercise discretion can be difficult with more serious infractions, but normal everyday traffic violations are much easier. It may seem more complicated if the scenario includes a fellow officer or maybe the mayor or a chief of police from another agency. If the traffic stop is for a routine traffic violation, don't cite any of these people. Make your answer come across as an easy decision. Here is a reasonable answer:

> I know an officer has great discretionary powers. Every situation is different and should be judged on its own merits. Not every person who violates the law gets a ticket or goes to jail. There isn't enough room in the jails or time in the courtrooms to process every violator.

I realize that a common goal of the criminal justice system is to deter crime. I would handle a traffic violator differently who disobeyed the law blatantly than someone who may have accidentally breached a traffic law. I plan to use my discretionary power as fairly as possible and for the right reasons. Sometimes a person changes behavior just from the fear that was experienced in the traffic stop. I feel that if I would give a break to someone I don't even know, I would surely give a break to the person who raised me, fed me, and drove me to soccer practice.

In the situation in which the question involves a fellow officer, stay with the same way of thinking, but you can also add that you know that an officer will be treated more harshly in court than a regular citizen would be. Judges must be careful with the appearance of favoritism, as must officers. They have less discretion and would need to be harsher in sentencing than they would for a normal citizen. This is just an additional reason why you might give a warning to an officer who should already know better than to speed.

Be careful not to refer to an authority figure as a hypocrite for violating a traffic law. Everyone violates traffic laws, whether it is intentional or accidental. In reality, every time an officer writes a ticket for speeding, it could be considered hypocritical. Stay focused on the concept that you will write tickets if you feel it is for the better good of society as a whole. If you feel that a violator needs a ticket to help deter future behavior, you should write the ticket. If you feel that a warning would produce the desired result, just issue a pleasant warning and leave that violator with a positive feeling about the police.

Officers will sometimes write tickets out of anger at the way violators talk to them. Although this type of ticket seems unfair, officers are only human and might feel that violators need a "behavior adjustment." If you are asked a question that includes a belligerent violator who lacks respect for the law and for people, remember the purpose of the ticket. If you feel that the ticket will help society as a whole, you should write it. If you feel that the ticket would make things worse, you might go a different route and use the stop as a way to change the violator's opinion of police through kindness. You have that kind of power out on the street. These decisions are totally up to you. Just make sure you don't write a ticket out of anger. Just as in raising children, discipline for the good of the child, not to make yourself feel better.

9. As an officer, you must be able to communicate and obtain useful information from people. Assume you are an officer dispatched to contact a suspicious person. You locate the subject, who is elderly and apparently disoriented. How would you handle this situation?

Much of police work consists of difficult situations, but not all are criminal. You could be assigned to handle almost anything. Luckily, there are other agencies out there to assist the police in cases that can be handled by other experts. Police are sometimes dispatched for "other agency assists" because the level of danger isn't known initially. Police officers have guns, handcuffs, radios, training, and authority. Thus, any situation in which danger is a possibility will involve police. This is one possible answer:

> Police often rely on the instincts and perceptions of citizens to detect activity that is out of the ordinary. Police have a duty and responsibility to follow up on reports of suspicious persons. Upon arriving on scene at such a call, it would be important to ask questions and determine what type of situation I am dealing with. In such a situation, an elderly, disoriented person could have Alzheimer's disease or some other related dementia. It is important to identify and understand the signs of Alzheimer's disease and related dementias and how to communicate with people who have these conditions. This helps better serve both people with these conditions and the community as a whole. I would communicate to my supervisor what I was dealing with and determine what services the police department could offer, if needed.

It is sometimes crucial to say that you would contact your supervisor, but never use that as an easy out on your answers. The interviewers might not let you off that easily. It is common for an interviewer to follow your answer by saying that your supervisor is busy at a helicopter crash. If this happens, the interviewer wants to assess your knowledge of the particular situation. Give general answers; do not be too specific. It is best to let an interviewer know what you would do under a variety of scenarios. For example, you could call the man's family, friends, or doctor. You could contact a crisis intervention team if your city has one. You could call an ambulance if the man needs to be assessed for dehydration or other common problems with disorientation. You always want to do something. It is okay to admit that you don't know what to do, but follow that with your best guess. It is better to admit that you don't know than to pretend you do and disqualify yourself with an inappropriate answer. If a weak answer knocks you out of the top list of candidates, you will have an advantage by knowing what types of questions to prepare for the next time you have a hiring interview.

10. An officer must accurately report information. Assume you are assisting another officer with an inventory of a prisoner's property by completing the impound form. You see the other officer take a quarter from the prisoner's property, put it in his pocket, and place a different quarter in the property bag. The other officer tells you that he is a coin collector and that that particular quarter is a solid silver quarter. What would you do?

What is the interviewer trying to find out about you with this question? Are you going to be a tattletale? Are you going to be unethical and just turn your back on what your fellow officers do? You are always safe to lean toward what you would say to the chief if he or she were asking the question. Answer this type of question something like this:

> This is an integrity issue. Police are expected by the public to be held to a higher standard than the general public. Police officers' ethics and integrity should be beyond reproach, because the public relies on police to respect civil rights. I would confront the officer and remind him that there are department policies in connection with handling prisoners' property. I would also advise the officer that this is an ethical issue. I would document exactly what happened in the police report. I would notify the officer that I am required to do so. I would make sure that the immediate supervisor is aware of the police report. It is important to document these things as a matter of record for performance review purposes and for future reference in case of repeated misconduct. Repeated problems or an accumulation of minor infractions of policy or procedure could become a problem. As such, this information must be available to supervisors.

Be careful of questions of this nature that might be assessing if you are too quick to jump to conclusions. Regardless of the scenario, you will normally be expected to take some form of action. Doing nothing is usually the wrong choice.

11. Department policy states that officers are not to accept gratuities, for example, free drinks or meals. You have just finished eating at a restaurant on your patrol beat, but the waitress is adamant in refusing to give you a bill. How would you deal with the situation and why?

With a few exceptions, police officers may not accept gratuities. Local and state police officers are first responders, and accepting a gratuity might make an officer feel obligated to favor the donor at a future time, when the officer should instead be unbiased. It might also make the donor feel that the officer owes him loyalty. You also want to avoid a scene at a restaurant. This is a possible answer, although a little over the top:

> Police departments have rules for a reason. Although the payment of free coffee is perhaps a commonly received gratuity in many jurisdictions, business owners might expect extra services in return for giving gratuities. When law enforcement officers offer additional services to private businesses in exchange for a free cup of coffee, they detract from other citizens within their communities. Police service cannot be perceived as going to the highest bidder; decisions must be based on need. Many argue that the coffee is inexpensive and that owners are showing appreciation by offering a cup and enjoying the fact that officers spend time in their shops. Therefore, what is the harm? On the

other hand, what happens in a discretionary issue when an officer stops the owner or an employee for speeding? The officer may base the decision of whether to cite on the fact that he received free coffee. Should the free coffee factor in the officer's decision? Police officers often face the dilemma of accepting gratuities. Some officers view the acceptance of free coffee and free or discounted meals as an entitlement, while others view it as an unethical act. Law enforcement agencies should consider the perceptions of communities, as well as business owners, when accepting gratuities. Where there are departmental policies against accepting gratuities, they should not be accepted. I think the best practice is to be diplomatic with the restaurant server, thank him and explain that I cannot accept a gratuity, and leave payment with the cashier.

Could you just leave the money at the table, plus a tip, and not say anything? This is a solution, but be careful in your answer to this type of question. You want to focus on what the interviewers are trying to find out about you. You want them to know that you understand the real issue. It isn't only about whether you will accept the gift. If you just leave money at the table to cover the food and tip, it might all end up in the server's pocket, and the owner might think you accepted the gratuity. Plus, other citizens who may have witnessed the conversation would assume that you took the gratuity and just left a tip for the waitress. Even though you personally refused to go down that slippery slope, other damage could still be done to the police department as a whole.

12. Police officers work in ethnically diverse communities. Please describe how diversity affects the role of a police officer in the performance of his or her duties.

This may be an easy question for you. Make sure to use proper terms when appropriate. If you are a Caucasian man, you wouldn't want to start out by saying "I don't have any problems with minorities. I married one." Use terms such as *African American, Mexican American, Native American*, and so on. Using these terms will demonstrate that you have had some kind of training in the area of diversity. Make sure not to downplay this issue. It is a very important and controversial issue in the criminal justice system. Here is a possible answer:

Historically, many minority groups have been treated badly by the government—some by officials in the United States and others by governments in the countries from which they came. Harsh treatment can create distrust and fear of the government and authority figures in some minority communities. That distrust may make it difficult for minority groups to trust police or other authority figures in society. When approached by police, a minority member may express alarm or doubt, or be coldly polite. It is important to keep backgrounds and experiences in mind as we reach out to different people. We may need to consider altering how we approach and interact with individuals from diverse communities. However, grouping people into categories such as these also can be misleading. We must be careful to avoid making broad assumptions about people based solely on appearances or ethnic or racial affiliation. Poor relations between community members and police can lead to feelings of distrust, anger, and fear. A situation involving the shooting of a minority citizen by a police officer, for example, could potentially cause heightened racial tensions. Citizens may think the police are prejudiced and have unfair policies. People from diverse backgrounds and experiences need to develop trust, understand one another's experiences, and work together on solutions.

You could also add comments about how important it is to have diversity within the ranks of criminal justice jobs to capitalize on dissimilar viewpoints and ultimately make better decisions for the community as a whole.

Dos and Don'ts

Some of the important dos and don'ts of interviewing have been covered, but here are a few more to help you succeed:

- Do get plenty of sleep the night before the interview.
- Don't chew gum during the interview.
- Do give a good firm handshake if the interviewer offers a hand.
- Don't have the smell of smoke on your clothes when you walk into the interview.
- Do listen to the last names of the interviewers and try to remember them. It would be impressive if you have the opportunity to insert a name or two later in the interview instead of saying "sir" or "ma'am." Remember to use "Mister" and "Ms." or "Councilwoman," "Judge," "Doctor," or "Professor" (along with the last name) if you know the proper title.
- Don't eat too much fiber or gassy foods (beans, broccoli, cabbage, cauliflower, brussel sprouts) within 24 hours of the interview. Your comfort is paramount to your performance.
- Do maintain a friendly and humble demeanor in your facial expressions.
- Don't slouch. Sitting up straight (yet comfortably) might take practice, but it is helpful to show confidence through body language.

- Do bring your portfolio to the interview. It might not be required, but having it will be impressive. There may also be opportunities to pass a recommendation letter around or a certificate of relevance.
- Don't let your cell phone make any noise during the interview. However, if you do forget to shut it off, just apologize and move on. You could even make a joke about it at that moment, such as "Wow, that's a good way to impress my interviewers." Well-timed and tasteful humor is always welcome, even in the most professional settings. You are especially okay if you are laughing at yourself.
- Do use good vocabulary and avoid slang and jargon or pause words such as "uh."
- Don't speak negatively about past employers or coworkers unless it is absolutely necessary to explain a bad report.
- Do tell the truth.
- Don't bring in personal issues and family problems to the interview if it can be avoided. However, you should always be honest if asked.
- Do focus on what you can bring to the agency, not on why the job is important to you.
- Don't rush to answer a question. It is okay to repeat a question to make sure you understood it. That will buy you more time for your response. A slight pause is fine after each question, so that you can visualize the path you want to take with your answer. Seasoned criminals use the pause technique during interviews; why shouldn't you?
- Do come across as appreciative and respectful without sounding desperate.

A Personal Note to Minorities, Women, Gays, and Lesbians

I have had the pleasure of working for and alongside minorities, women, gays, and lesbians during a 27-year law enforcement career. The police department was better because of them. We became like family through the years, but these remarkable individuals all had their share of depressing experiences dissimilar to my own, as a straight white man. There will always be some prejudice and bias in the workplace. Cultural and religious issues will be present as well. Caucasians, men, and heterosexuals who don't see it may never see it. Remember the serenity prayer: "God, grant me the serenity to accept the things I can't change, the courage to change the things I can, and the wisdom to know the difference."

Hopefully you will have the courage to aggressively seek the job you want and not be dispirited by the unfortunate past or the imperfect present. There are a good, a better, and a best in many areas of our lives. Be the best you can be at the best job you can earn, and persist in making the world better.

Summary

You should expect an interview for any job you apply for. In a perfect world, the best candidate would get the job. In our world, the best interviewer often gets the job. Some important hints for success are to be about 10 minutes early, have the proper appearance, use body language tricks to help show yourself off, and make a good first impression in your introduction, which includes a smile.

There are two types of questions in the interview. The first part of the interview involves questions that you might expect, such as what you have done to prepare yourself for the job, why you chose this career, and what you know about the agency or firm. The second part involves situational questions to assess your thinking process. You can prepare for these types of questions by learning about use of force (in police and corrections interviews); knowing the firm's or agency's policies; and having examples in your mind of situations you have been in, such as handling difficult people, crisis situations, and teamwork experiences.

Historically, women and minorities have experienced inequality in the workforce. Women continue to enter jobs that have traditionally been carried out by men. Although there has been significant progress in welcoming women to police and correctional jobs, there is still more ground to cover. Although not many, there do remain a handful of men in police agencies and correctional facilities who are skeptical about women's abilities to perform all facets of the job.

Women need to be mentally prepared for interviews by men. The vast majority of men have no issues, but there is always a chance that a male interviewer could be a skeptic. Men change their views of women in law enforcement as they witness outstanding female employees do the job well. The interview is not the right time to make a statement about women's rights. Women should portray in interviews that they are team players and can work with anyone. Once women are hired, they can prove to any skeptics that they belong there through their performance.

There will always be some prejudice and bias in the workplace. Cultural and religious issues will be present as well. Caucasians, men, and heterosexuals who don't see it may never see it. Hopefully you will have the courage to aggressively seek the job you want and not be dispirited by the unfortunate past or the imperfect present. There are a good, a better, and a best in many areas of our lives. Be the best you can be at the best job you can earn, and persist in making the world better.

DISCUSSION QUESTIONS

1. Are there any suggestions about your appearance for an interview that you strongly agree or disagree with? Explain.

2. Do you agree with the level of importance placed on smiling? Why or why not?

3. Do you agree that it is better to let the interviewer offer a hand for a handshake instead of being the first to do so? Why or why not?

4. When answering questions, the author suggests that you make eye contact with all the interviewers, not just the person who asked the question. What is the reasoning behind this strategy? Do you agree or disagree with this reasoning? Why or why not?

5. What are some things you can do to prepare for the hiring interview questions?

6. Do you agree with the author's assertion that there will always be some prejudice and bias in the workplace? Why or why not?

Index